CONFESSIONS OF THE GREEN RIVER KILLER

CONFESSIONS OF THE GREEN RIVER KILLER

A TRUE STORY OF MANIPULATION, MADNESS, AND A SEARCH FOR JUSTICE

Maria DiLorenzo

NEW YORK

Books should be disposed of and recycled according to local requirements.
All paper materials used are FSC compliant.

Published in the United States by Crooked Lane Books, an imprint of The Quick Brown Fox & Company LLC.

Crooked Lane Books and its logo are trademarks of The Quick Brown Fox & Company LLC.

Library of Congress Catalog-in-Publication data available upon request.

ISBN (hardcover): 979-8-89242-396-0
ISBN (paperback): 979-8-89242-397-7
ISBN (ebook): 979-8-89242-398-4

Cover design by Lauren Harms

Printed in the United States.

www.crookedlanebooks.com

Crooked Lane Books
34 West 27th St., 10th Floor
New York, NY 10001

First Edition: July 2026

The authorized representative in the EU for product safety and compliance is eucomply OÜPärnu mnt 139b-14, 11317 Tallinn, Estonia, hello@eucompliancepartner.com, +33757690241

10 9 8 7 6 5 4 3 2 1

To my mother, Christine

I will tear the petals off of you
Rose red, I will make you tell the truth
Was she asking for it?
—Courtney Love (singer and guitarist
for alternative rock band Hole,
in "Asking for It," 1994)

CONTENTS

AUTHOR'S NOTE

Confessions of the Green River Killer contains research I conducted over a span of five years. What was initially intended to be a concise blog post for my website, Beyond the Crime, turned into a long, complex, unsettling journey of conversing with Gary Ridgway—one of the most prolific serial killers in United States history—over the course of two years from 2020 to 2022. This book is my best attempt at providing an honest profile of Gary Ridgway and making sense of the most disturbing, yet fascinating, experience of my life.

All the conversations between Gary and me included in this book are true, and in some instances, completely unfiltered. However, due to Gary's nature to lie pathologically, the veracity of his words will never be entirely proven.

Other statements made by him were retrieved directly from transcripts of his interviews with law enforcement that took place in 1985 when he was an initial suspect and then, from June 2003 to December 2003, after his final arrest. Statements from those who knew him and/or interacted with him were pulled directly from witness statements on file with the King County Sheriff's Office (KCSO). Over these five years, I also spoke with anyone connected to this story who was willing to give me their time—surviving victims, law enforcement, family members, medical examiners, etc.

A lot has been written about Gary through the years, but very few people have actually interacted with him to gain a better understanding of him. Who is Gary Ridgway the person? Who is Gary Ridgway the serial killer? Where do the two collide and blur together to become what most of us would only define as a monster? I intended to find out, but the process of trying to extract the truth from Gary would prove to be an exhausting and daunting task. Yet, I became committed to trying to understand the inner workings of his mind and seeking justice for victims of cases that have remained unsolved for decades, sometimes working as many as four jobs to afford the daily phone calls with Gary and the trips back and forth to Seattle.

The romanticized version of some serial killers created in drama series and films does not exist within these pages. Sometimes there's no cooperation, no mercy, no kindness—a serial killer rarely does the right thing because we want him to. The conclusions we seek do not always prevail—in this case, solving 32–42 cold cases. Sometimes there's no happy ending. Serial killers will often do what they want and what only benefits them, making all of their interactions with others self-centered and transactional. I'm sure readers will share my frustration as they also come to this realization. With that being said, I hope this work will provide a more realistic insight into the mind of a serial killer.

Some readers may find the content of this work disturbing, but fictionalizing Gary to soften his character or sugarcoating my own experience with him I believe would do more harm than good. Instead, it's better to know the bare ugly, gut-wrenching, nauseating, horrific truth; anything less than that would be a denial of my own experience and a betrayal to those who desire to remain steadfastly unshielded to stare this reprehensible evil dead in the eye, if only to try to understand it.

FIRST CONTACT

CHAPTER ONE

The Call

I was folding laundry the first time the Green River Killer called me.

I had mailed a letter to him not even a month ago, but from what I understood, the chances he'd answer it were slim. Within the past nineteen years, the man was only known to give two interviews. He barely replied to anyone, especially not journalists. He was not like other incarcerated people, engaging with a multitude of pen pals.

But a part of me had *known* this day would come, no matter how unlikely it had seemed.

The day I sent him that letter, the thick, malted air made walking anywhere tedious. Still, I decided to venture to the mailbox a few blocks away. Since the onset of the pandemic five months prior, keeping me captive in my one bedroom apartment, I had made a diligent effort to get my steps in each day.

The humidity was typical for New York City in early August, one of the few things that managed to stay the same during this dystopian-like year of total isolation. As I stepped out into the night, it felt the same as summers before. As I quickened my pace, sweat began to line my forehead, but it felt good to move, to be outside.

I clutched the envelope I was holding in my hand, wrinkling the face of it with my palm sweat. As I turned down the block lined with tall trees, I wondered what Gary Ridgway—his name I had written in black ink so firmly I could feel the indents of the letters beneath my fingers—was able to see from the window in his cell. Or maybe he didn't even have a window. But if he did, were trees part of his view? What about the sky freckled with stars that seemed to throb with painful light? Could he see any of this?

The entire world had come to experience a form of isolation during the past few months, leading to loneliness, depression, and other mental health issues, but what had his life been like the last nineteen years living in a solitary cell? Were the conditions so horrid to move him to regret his actions? Did he miss breathing in the air of an uncaged space?

I intended to ask him all these questions—if he responded to me.

When I typed his name into Google and was faced with an image of his mugshot from his final arrest in 2001, I felt oddly sure that I was meant to talk to him. But as I stared at his face, which appeared mean and unapproachable, his eyes squinting back at me with an expression of utter annoyance, I double-guessed my intuition like I always did. *Why would he ever want to talk to me? Come on, Maria. Probably a million writers have reached out to him through the years.*

Yet, I still felt sure. I scrolled through the thumbnails of his face and stopped on one image where he was smiling a wide, toothy grin. There, he looked like anyone else caught on the rare occasion of having a good day. Suddenly, it felt like I was surveying the photo of an old friend I had lost contact with due to time and forgetfulness, one you regret disconnecting from in the long run. I couldn't explain it. Talking to him somehow seemed imperative, as though if I didn't, my life would fall off course.

So, I wrote my letter, explaining that I was a writer from New York who had just started a website called Beyond the Crime. There, I provided those who were incarcerated for murder with a platform to discuss any topic of their choosing, whether it was related to their crime or not. I made sure to specify that he would have total freedom within our potential conversations, and that I was willing to publish an uncensored version of whatever he wanted to share, something most writers were not willing to do. I signed off the letter, including the address of my PO box and phone number. Even though I had sent a similar version of this letter to a few others, as I folded up the typed page into three neat rectangles, this time it felt more important, as though my life or his life depended on it reaching him.

As I passed a desolate bus stop—I was now nearly a mile from my apartment—loose strands of my hair that had escaped from my messy ponytail stuck to my face, which glistened with sweat. I could taste the salt of it like balm on my lips as I sucked in the humid air. The mailbox was only a few feet away.

I stood before it and stared down at the envelope in my hand. Every other letter I had sent out so far—six in total—I did while barely thinking about the outcome. This one felt different. Once I pushed the envelope through that slot, I knew my life would somehow be changed. I just didn't know in what ways, for better or worse, or both.

As I stood in contemplation, I surveyed the empty street that glowed a dim orange beneath the streetlamp. I considered his reaction upon receiving this letter that was still pressed firmly between my fingertips. Would he want to talk to me? The logical side of my brain reminded me that he *never* responded to anyone. But my heart knew something different, something foreign to any common sense. I was meant to do this.

I took a deep breath of the heavy air and watched the last edge of the white envelope become swallowed, disappearing into the belly of the box.

As I turned to walk home, leaving my words to Ridgway there in the pit of that box seemed so final. Much like his decision to kill, the certainty of death by his hands, there was no reversing it.

* * *

Weeks passed, and I barely thought about receiving a response from him. I simply lived my life, which consisted of adjusting to teaching in a post-pandemic classroom and corresponding with a few others who had expressed interest in sharing their stories on my website.

Toward the end of September, just like any other Sunday night, I folded laundry I had neglected for most of the week. Using my bed as a space to sort and organize each garment, I sifted through the heap of socks, trying to match them. Lost in my thoughts of the asshole guy that had stood me up a few nights before, the buzzing of my phone vibrating through my mattress shifted my focus. I glanced down at the screen to find an area code I didn't recognize and the words "Walla Walla, Washington" beneath the number. *Another annoying telemarketer, I bet.* Normally, I ignored such calls, but I had an instinct to answer. When I slid my fingers over the screen and pressed the phone to my ear, before I could say hello, a woman's robotic voice greeted me, "This is a Global Tel Link free call from—"

A name was spoken by a man—a prerecorded message most likely made by the caller—but it was too muffled to understand.

"—an inmate at Washington State Penitentiary. This call will be recorded and monitored. If you wish to block any future calls of this nature, dial seven now. To accept this call, press five now—"

It had to be Gary Ridgway: also holding a phone to his ear, somewhere within a prison, almost three thousand miles away, where he had remained confined for about half of my life, and he was waiting to speak to me. I couldn't believe it.

Even with the part of me that had intuitively known something would come of that letter, I had never anticipated he would reply so quickly, and especially not with a phone call. Usually, the people I reached out to in prison began the correspondence with a letter before ever deciding to call. This time, there was no warning except the few seconds I had before the robotic message would end. I took a deep breath and tried to prepare for what he was about to say.

"Hello, Maria?" a soft voice on the other end responded. "It's Gary," he said, as though we had been friends for years.

"Gary Ridgway?" I questioned. I had to be sure. *He never responds to anyone.*

"Yeah, Gary Ridgway," he repeated.

"Oh, hi. How are you doing?" I was stunned but attempted to sound nonchalant. As I stood in my bedroom clutching a sock, I tried to redirect my brain from the mundane task of folding laundry to now possibly conducting an interview with one of the most prolific serial killers in United States history.

Although there's probably an expectation that in a moment like this I should feel fearful, my heart beating as if I had just run a marathon, my voice shaky—after all, this man was convicted of killing forty-nine women and suspected of killing more—I felt ready for the conversation.

Over the years, I had grown accustomed to those kinds of calls. Besides, with him in a prison yard across the country, was he really a threat? It wasn't like he was standing beside me in my bedroom, or I was standing beside him in his cell. What harm could he actually cause me?

"Not bad," he mumbled. Before I could ask him anything else, he switched the topic away from pleasantries. "So, what's your blog about?"

I had explained this to several others by now, so my response was starting to feel scripted. "Basically it's a website for incarcerated people to share their stories. Whatever they want to tell, whether related to their crimes or not."

"Uh-huh. Do you know about my case?"

My mind raced—*what details does he expect me to know?* I was no expert, but I was aware that forty-nine young women or more—mostly prostitutes and runaways—had died by his hands, and he had managed to escape detection for nearly twenty years. "I know some things about it," I said. I had a feeling it was wise to keep my answer short and simple. By doing so, maybe he would state what was on his mind. *Always let them talk*, I had learned over the years.

"Uh-huh. Do you know about the Jane Does . . . the ones still missing?" There was no emotion behind his words, just matter-of-factness, like he was asking me my thoughts on something as banal as a TV show. There was no way to tell what his motives were for bringing up the women who were still missing, the women he had killed. Did he want my help in finding them? If so, how could I possibly do that, especially from New York? On the other hand, was he only looking for more attention, a way to increase his death toll to have as "prolific" a record as possible? Or by some shock to his conscience, was he now desiring to do the right thing and wishing to bring closure to families? By bringing up his case right away, was he checking for my immediate reaction to the violence he was capable of? It felt like a test.

"Yes, I have heard some things, that there are still unsolved cases." I remained neutral, unbothered, unflinching.

"Yeah." He seemed pleased with my answer. However, it was impossible to gauge if he was being agreeable or actually admitting that there were more victims to be found.

"Is this something you'd be interested in talking about?"

"You're going to have to set up a GTL account," he directed.

"A phone account—"

"Yeah, a phone account."

"Okay. That's not a problem—"

"You have sixty seconds remaining," the robotic woman interrupted.

"I'll set one up this week," I finished.

"They only give a couple minutes on these free calls, so you'll need a GTL account so we can talk," he reminded me again.

"Yes, I will make one," I reassured him.

"You have thirty seconds remaining," the robotic woman chimed in again, counting down to when she would disconnect us.

"I'll call you again soon," he added.

"Okay, have a good night."

"You—"

Before he could finish his sentence, a dull click cut him off, and I was listening to silence. I stood facing the wall, staring into the shadow of my headboard that ironically resembled prison bars. For a few moments, I could not move. With one hand still holding a sock and the other the phone, his soft voice and his words that alluded to his ruthlessness replayed in my mind.

I couldn't help but wonder, what was it about my letter that had prompted him to dial my phone number? He usually turned down every interview initiated by anyone within the media. But more importantly, what was he hoping to get out of communicating with me?

I tried to anticipate our next call, imagined what he'd say, but someone like him, not only a serial killer, but someone who had been a recluse all these years within a solitary cell in prison, seemed impossible to predict. He had already caught me off guard with his call, the subject matter of it, and his aloof demeanor. I couldn't speculate what I would learn about him or the lessons about myself that I would be forced to accept through conversing with him. It only felt inevitable.

CHAPTER TWO

Unprepared

Four days later, my phone vibrated atop the smooth surface of my wooden kitchen table. "Walla Walla, Washington" flashed beneath the number I now recognized.

Fuck.

Although he said he would call again, I did not expect it so soon. During the entire week, the first phone call had replayed in my mind with the same fervor as a song I loved. I could barely focus on teaching personal narrative to the many ceiling fans that had replaced the faces of students in the small Zoom squares. The only story I cared to know about was the one Gary Ridgway had started telling me. How many women was he really responsible for killing? Would it ever be possible to uncover the victims that were still missing?

While I obsessed over these questions, I idiotically had forgotten to open and put money on a GTL phone account so I would be able to accept his calls. It was still hard to believe he had called at all, so the idea of him reaching out again within the same week seemed unlikely.

As I stared down at my quivering phone, I learned an important lesson about communicating with Gary: he would never be entirely predictable. What I expected him to do he would never do; in fact, he would usually do the thing that did not even cross my mind. However, it would take years to grasp the latter of this lesson.

I took a deep breath and slid my finger across the phone's screen to answer the call, unsure if I would even be able to speak to him without a functional GTL account. Entirely unprepared, I felt like a failure of a journalist. However, just like last time, he had used one of his complimentary five minute calls.

As soon as I greeted him, he asked the question that would become one of the many factors to fool me into thinking he was predictable, the question I would eventually become so accustomed to hearing right after pressing five, the one he'd begin every call with, like old friends settled in a routine: "So, what's new in New York?" His voice was upbeat and full of the same energy as a kid amid a sugar rush.

At the time, I suspected this question was simply a pleasantry. After all, hadn't the media dubbed him as "mild mannered" and polite? I didn't anticipate that he actually wanted to know about New York or my life there. So I dodged it, and maneuvered into my own basic question, "How are you doing, Gary?"

"Pretty good." He rushed his words, making sure to move the conversation far away from how he could possibly be feeling, another thing he'd often do that would eventually become familiar.

He seemed guarded, and even bothered, if ever so slightly, that I had inserted my own question into our exchange. If he didn't like answering a simple "how are you," how would I ever be able to ask him anything more pertinent? But he wasted no time before picking up where we left off, about what seemed to be his only concern.

"About the women—there are still Jane Does out there," he asserted.

"Yes, you started to tell me about this when we last spoke. Is this what you would want the blog on my website to focus on?"

"Uh-huh. The Jane Does that are out there, so finding them. Could you help?"

"I would like to help, yes. What do you have in mind?"

"If you can research the dates and locations of the others who have not been found—the Jane Does—and compare them with the forty-nine." He seemed to have a well thought-out plan of my role in this investigation. But just like the first time we spoke, I couldn't help but wonder if his expectations were realistic or even genuine. Could this all be a game for his own personal entertainment?

Over the past few days, I had begun to conduct preliminary research to find out if there was any truth to his claims. Although he confessed to seventy-one murders, and some of the detectives who had interrogated him seemed to believe this number could even be closer to one hundred, I had also learned that in 2013, he had sent a former air force criminal investigator, Rob Fitzgerald, on a wild, aimless hunt for bodies that were never recovered.

By the end of their work together, Fitzgerald had utilized over $100,000 of search gear, hired volunteers, and included a bloodhound in his search efforts, which took place every weekend. Gary would provide him with locations of where he left victims that were yet to be found, claiming there were at least thirty-one more, and Fitzgerald would search relentlessly, only to find nothing. Eventually, Fitzgerald seemed to give up. From what I understood, he was no longer involved in this investigation in which Gary seemed to be the maestro, leading him, and now possibly me, into an endless chase.

Still, I decided to give Gary the benefit of the doubt. What harm could there be in listening to what the man had to say and maybe conducting some research? I had no intention of booking a flight to Washington anytime soon to finish where Fitzgerald left off. Gary would have to provide me with something more substantial. However, I wasn't sure what I would consider substantial, or how I would ever detect his truth from his lies.

If I had listened to logic, I would never have answered his calls again. Since he had already led Fitzgerald on a wild goose chase, why wouldn't he want to do the same thing to me? Worse, his intention could have been to put me in danger when sending me off on said wild goose chase. After all, he was a serial killer responsible for killing forty-nine women, if not more, so wanting to hurt me, even if it was indirectly, could have been his only reason for responding to my letter. However, my curiosity was more powerful than logic.

What could be unearthed from his seventy-two years of unusual, wicked life? I felt on a deep level that I needed to listen to him. Besides, wasn't that why I had started my website, to listen to what incarcerated people had to say, regardless of my feelings about it?

"Well, how many are still out there?" I asked.

"How many?" he repeated my question, another of his idiosyncrasies I'd come to learn. Did he do that to show he understood the question, or was he trying to come up with an answer, whether it was true or not? "There's the forty-nine I was convicted for, but there's more. Jane Does," he repeated.

Once more, it felt like he was presenting me with a riddle I was unsure if even he, the mastermind inventor of it, could solve. The conversation seemed to go nowhere, like a fish swimming back and forth in a tank or a caged animal pacing the same steps for its entire life. Interviewing him and researching anything would be difficult, yet the challenge felt worth it. Intuition maintained a powerful grip on me, keeping me in its custody. I knew I had to see this through, wherever it took me. Right now, I simply needed a starting point, which Gary could not seem to provide.

Instead, I circled back to the initial purpose of my letter: Was my website even a thought in his mind? He had failed to give me a direct answer, something I'd come to realize he'd often do whenever I'd ask him almost anything.

"Gary, is this the story you'd want featured on my website, finding these missing women?"

Before he could answer, we were interrupted by the mechanical woman announcing that we only had a minute remaining before we'd be disconnected.

"I'm really sorry I didn't set up a phone account in time. I will get a GTL," I assured him.

He neither forgave me nor acknowledged what I had said.

"This call's going to end," he cautioned.

"Can you call me again tomorrow?"

"Uh—tomorrow. Uh, let me think." He seemed to have forgotten the day of the week or if he had already made plans to do something else.

I briefly wondered what schedule he kept and how much freedom he had to choose his own activities. As he continued to scramble for an answer, I reminded him, "Tomorrow's Friday."

"Yeah, I'll call you tomorrow," he finally said as the robotic woman's voice spoke over him to inform us the thirty-second countdown had begun.

Later, I'd learn that Fridays were one of his designated shower days. He never even had the opportunity to make a call on a Friday, unless there was some monumental disruption to the otherwise clockwork prison routine, like a holiday or the mistake of a new officer.

After we hung up, I stood in my kitchen for an indeterminate amount of time, staring at dishes piled in the sink. It felt as though I was intruding upon a scene from another person's life, as though I had been transported somewhere else during those previous five minutes.

Would I ever learn anything more from him about the "Jane Does" he seemed so adamant on finding? What had their lives been like before he had taken them?

Nearly an hour passed, and my kitchen still remained a mess. I had finally managed to sit down at the table, running my fingers over the dribbles of sauce splatter now dried to the wooden surface. By this time, I had started to berate myself. *How could I not have set up a phone account in time? I'm so fucking stupid. I had all week*, I thought, tapping my fingers on the edge of the table.

Although he seemed indifferent about the phone account and said he'd call back tomorrow, on some level, I believed my unpreparedness had caused him to doubt my investment in his story, the worst possible impression you could ever make on a potential subject.

But he did say he'd call back, I reminded myself. This time I'd be ready. Still sitting at the kitchen table, I put my phone down in front of me. I googled GTL, and within minutes set up an account and purchased fifty dollars' worth of minutes.

* * *

In between classes on Friday, I checked my phone obsessively. Both times he had called in the evening, so I expected to hear from him much later. However, I did not know his schedule, so I figured he could call anytime. I imagined what I'd do if he called while I was teaching. No one seemed to be listening anyway, so I would mute the screen like a boring TV show.

But he didn't call.

When I returned home I did everything I could to calm the anticipation that grew each hour. I dusted the living room furniture, put towels in the washing machine, and ordered a pizza I barely ate. I was certain he'd call by dinnertime. I practiced what I would ask him about the other women he claimed to have killed. Where did he leave them? Did he remember anything about their physical features? Did he know anything about their identities, their lives, or how they ended up on the streets?

The departing sun left behind a sky tacked with stars. On my balcony, I sat in a rocking chair, trying to connect the dots of a constellation, but found no shape. I clutched my phone, waiting. By this time it was ten PM in New York, but it was seven PM where he was across the country. Could he still call? I had no idea, but I waited anyway, expecting him to. Why I had put so much stock into his word, I had no idea. Serial killers were known to be pathological liars.

But he seemed adamant about speaking with me. Why would he ask for my help and then never call back?

Maybe a lockdown in the prison prevented him from leaving his cell, I reasoned. As I explored the possibilities why a lockdown would occur—a fight on his unit, a Covid outbreak, an assault on an officer—the hours passed. By midnight, I knew I wouldn't learn anything else about those unsolved cases that day.

* * *

Weeks passed without a word from him. I wrote him letters, but they remained unanswered. In each one I reminded him of our conversations about the missing women and informed him I now had a functional GTL account. I even sent him pages from my website, including my bio. I hated the idea of him having a photo of me, but I tried to put myself in his shoes—not those of a serial killer, but someone who had no freedom and no way of googling who they were speaking to. If I was going to divulge important moments from my past to a stranger, I'd want to know what that person looked like, I reasoned. A lot could be understood from a face—intentions, kindness, warmth—eyes, especially, reveal truths otherwise hidden. Maybe seeing me would lull any doubts he might've had about corresponding with me; if anything, I'd become more real to him, a face to match my words, my name.

But it was as though we had never spoken at all, like I was writing to a person that didn't exist. *Could he have died?* I wondered one night in November. I was certain his death would make the national news, but then again, prisons had extraordinarily high death rates during the pandemic, and they were almost certainly trying to understate those numbers or were at least disorganized enough that someone might slip through the cracks. Why would he be exempt? Just because he was the Green River Killer? His notoriety could be even more of a reason for the prison to keep any news of him quiet. They'd probably hate for him to receive more attention.

The more I thought about it, the more it seemed possible that he could be sick or dead. He wasn't exactly young. I decided to call the prison to find out.

An officer answered, his name sounding like gibberish in the static reception.

"I'm wondering if you'd be able to tell me if someone over there is doing okay, ya know, with Covid and all," I clumsily managed to question.

"DOC number?"

"866218." I read my scribbled writing from a Post-it and could hear the *click-clack* of the officer typing on a keyboard. I felt squeamish and uncomfortable at the thought of Gary's name flashing across a screen due to my inquiry.

The officer paused, and I contemplated hanging up. I imagined him shaking his head in disgust or rolling his eyes in annoyance.

"He's fine."

"He's able to make phone calls?" I didn't know what I was expecting to hear; no matter what he told me, it seemed I'd be left surprised.

"Yes, he is."

"Okay, thanks," I said.

Sure, it was reassuring to know he wasn't ill or dead, since that meant we could still finish our conversation about the Jane Does, but it also confirmed that he was deliberately ignoring me. Maybe not setting up a GTL account in time really did piss him off. Whatever it was, it seemed unlikely he would ever call me again.

Still, I felt compelled to reach out to him one more time. There was a reason he answered my first letter, and the desire to find out why consumed me. It didn't make sense that he would eagerly seek out my help only to ignore me, but this was also a man who was suspected to have killed close to a hundred women for his own personal satisfaction. Perhaps ignoring me now satisfied him, too.

When I opened my mailbox at the post office one day in the middle of December to find an envelope typed with his name in black font, my belief that I should persist was affirmed. I hid the envelope under my crossed arms, not wanting anyone to see it. Pushing my way through the crowd of last-minute gift senders, my heart beat fast. Cold wind slapped against me the quicker I walked. The muscles in my legs burned as if I was running for my life. I couldn't wait to be in the confines of my car to tear open the seal.

The neat fold of the paper caught my eye first and then his signature, black and precise cursive, like an example from one of those old penmanship school workbooks, as though he took his time weaving his letters together. But I knew he didn't.

As I read the typed letter, I knew I had not made any progress at all. This was not a direct response to any of the letters I had sent him over the last two months. I had seen this letter before on murderabilia websites; it was the generic one a third party—a Seventh Day Adventist group in Michigan—sent to just about anyone who wrote to him. Apparently, since his incarceration, he had been flooded with so much mail he needed to recruit people to help him manage it. From what I understood, he would send bundles of his mail to these go-betweens, who would then write responses on his behalf. The only thing that changed from one letter to the next was the name of the recipient. The rest was a template of his spiritual journey and his supposed poor health that I knew was a lie, since the prison had confirmed to me he was perfectly fine.

I studied one of the paragraphs at least a dozen times: "After many years of serving the god of this world, and sinning against the God of Heaven as well as my fellow human beings, I turned my entire life over to Jesus. I am a 'new creature IN CHRIST JESUS' and my heart is full of joy."

You've got to be kidding me. I recalled his voice during our phone calls full of enthusiasm. He was eager to talk about the women he killed, not Jesus. Was it even possible that he was truly religious?

I then reread the line: "Although I am not able, due to health reasons, to personally answer your letter, I wish to share briefly what is happening in my life."

What a crock of shit. You already responded and with a fucking phone call!

Clearly, he was lying about his health to avoid responding to anyone. For most people, this generic letter would be enough, a conversation starter among friends, something to show off on Instagram. But I was not most people. I needed to know about the other cases he mentioned. I needed to understand something about him. Anything.

Besides, he *did* "personally answer" my letter already. What was it about that first letter that caught his attention enough to call me, a writer, the type of person he normally avoided at all costs? And what had happened in the interim for him to now ignore me, and worse, cast me off into the pile of others who wrote to him, unworthy of a thoughtful response? It didn't make sense.

As I slid the letter back in the envelope, I noticed there was something else stuffed inside. Pocket-sized religious tracts littered my lap as I shook them free. Each of them were titled *Signs of the Times* with unique subtitles: "Someone Cares About You," "A Love Letter from Jesus," "Bible Facts about the Sabbath and the First Day of the Week," "When Jesus Comes Again," "Adventist Christians," "Economic Crisis and Your Future," "You Can Trust the Bible," and my personal favorite, "Judgement Day: Are You Ready?"

Was he really just another prison cliché finding Jesus in the confines of his cell? On the surface it seemed like it, but the more I thought about it, I wondered if his "transformation" revealed something else about him. Whatever it was, I would never figure it out by this meaningless, impersonal blueprint of a letter.

As far as I knew, prior to confessing, he was able to fool nearly everyone in his life into believing he was a decent person. Was he trying to do the same thing now with public opinion?

Rather than being angry, I was intrigued by his fucked-up thought process and his agenda I could not grasp, no matter how hard I tried.

Although this letter felt like an enormous *fuck you*, as I started to drive home I decided I'd answer it anyway.

For the rest of the night I scrolled through Amazon for a religious gift to send to this new man of God. My search ended on an adult coloring book, *Psalms in Color*, which consisted of sixty-five pages of complex pictures of religious symbols and scripture to shade in with colored pencils or markers. I figured since he painted trucks for a living he might have the patience and meticulous attention to shade in the looping patterns of font and intricate designs of flowers and crosses for hours on end.

I attached a holiday card thanking him for his letter and wishing him a Merry Christmas and to feel better soon. I played along, something I'd find myself doing for the next two years as I was assigned to a variety of different roles, both as a character in a theatrical act and a pawn in a sadistic game.

A few weeks later, he called.

CHAPTER THREE
Unsolved Cases

The sliding glass door—opened to a slit—let freezing air infiltrate the room. Nestled on the couch with a blanket wrapped around me, I was too tired to move. I'd deal with the cold, I decided, hugging a pillow to my body.

It was Sunday night, and dread for the upcoming week started to consume me. The thought of those brain-dead Covid classrooms, empty and drab, made me contemplate calling out sick. What excuse could I give this time? Before I could ponder the most convincing lie, my phone buzzed.

I expected no one and intended to reject the call. But then I saw *that* number, the one I had been waiting on for months. I accepted the call and let the blanket fall from my body as I stood up. Suddenly, the room felt like an inferno.

The same automated message greeted me, but this time there were pauses between the words as if the robotic woman had forgotten her script. I said "hello" over and over to dead air. *Please don't disconnect. Please don't hang up.*

But then I heard his voice. Just like the times before, he sounded cheerful and spirited, like an old friend basking in a reunion, except the reception was muffled, making some of his words inaudible. I was left no choice but to ask him to repeat himself; I couldn't be sure if he asked me if anything new was happening in New York.

However, he quickly moved on; whether out of annoyance, impatience, or nervousness, it was hard to tell.

"I was just wondering, do you have any more information on my case?"

Straight to business.

I expected him to acknowledge the months that had passed since we had last spoken, to provide some type of reason for his silence, an apology for not calling when he said he would, but he acted as though no time had elapsed at all. Did he truly have no concept of time? I wanted to ask why he didn't respond to the mail I had sent him the past couple months, but instead, I responded, "What do you mean, exactly?"

"I was just wondering, did you get a chance to look at the forty-nine convicted—convictions of my case? You ever see that?"

"I know about your convictions," I assured him. "But I'm not sure what you're asking, exactly."

"There's forty-nine. It tells you about when they disappeared." He continued talking in circles, barely making sense before he went on to complain that the printout in his possession with these details happened to be typed in such a small font, he'd need a magnifying glass to read it. In prison, he lacked this resource.

"The printed convictions has the date the person disappeared . . . what day of the week of the disappearance—write that down on a piece of paper," he commanded.

I yanked a notepad from the side of my refrigerator, ripping away the grocery list for the week, not sure what he was about to tell me. But I soon realized he meant for me to research this later on the internet and then send those dates to him, as a way to possibly trigger his memory.

Then it dawned on me: he wanted me to help him sort out his kills. *What a fucking task.* I couldn't quite believe it, nor did I know where to begin or how to accomplish such an endeavor.

"Can you also send me the convictions, the forty-nine confirmed convictions and thirty-two other cases? Can you get that, too?"

Did he just say thirty-two? Did I hear him correctly? I knew he had admitted to this before, but to hear it in his own words changed everything. It was like looking at a knife from across the room and then feeling the sharp blade drawn to my throat. I wanted to ask so many questions—who were these other women, when did he kill them, and why, why, why? But it seemed he didn't even know these answers, which was the reason he was seeking my assistance.

"Sure, I can get that for you."

At least I hope I can.

"The idea is you have many cases that come up on my case. Did you ever notice that? Did you ever see that?" He pushed in a way that felt like he was backing me into a corner, like he was the one seeking a story from me.

"Well, I—"

"It tells you that a body was found a mile away from some of the convicted kills. Someone else is out there putting them in my spot . . . did you notice that?"

"No, I did not."

Just like the last time he called, it felt as though he was testing me, and I was failing miserably. Yet, he didn't seem to mind, as he continued his attempt at an explanation that ended up a long-winded ramble I was committed to deciphering.

"It's surprising. I put them in private sites, right? Why are other people killing people and putting them in my sites? Do you know that?"

"So you're saying other people killed in the same area you did?"

"Yeah. At the same time I killed—so they got two people [who] killed in the same area I had for twenty years or whatever it is ya know, and they're all in the same area I was. Do you know other serial killers out there killed people and put them in the same sites? Do you know that? . . . Why do other serial killers kill people in the same sites as mine, ya know?"

I'd learn much later that during the late '80s and throughout the '90s and early 2000s, several bodies of young women involved in prostitution were, in fact, discovered strangled to death in locations close to his "cluster" sites, as he'd often call them. However, those cases would remain unsolved, despite the evidence pointing to him. The local newspapers would also claim another serial killer was responsible, not the Green River Killer, which I suspected could have been an attempt to lessen the public's fear and salvage the reputation of the King County Sheriff's Office, who took nearly twenty years to arrest Gary.

At the time, I didn't realize the subtle confession he might have been offering to me. It would take years of research to understand much of what he told me, to pluck the truth from the lies.

"Why do *you* think they put them in the same areas?"

He tried to clarify his intangible, jumbled logic, instructing me to "Write down the date they disappeared—if it [was] a Sunday or a Monday—the day of the week . . ."

"And you want this information? You want me to send it to you?"

"Yeah, go and get me a copy and put down—look at the dates 1982, '83, '84, whatever it is, and write down the day of the week, Monday or Tuesday—their disappearance . . . the date of the disappearance of the person," he ordered.

How many dates could he actually remember, and how many of these mysteries would I have to piece together on my own? I wanted to ask these questions and a million others, but he barely stopped talking.

"I killed mostly on the weekends, ya know," he recalled. "But ya know, write down a Sunday or a Monday or whatever day it is," he instructed. "You might come up with why somebody would kill in the same area that I killed."

"Wait. I'm a little unclear with what you're saying," I said.

"Well . . . why is there other unsolved killings in the same area? . . . The other forty-two victims were in the same area that I was killing people and dropping them off, ya know." As though he expected me to not notice, he changed the number from thirty-two to forty-two. I suspected he really didn't know the exact number, that he had lost count a long time ago.

"So what do *you* think that means?" I spoke firmly, without consequence, like a parent interrogating a rebellious child, hoping this tactic would lead to a more direct answer.

He paused, and for a few seconds I listened to him breathe. I couldn't tell if he was surprised or annoyed by my sudden boldness. Was he at work trying to come up with a lie, or was he contemplating the outcome of the truth, if he were to tell it?

"Well, I think why is everybody killing people—somebody else in King County and Washington killing people and putting them in my places? Why is other people doing the same thing?" Then, the truth, finally: "They're all mine," he said.

Everything he had asked had been rhetorical: *Why would someone else dump their kills in the same place as me, at the same time?* The answer was, "They wouldn't." Another serial killer wouldn't have the exact same dump sites he did, and he had wanted me to come to that conclusion through his vague questions rather than him admitting it from the start.

I couldn't help but wonder why he was confiding in *me*. What was his process in choosing me, or was it pure impulse? Dialing *my* number, *my* name falling from his tongue felt intentional, although I couldn't prove it. I knew I couldn't ask any of this in that moment, so I continued to listen, starting to believe him.

"I told them I had a lot more than eighty people, ya know," he explained. "Somebody was killing people in Seattle in the '80s. A hundred people. Okay. They think somebody was killing them in the '70s, but no bodies were found in the '70s."

Another admission of guilt? 'Somebody,' or him?

"Bodies weren't found until the '80s. It was '82, when you started, right?" I hoped he'd elaborate on whether he had killed before the '80s. But this was wishful thinking.

If Wendy Coffield was not the first woman to be strangled—her own pants tied around her neck like a noose—in the Green River, then who was his first victim, and where did he leave her?

His life during the 1970s had been a lot different from in 1982, but whether he was single, married, or a divorced single dad, it didn't seem to matter. Later on, in 1982, he killed while his son, Matthew—seven years old at the time—slept in the car. Having sex with women and killing them as soon as he climaxed, and sometimes not even climaxing at all, was something he continued to do throughout his marriage to Judith Mawson, his third wife, so he could have been doing the same thing during his marriage to Marcia Brown, his second wife, as well. There were no limits, nothing to keep sacred, except the invisible boundaries that divided both of his worlds: his perfect home life and his killing expeditions.

"Yeah, '82 is when it started. In '82," he repeated.

Before I could question him further about his actual start date, he trailed off, something I realized he did quite often. However, was he being strategic to dodge my questions, or did he really lack the ability to focus? It was hard to tell.

As much as I wanted to focus on his number of kills and what years he was active, he didn't linger on the subject. He moved on to talking about prostitutes and STDs, while I did my best to be agreeable and build common ground even as he said horrible things about women. Finally, the conversation circled back.

"Send me the list of the disappeared," he said at last. He seemed to have one motive, one use for me.

"The location with the dates and eighty-two other sites, study them yourself and basically disappearances of the case of the Green

Killer and [get] a copy and send [it] to me," he rambled his instructions to me again. "And . . . why in the hell is some of them at the same places of mine, of the other cases?" he pleaded as if I had some secret knowledge I was hiding from him, like I had been conspiring against him all along, in cahoots with an invisible enemy—as if he hadn't already said that these kills "in the same places" were his own.

Before I could ask him anything else, we were interrupted. The robotic woman cued us that the call would end in sixty seconds.

"You want to call me back?" I asked. From my previous work with inmates, I knew most phone time was extended over an hour, and sometimes even longer. With Gary it was no different.

"Yeah, I'll call you back . . . you wonder why so many people were killed at the same area I killed, " he repeated, still focused on our conversation.

"Yeah, I know," I agreed.

If the call wasn't about to be disconnected, I wondered for how long he would've continued talking about these other cases.

"I'll call you back," he repeated, "but it might cut off early . . . I'm halfway through my yard."

So, he really only gets one hour out of his cell each day. Even though I already knew this was the truth, it seemed hard to believe.

"I mean, it's up to you," I said, worried I was somehow wasting his time.

A minute later he called me back.

"There's a list—I don't know how you get it—but yeah, there's cases of [other] women who disappeared. I told them, ya know—why in the heck is other people's bodies put in the same . . . Washington parks . . . has to be Ridgway's, basically," he continued, his brain, a carousel, circling and circling the same tired ground.

Except now he was also speaking in third person. I recalled hearing Ted Bundy do this on his confession tapes years ago, and I wondered if Gary did it for the same reason, to disassociate himself from his crimes. But why only disassociate sometimes? Just minutes ago, he had no problem telling me, "They're all mine" when discussing the victims of the unsolved cases. But now he was speaking as though "Ridgway" was a stranger neither of us knew and this was a random case we had been bantering about, like we were both some kind of true crime sleuths sharing an obsession. I couldn't figure him out.

"I think they ignored the cases because they didn't want Washington to be known as the killer capital of the world," he blurted out.

By "they," he meant law enforcement.

Years later I'd seriously consider the validity of this statement, but in that moment I only began to skim the surface of his chaotic depths, not realizing how far his uncharted undercurrents would eventually throw me. I knew it was crucial to start slowly with him if he would ever tell me anything significant.

"Do you know how many people you killed?" I asked. I genuinely wondered if this was a number he precisely kept track of, like the amount of money owed in a paycheck.

"Yeah, it's more than forty-nine," he said proudly.

The exact number he kept secret. I was ready to bang my head against the wall at his discretion, his vagueness. Was it possible he really didn't know how many women he had killed? Or was he safeguarding this detail for when it would benefit him to reveal it? Would I ever be privy to knowing anything specific, actionable? If so, what would it take?

He chattered on without any real direction. His mind felt abstract, something I'd always want more time to deconstruct and dissect but never would. He'd always leave me with what he gave me, nothing less or more. Puzzle pieces that may or may not fit, that he had recruited me to piece together until I found some resemblance of a picture. I tried to keep up.

"You have people—you have women—let's say prostitutes. Dancers . . . they dated a guy, and somebody kills them, ya know. When people are in the apartment, they don't give a crap—in the motel, they don't give a crap. They just want to empty out the room and throw everything away," he explained, his attempt at denoting the aftermath of killing these women. According to him, no one cared when any of these women went missing.

I pictured the motel rooms, the kind no one wants to stay in. Last-minute options after a delayed flight or fucked-up plans. The kind that forced people to sleep in their cars or the airport instead. The kind in nearly every city reputed as where men go to fuck sleazy women. The strip along Highway 99 in SeaTac was littered with places like these. Carpeting so dirty you never rake your toes through it, a bed concealed by a stained comforter, the walls mucked and slowly falling apart, ceiling paint chipped and flaking, smoke floating in every room even when no cigarette was lit, the outdated furniture, worn fabric greasy to the touch, windows that remained closed, curtains the color of rotting teeth, hiding the ugly truth of those tiny worlds.

I hated to imagine him being right, that no one would care when a woman stopped returning to one of those rooms, that her belongings could simply be tossed into the dumpster in the back parking lot; it would be as if she had never existed at all. But I knew sometimes that could be the harsh truth. Still, did he think the uncaring of others excused his cruel actions? If no one cared about these women, did that make him feel justified to kill them? I couldn't wrap my head around what he intended to be the message of his storytelling, but it seemed he really wanted to highlight the fact that no one cared about the women he killed.

"You have a birth certificate, you have your pictures of your brothers and sisters, you have a marriage license or divorce or death certificate or something like that. Why in the heck would you leave them in the apartment? Why would you leave your personal information in the motel? Wouldn't you . . . call [the police] and say this woman's missing?" He critiqued those involved in these cases as though he had not been involved himself, as if he had not killed anyone.

I couldn't believe his disassociation. All I could muster up was, "I don't know," and I truly didn't.

He continued to argue his convoluted point as if it was his goal to get me on his side, but for what reason, I had no idea. What was he trying to prove?

"Why—half the people there—you got—let's say you got, what is it, forty-nine—let's say eighty people, ninety people, ya know. That is a lot of people killed that are prostitutes in [King County] . . . so you look at that and you study it—why in the heck—how many of those, the women, the forty-nine killed, were they ever reported missing? If they were reported missing, that's fine, but most of them probably weren't reported. . . . If they were reported missing at the motel . . . they'd probably say well, this woman left all her . . . weed or drugs, or heroin, and their clothes and their kids' pictures and their family album or something like that. Why didn't the task force go to the motels and find out who was missing from their property, ya know?"

How easily he blamed everyone else—roommates, motel workers, the task force—for not finding these women. Didn't he realize all this could have been prevented if he simply didn't kill them? I wanted to ask this, but I couldn't find the courage. The last thing I wanted was to offend him.

The more I listened to him point the blame at everyone else, he made it seem as though killing was unavoidable for him, something he couldn't do without, much like consuming food and water and breathing air, something out of his control.

To oblige him, I asked, "So do you think it wasn't properly investigated, that it went on longer than it needed to?"

"Yeah, that could be, that could be—you gotta ask yourself, why did somebody hide that from the public, ya know? And why do you think—why did they hide it? . . . Because they didn't want the public to know that someone . . . killed more than what he said he did," he pressed on, like he was trying to win a debate against an invisible opponent. I was certain he had killed more than forty-nine women, but aside from that, it was hard to say what else I believed.

"In the papers there, one of the women missing was this ten-year-old—nine years old." Without warning, he had shifted the conversation to a new subject. I tried hard not to have a reaction, but how could I not?

"Wait, you said a nine-year-old girl?" He could sense the disgust in my voice despite my efforts to conceal it.

"See, I was going to say there was a nine-year-old woman—girl—I'll tell you what. I think my ex-wife was living in the same apartment."

"Wait—what?" Sucking in my breath, I braced myself for whatever convoluted story he was about to tell.

"Yeah, my ex-wife was living in an apartment—the same apartment that a nine-year-old girl [went] missing, and it's strange . . . I called the sheriff's department on a nine-year-old or ten-year-old girl, ya know. I tell myself . . . you don't want a nine-year-old, but a lot of guys will take a nine-year-old," he said, his tone mellow, as if to buffer the ugly truth of his words. Yet, the way he told me this was like a parent telling a child something they didn't want to hear—something as trivial as an early bedtime—he couldn't seem to avoid the responsibility of being the one to inform me of the nauseating, crude nature of some men, of most likely himself.

Had a nine-year-old girl actually gone missing? And if so, had he actually called the police to report it? Was he trying to convince me he had some kind of conscience, that his violence had boundaries he wouldn't cross? A nine-year-old was where he drew the line.

"I was pissed off, and I said I think I'll go out and get a gun and shoot him," he added.

* * *

In that moment, I desperately wanted to have faith in him, that he could possess even a shred of decency. To believe otherwise, the totality of a monster in human form, was too hard to accept.

I would eventually learn that a nine-year-old girl never went missing from the Edgewood Apartments in Tukwila where his third wife, Judith, had lived in 1985. He had made up the entire story. However, he did come across a young girl—eight or nine years old—on the street. He later admitted to detectives, although he felt she was too young to be a prostitute, if the opportunity presented itself and he had enough time when he passed her, he would have been tempted to pick her up and possibly have sex with her and kill her. It wouldn't have been any more special than "killing a thirteen-year-old or fourteen-year-old" that he already killed, he noted.

Years would pass until I could detect a pattern, his tapestry of what he *wanted* me to see, his imperceptible mission to convince me he was a "good guy," dependable as a bird's morning song, someone I could trust with my life, even though he was one of the country's most infamous serial killers.

On the early calls with Gary, it was difficult, if not impossible, to parse out what he was really saying underneath his labyrinth of rambling, disconnected asides. But what became clear was that he was telling me that after the Green River Task Force disbanded in the late 1980s, he hadn't stopped killing like the police and media claimed. It wasn't another serial killer with a similar method, victimology, and dump site: it was all Gary, and the claim that it was someone else seemed only an effort to preserve the reputation of the police and try to make people forget the Green River Killer.

Even during Gary's interrogation, he asked why they only focused on those forty-nine cases, and he was told it was for "political" reasons that those with more authority seemed to want to keep that number the same.

After that early call, I understood what Gary was really saying, and what he was asking for regarding my help in identifying the Jane Does. He was claiming that if a woman involved in prostitution was found strangled to death in or near his dump sites through the late '80s to 2001, then he killed them, and he wanted my help to prove it.

BACKGROUND AND VICTIMS

CHAPTER FOUR
His Origins

The water tower ascended toward a sky blotted with thick white clouds, the kind that if you stare at them long enough will start to resemble animals and dinosaurs or any other shape conjured by the wildness of imagination. The tower's legs crisscrossed with beams to create a makeshift ladder that ran up the steel body like a perfectly straight spine. *This has to be the one he climbed*, I thought as I slowed the car to a full stop.

During one of our conversations, Gary described that when he was a teenager he watched his brother and his friends climb the thin rails to the top, where the tank full of water sat like a bulbous head. He chickened out, refusing to follow them. The defeat and embarrassment stayed with him, the other kids' ridicule churning in his mind, tormenting him. A few nights later, instead of going to the movie theater with everyone else, he returned to the water tower alone. He hopped over the fence, the flimsy chain links wobbling under his feet. As he stood on the grass, he beheld the height of it, how far he would have to climb. What was he so afraid of, anyway? Breaking every bone in his body? Becoming paralyzed? Falling to his death? Living in fear was worse. It didn't matter that no one else was there to witness him doing it; proving to himself that he was not a coward was more important.

He latched his hands onto the steel beams, the same way he would grip monkey bars at a park, and he pulled himself up. He steadied his feet on each step, taking his time, but climbing higher and higher. Then the grass below him was the farthest it would ever be. The entire city glowed in the distance as if the stars had fallen atop of it, blanketing it with indestructible light. As he began to descend to the ground, he felt unbreakable. The night and the universe belonged to him, but he told no one.

As he recounted this story to me, over fifty years later, I marveled at his once-upon-a-time innocence. I stared at the water tower as if it could resurrect the child he described to me, as though if I stayed long enough, he would appear in front of me, nimble and free, not caring about anything but making it to the top. What had changed him?

Was Gary born to be the Green River Killer, or was it his childhood that turned him into the man he was today?

I thought of the seventeen-year-old girl, Shawnda Summers, that he had nicknamed "Water Tower Lady" during his confession to police. He had choked her to death after having sex with her in October 1983 and buried her in a shallow grave across from a different water tower north of the airport.

How had he gone from a boy climbing a water tower to a man trying to hide the body of a woman he had killed? I could hardly reconcile these two versions of him.

But his faulty conscience dated back long before he became an adult. Even as a child he was unflinching at the outcomes of his offenses, like they were things that just happened rather than things he *made* happen. Really, he had been doing whatever he wanted, acting entirely on impulse, and not concerning himself with consequences long before he became a serial killer.

The matches he played with as a small boy in Pocatello, Idaho, that caused a fire that burned down a garage close to where he lived, and then later, a field of grass he set ablaze near Long Lake in

Washington, where his grandfather owned property, were only two incidents that reflected his early carelessness.

When he was a kid he suffocated one of his family cats in an icebox, an act he claimed was done out of anger about the way his life was going and had nothing to do with the cat itself. "This is all the time I was wetting the bed. This is all the time I was having trouble with school," he explained to a psychologist years later, after his arrest. "I just wanted to fade away—wanted not even to be in the class," Gary said as he recalled the difficulties dyslexia presented, especially when forced to read in front of his peers. "I didn't have control over my school work . . . things that happened to me . . . but I had control over putting the cat in there," he reflected.

Around the same time, when he was about fourteen years old, he bribed his eight-year-old cousin with a penny so she would show him her vagina, and when she did, he ran his fingers over it. Shortly after, she told on him, and he received a spanking from his mother and was forced to stay in the car until his family went home. Aside from a brief conversation about why boys should never touch girls inappropriately, the incident was forgotten and never spoken about again.

Although his parents would try to teach him right from wrong, he would find his own loopholes and ultimately do what he wanted. For instance, growing up, they would tell him never to hit a woman, and he would abide by their advice, years later, strangling women instead, since technically it was different from using his fists.

As I continued to drive around his childhood neighborhood, I tried to imagine his life then, if it would have been possible to stop him from hurting anyone, a question he would even ask me sometimes. In front of Chinook Middle School, which he attended, I stared at the wooded area on the other side of the street where he had lured a six-year-old boy to stab him just to know what it felt like.

The boy had been playing cowboys and Indians alone and unsupervised when Gary ran into him. *How easy it would be to stab him with the knife he had been carrying in his pocket*, Gary thought.

"There are other kids out to kill you," Gary lied, trying to invoke fear into the kid. Terrified, the boy listened to Gary's advice, that he should hide by lying down in the tall grass across the street. As Gary laid beside him, he drew his knife and pushed the blade deep into the boy's stomach, puncturing his liver. As blood soaked through the kid's clothes, he stared at Gary, horrified, while trying to make sense of why anyone would want to harm him, let alone kill him.

But Gary had no reason besides his own curiosity coupled with the anger he had been harboring. As if he had been told a good joke, Gary stood over the kid, laughing. "Don't worry, you'll be dead soon," he taunted before wiping the blood from the blade on the kid's shirt and walking away. But rather than dying, the kid spent a month in the hospital recovering, and as usual, Gary never faced any consequences but his own fear of being caught, which subsided as more time passed. Not getting caught became a regular occurrence, and his violent behavior only worsened.

During one of our phone calls, he admitted that he should have been arrested long before he ever became the Green River Killer. When he was a teenager, he had been "playing around" with a girl while they were watching a movie together. Not caring that she was trying to push him away, he did not stop putting his hands down her pants, his fingers inside of her.

"I probably would've gotten arrested if the parents found out . . . Fingering . . . with your body parts. You're raping her, basically," he reflected.

"And she wasn't consenting?"

"No . . . she didn't want it in her vagina, basically."

"She didn't? She said not to do that?"

"So, I put another one further up. But the idea is you're messing around with a damn thing like that . . . you're watching a movie, and you're playing around with her, and you stop because you can't do anything in a theater. You can't hop on top of her—but that is rape. Because you're entering her body. That's rape," he acknowledged.

But he didn't seem the least bit remorseful. He was able to understand why fingering a woman against her will would be considered a criminal act, but he couldn't seem to grasp why it would be deemed vile and reprehensible.

I wondered who the girl was—if he was telling the truth. It wasn't difficult to believe, but with him, you never knew. Sometimes he lied just for the fun of it. However, since he also told law enforcement a similar story, it seemed more plausible. The only difference was in that version he blamed the girl for "leading him on."

By now, I was only a couple blocks away from South 175th Street, where the house where he spent most of his formative years stood. From the time he turned ten years old, that was the place where, behind tears, he'd talk to his dog because he felt no one else would listen to him, where he would wet the bed only to be paraded naked in shame down the hall by his mother to a bathtub filled with cold water, where his feelings of isolation grew, making him feel like he didn't "belong to the family" so he'd wonder if "they picked the wrong kid up from the hospital."

As I drove through his neighborhood, the place he told me he would always call home, I tried to find the tree he fell from when he was about sixteen years old. He recalled he had been "upside down, hanging by his feet," when he fell, slamming his head onto the pavement. "I fell down and hit my head, and I did see stars or speckles, and it hurt for a while, but five hours later I got up and started moving around," he recounted. "Maybe [I had a concussion], but I didn't give a crap. Just showing off I can do it."

It was possible his head injury could have been one of the catalysts of his increased aggression, even though he thought nothing of it. In 2011, a study showed that one in four serial killers suffered a head injury or brain condition in their early years. According to the study, when someone suffers from a traumatic brain injury, or TBI, they risk developing long-term neurocognitive issues such as loss of executive function, impulsivity, and aggression. Several other serial killers also had a history of head trauma: Keith Jesperson fell from a rope he had to climb in a high school gym class, and Richard Ramirez, Jeffrey Dahmer, John Wayne Gacy, and Ed Gein all admitted to experiencing some kind of head trauma when they were young.

Maybe Gary was no exception, and his violence was an inevitability after that fall. Or could it have been a combination of everything—his upbringing, a genetic disposition in his brain never allowing him to feel empathy, his ability to evade punishment and consequences, his anger at his learning difficulties and the way he was belittled because of them—that led him to become a serial killer? If he had lived somewhere else and had been part of a different family, would he still have become the Green River Killer? There was no way of knowing, but I couldn't stop imagining all the scenarios that could have made him someone else.

—

It wasn't until Gary was in his thirties that he killed a woman for the first time, or so he claimed. But like his childhood, his early adulthood was marked with violent indicators of the killer he would later become.

In 1972, after Gary's first divorce, he joined a singles club called Great Expectations, an antiquated version of Tinder. For fifty dollars, the guys who joined would get to meet at least three women a month, dates that would start out at a coffee shop or at his apartment drinking wine and would end in his bed. When he suggested to one woman that they spend the afternoon at a small lake in a wooded area in Maple Valley, he assumed sex would be guaranteed.

After spreading a blanket on the grass, they talked for a while with the sun beating down on them. As the woman spoke, Gary noticed she slurred her speech, although she did not appear to be drunk. He wondered if she was maybe mentally handicapped or if she had a speech impediment. Either way, he thought she was beautiful, so it didn't really matter to him.

When it became too warm, Gary removed his shirt, believing they would both be naked soon. Aside from a woman who had passed walking with a horse, they seemed to be completely alone. When minutes went by without seeing anyone else, Gary began to kiss her, moving his hands over her body. He began to unbutton her shirt and pull her pants down, but the girl pushed his hands away. He couldn't believe it. He continued to try to remove her clothing, even ripping her blouse in the process, while she attempted to control his hands, which were now around her throat. He squeezed tighter and watched her face redden.

When he realized he was actually hurting her, he "caught" himself and relaxed his hands, letting her jump up from him. As she gasped for air, he repeated he was sorry and offered to buy her a new blouse. "I've never done that before," he said, upset with himself. From what he recalled, that was the first woman he had ever choked.

Although it looked like she was crying, he couldn't be sure if her face was red from the lack of air in her lungs. When she didn't say anything, he suggested they leave. Rather than drive her directly to her house, he asked if she would prefer to be dropped off somewhere else. "I didn't think I was gonna be able to get another date from her. And I didn't want her to be feeling that I know where she is and I'm gonna come back [to] hurt her," he told detectives after his arrest decades later.

By the time he was married to Marcia in 1973, he had also held a knife to a woman's throat after picking her up in Renton. Since he didn't want to pay her for sex, he forced her to give him her purse before kicking her out of his truck. It seemed that his violence was becoming a regular occurrence, something he resorted to whenever he didn't get his way, and his anger consumed him. During his marriage to Marcia, it only escalated, but when we talked about those years, he portrayed himself as a good husband.

Ater accessing Marcia's unredacted witness statements from 1986 and 2001, I would learn that Gary was, in fact, distorting the truth as he told it to me, excluding all the things that would define him not only as a shitty husband, but someone who evoked fear. He did not tell me that when returning home from a party one night as Marcia was entering the house, he snuck up behind her and began choking her. "It was getting tighter and tighter, and I thought it was somebody else . . . and I started screaming, and then I realized it was him, and I started fighting him, and he finally let go, and he kind of pushed me. By the time I got my balance back, he had walked around the other side of the van and tried to convince me that there was somebody else there and that they had run off, so I tried to get him to call the police, but he wouldn't do it. But I knew it was Gary," Marcia reflected.

Marcia described that throughout their seven-year marriage, "There were a lot of times he'd get mad and start to hit me and stop, and just that last time after we had split up and he got mad and he hit me, and I threw the vacuum cleaner at him." Following that altercation, Gary filed a report with the police, trying to be perceived as the victim.

When Marcia agreed to let him tie her up during sex, she said, "He put his hand over my mouth and nose . . . kept me from breathing, or a pillow once or twice." These encounters would serve as precursors to killing prostitutes a few years later. Yet, in Gary's recollection, he erased these parts of the story, revising his own history in real time as we spoke.

Following his divorce from Marcia, he would continue to take out his anger on the women he perceived as the most vulnerable: prostitutes. However, in the beginning, he would try to "catch" himself and stop before the point of death.

When he picked up a woman in 1981 and parked in Skyway or Central District—he couldn't remember—and had sex with her, he wondered if he had kept his arm wrapped around her neck for too long. Since she did not let him "ejaculate in her," he couldn't reach a climax. He'd be damned if he was going to pay for it when he got nothing out of it.

As the woman dressed, he watched her zip up her red boots, a detail vibrant in his mind. As soon as she turned her back to him to exit the truck, he began to choke her. "I pulled her out of the truck and left her in the street . . . I laid her down so she wouldn't have a headache . . . dropping on cement you'd get a headache and get pissed off and turn me in . . . but evidently I choked her too long and . . . she wet her pants . . . and I thought she was alive," he recalled, unsure if he had killed her. During this time when he would choke women, he did not plan on killing them. If this one had died, in his mind, it was an accident.

If he only choked them unconscious, he figured what harm was he really causing except the trouble it could mean for him later on? If anyone reported him, he would end up in jail. Still, that didn't deter him. He reasoned that most prostitutes feared the cops and the repercussions they could face for working on the street. That alone was enough to cause any desire for justice to fall to the wayside.

By 1982, his violence had become almost like a habit. In the winter in a parking lot in downtown Seattle, Gary choked a woman and "left her unconscious and took her money," he explained during his interrogation. "I think I was panicking. And I put my clothes on really fast, and I think I threw my underwear out driving down the road . . . I never planned on [it]. But the opportunity was there, and she was unconscious."

The first time I visited Seattle in 2021, I walked along the same street, wondering which parking lot was part of his memory of that night. I tried to picture his truck idling, him pushing the woman out, and then speeding off, leaving her body sprawled on the pavement. Alive or dead, it didn't matter to him. All that mattered was the rush it gave him, an outlet for his anger. By then he'd found a way to find relief, to feel in control, as he tightened his grip around the woman's throat. Her feet kicked at him as she floundered beneath him, but his hands wouldn't let go. Not until her eyes shut and her entire body grew limp, no longer something he had to conquer.

When reality set in that he could get caught, he took off. "I was panicking and never thought about a pulse. I didn't think about putting my head on her chest. I had to get out of there," he admitted.

He realized that using his hands wasn't fast enough, and the woman could have leverage to grab his fingers. She was too unrestrained, squirming beneath him. He pondered his mistakes and thought about how he could fix them.

In May 1982, after drinking a few beers, he drove past a woman he believed was a prostitute. In what had become his routine, he waved at her, and she waved back, insinuating she was interested. He drove around the block to where she stood in front of the Vance Motel. He pulled into the parking lot, and she walked over to his truck. They discussed what he wanted—a blow job and sex—and she led him to her room at the motel. Once he sat on the bed, she revealed that she was actually a cop, and he was arrested.

By the next morning he was out of jail, angry for getting duped by the decoy, and still in need of a woman. On his way to work that day, he picked up two prostitutes, "a stupid mistake," he reasoned. "In the process, they pickpocketed me, took my wallet, and hopped over into the bus," he later told detectives. "That really pissed me off and was a big reason—probably one of the big reasons why—after that I started—I choked one during sometime between there, but I didn't kill her."

After that, he picked up several women he choked but didn't kill. On PAC Highway two blocks north of 188th, at around three o'clock in the afternoon, he picked up a woman and explained what he wanted and how much he was willing to spend. He then pulled alongside the wooded area behind a newspaper stand. He brought a blanket that was folded in the back of his truck and laid it on the ground. They took off their clothes, and he climbed on top of her and proceeded to have sex with her. "I come faster from behind," he told her, the same line he'd use on most of his victims. With her on all fours, he continued to have sex with her until he came. He thought of the two women who had stolen his wallet, and he felt justified in what he was about to do. *They're only gonna do it again.*

He wrapped his arm around her throat and choked her, telling her not to talk and that he would let her go if she stopped fighting him. He began to count to sixty in his head, something he would do when he was younger when he would swim under water. "I knew I could hold my breath for sixty seconds, [so] I knew I could kill her as long as I could count to sixty seconds," he recalled. But this time he didn't count long enough. She was unconscious but still breathing.

He dropped her naked body to the ground and left her there, unsure if she would die. But he was confident he had found "a better way" to choke the women. He realized if he choked them with his arm and wrapped his legs around them, he had more control over them. "I learned my lesson. No scratches," he boasted about this new choking method.

Later that night when he drove by there again, she was gone, along with all her clothes that he had left strewn beside her. He assumed she had gotten up and walked away, and for a moment he was relieved. He had not really tried to kill her. He just wanted to get some of his frustration out. Then a wave of panic came over him—what if she reported it? But like all the others, she never did.

However, by July 1982, he was doing whatever he could to never give any woman that chance again, and according to him, it was the women that were to blame.

CHAPTER FIVE
Catalysts to Kill

When I first began speaking with Gary, like most people in my position would, I asked him why he had killed so many women. "My ex-wife," he said and sighed, as he seemed to recall the sheer revulsion he felt nearly forty years ago when his first wife, Claudia, left him. I imagined him holding the phone to his ear and shaking his head in disgust at the thought of her.

"So, that was a hard time for you," I sympathized.

"Yeah, a hard time . . . The idea is you have that in your mind all the time—what the hell—a lot of times you blame your problems on your wife in a divorce . . . guys will do that . . . people that do that, they get divorced, and they take it out on the people, basically. You talk to yourself, these kind of things, ya know when you're alone by yourself, your brain's going and going," he said, trying to describe his torment.

But was her betrayal truly the catalyst for his violence? Were all the women he killed then like props to him, representing other women who hurt him, to take his pain out on, perfect recipients of his rage? I knew there was more complexity to it, that there were many factors that went into his decision to kill. Whether he was aware of them or not, was something I hoped to clarify.

"Was it a craving, want, need, passion, goal, thrill? I don't know. I'm trying to figure out myself what it was," he once told detectives.

However, by the time he and I began conversing, almost twenty years had passed since he made that statement. I wondered if by now he had more answers.

The rejection and pain he experienced as a result of women leaving him was something I tried hard to understand, a starting point, as I retraced some of his steps. I turned the corner onto 317th Street in Federal Way and pictured the scene Gary had once described to me: a moving truck parked in front, and all of his second wife's, Marcia's, possessions filling it up, the life he had built with her the last seven years disappearing. He remained powerless, incapable of stopping her. Instead, he was forced to watch his world crumble before his eyes, while someone else had all the power.

I stood in the middle of the street staring at the same quiet house, now shrouded in overgrown shrubbery that concealed all the front windows. The way he described it, moments like what he experienced in this very spot had turned him into a monster. I knew his version of reality wasn't really the case, that his cruelty grew over time, but the sobering reality of another woman leaving him, exerting her control over his life, was undoubtedly a piece of it, sending him down a path I would never want to cross.

The more I learned, the more I understood everything in his adult life that, in combination with his predisposition and his childhood, led him to kill—even though he wouldn't always say it directly. Embedded within his stories and contradictory life philosophies, the reasons he killed so many women would stare me in the face so intently, revealing the ugliness that I knew still festered inside him.

Paying child support to Marcia, making a mistake while painting a truck at work, a prostitute not performing up to his standards, having to pay for sex when he didn't want to, and anything else that would constitute as a bad day in Gary's world were all reasons for his anger, coupled with his general hatred for women. Then, there was the woman he dated from 1982 to 1984, Roxanne. Despite cheating on her with prostitutes, many of which he killed, and dating several other women behind her back, he had planned to marry her. However, during his confession to police, he would blame part of his rage on her, complaining he had gone from dating a beautiful woman, Nancy, who satisfied all his sexual needs, to Roxanne, who he did not find attractive, mostly due to her stout figure.

When Gary first told me about his experiences with his ex-wives and ex-girlfriends, the only pattern I could detect was that they had all left him. I didn't understand the complexities of their reasons nor his role in each ending, except for Judith. It was common knowledge that the exposure of his secret life as a serial killer had destroyed that marriage.

He told me only what he wanted me to know, like a politician attempting to win me over. Maybe it was his hope that if I understood the pain and rejection he endured, and the control women had over him—all the source of his rage—that would justify his reasons for killing so many of them. But, whether he knew it or not, that could never happen, no matter how sorry he tried to make me feel for him. That was not to say his partial honesty did not teach me more about who he was below the surface. Within his revisions of his own history, if I looked closely, his insecurities, anger, and need for validation became more recognizable, like grime on a dark surface under an intrusive light.

"My first one I married because she wanted to get a house," he disclosed to me one day.

By his "first one," he was referring to Claudia Kraig. They had met while both working at the Gov Mart Bazar in Burien in 1967. While he worked as a box boy stocking shelves, she was stationed at the snack bar; on breaks and throughout their shifts, they would end up chatting with each other at the counter. As their friendship progressed, Gary eventually asked her out. For the next couple of years they would date, often going for long drives in his green two-door Rambler on the weekends, sometimes as far as Snoqualmie.

Other times, they'd stay more local and go for long walks through the trails at Seward Park along Lake Washington. During many of those dates, they would have sex in his car or outdoors at a park behind Alki Beach in West Seattle. Nothing unusual or violent ever occurred during those encounters that could predict his future behavior.

When Gary graduated from high school in 1969—two years behind due to learning difficulties stemming from dyslexia—he enlisted in the navy to avoid being drafted into the army. By 1970, he had moved to San Diego, close to the navy base where he was stationed, and had asked Claudia to marry him.

"She wanted to get away from her parents. Her parents were Catholic," he explained.

In 1970, in most Catholic households it was forbidden for a woman to live on her own. Marriage ended up the only acceptable solution for a woman to gain a sense of independence, and Gary obliged.

"I wanted it to last. I wanted the marriage to last," he admitted regretfully. For him, marrying her was not just about breaking free from their parents. He envisioned a traditional family with her, one in which they raised children while he worked and she took care of the house.

"But after I married her . . . she just loved to party. And [it] led to [her] never [being] home when I was married to her. If you marry a woman, you have . . . you need roadblocks a lot, but with her, that was—every day I'd come home to—I made my mistake of thinking about it and asking her to be my wife. I don't think I married her to have sex with her, but [she] loved to party. I'd work at four o'clock and take the bus back to my apartment in San Diego. And they would go and have a party, go out and buy alcohol and beer, and she slept with the damn—like I said, she married me because she wanted to get out of the house. Well, that marriage lasted for three years," he reflected.

As Gary remembered that time in his life, I could sense his frustration. He rarely cursed, so for him to use words like "damn" or "hell" and sometimes "shit" usually meant he was pissed off. Although the tone of his voice never changed and he remained soft spoken, when he revealed that Claudia had cheated on him, he stopped himself from elaborating any further.

However, what he failed to mention was that while he was overseas in the Philippines, he also cheated on her with several prostitutes. I had stumbled upon this information years prior while watching a documentary about his case, long before I was in communication with him. It was unclear if he was aware that I possessed knowledge of his infidelity, and I didn't say anything. I waited, curious, if he would tell me that he, too, was unfaithful, that she was not entirely at fault for their failed marriage. But he continued to blame her. It seemed he wanted me to think he did nothing wrong, that he was an innocent bystander.

"I didn't divorce her until I got out of the service," he said.

On the morning Gary left San Diego, he didn't slam the door behind him to make his exit known. He didn't curse, yell, or mutter any insults under his breath. He didn't even slip into the bedroom where Claudia slept—*their* bedroom—to kiss her goodbye. He doubted she would care one way or another. The couch where he had been sleeping since he had returned home would be empty whenever she did wake up. If she did hear him rustling around the house, she would think he was only going out for a walk or a jog, his typical morning routine.

He glanced around the small, cramped rooms of the apartment they had shared whenever he wasn't deployed. Somehow he had become a guest in what was supposed to be their home. Instead of a homecoming after six months of being away, his presence was regarded more like an intrusion, unwanted and inconvenient. It was as though he had walked in on someone else's life that he was trying to take over, but it was no use. As if they were strangers rather than newlyweds, Claudia wouldn't even have sex with him, let alone return to Seattle with him. He remembered the long talk he had with his parents when he got engaged to her. They had pleaded with him not to go through with the wedding. What did they know? But now he wondered if they had been right all along. Was he really so stupid to marry the wrong woman?

He had at least expected to feel her body next to him while they slept, even if he couldn't make love to her, what he wanted more than anything else. The thought of her preferring the company of her roommate, another woman, in their bedroom while he was forced to sleep alone on the couch felt like a whip beating against his pride, bludgeoning it raw. He refused to stay there another minute.

The July San Diego air was neither warm nor cool but something in between, what anyone would consider perfect. He walked toward his blue Ford Fairlane that was parked in front. He slumped into the driver's seat, turned the key in the ignition, and pressed on the gas. He didn't look back at all.

He drove north toward Seattle, what would always be his real home—Midway, to be exact. It would take him days to get there, but it didn't matter. He looked forward to the long drive. But instead of thinking about everything that had gone wrong, he would make up for the hell he was put through. The only thing he wanted since he stepped off the ship was to have sex. In the Philippines, he had become accustomed to having sex whenever he wanted. On most nights, he would end up in a tavern, drinking with the guys. It became a routine for him to flirt with one of the barmaids until they settled on a price, usually about five to ten dollars, and she agreed to bring him home with her.

In her house that was little more like a wooden shack, they would have sex several times throughout the night before falling asleep. The woman had sex with enough sailors to know he would have to return to his ship before roll call, so as the sun began to rise, she shook him awake. "She kicks you out the door, and she goes back to sleep," he said with a laugh. "I had to be back and change from the civil clothes, the street clothes, and put on [my] uniform. And then you go to the roll call, and they can book us on the ship for the rest of the day, until five o'clock . . . and then we go back out to another tavern or the same one," he remembered.

With Claudia over six thousand miles away, it didn't matter how many women—six in total, he estimated—he had sex with over there. He still sent home his checks so she could pay the rent and the bills, so it wasn't like he'd completely abandoned her, he justified to himself. He liked to have sex at least twice a day, so what choice did he have if she wasn't there?

He figured he would be returning home to a wife that wanted him just as badly, and they would have what felt like a honeymoon, since they never really had one. After they were married, he shipped out soon after. If she wouldn't give him a real honeymoon now, he would just have to buy one, he decided.

With fifty dollars cash and a navy check for one hundred and ninety dollars in his pocket, he wouldn't have a problem. He didn't expect it would be much different in California than the Philippines, except he would have to find a woman on the street as opposed to a tavern.

A few hours later, he ended up in Los Angeles. The perfect place to find a streetwalker, he figured. He drove around a few blocks and pulled up next to an attractive young Black woman who was casually standing on the corner. She went up to the window of the car, and he told her what he wanted, a blow job and sex, and then flashed his navy check at her, proving he could afford it. He tried to negotiate a fair price, nothing more than twenty dollars, but she wouldn't consider it. She wanted his entire check. *What a greedy, racist bitch*, he seethed. But before he could cancel the date, she began to threaten that if he didn't give her the full $190, she would yell that he was raping her. Her screams would be so loud, everyone in earshot would hear her. Surely, someone would call the police, and then he would be arrested and hauled off to jail. He was terrified.

All he could think to do was appease her. He told her how badly he wanted to date her, and that he would get them a motel room. Afterward, she could have all the money. But first he would have to cash the check. As soon as he did, he would come right back and pick her up.

She seemed to believe him. But as soon as she stepped away from the car, he took off as fast as he could. Speeding along I-5, he couldn't put the thought out of his mind that she would run to the police, tell them he raped her, and give them his license plate number. It wasn't until he was out of California and in Oregon that he started to relax and consider his anger. *I just got through driving away from my wife. She didn't want to go back to Seattle. And here, I meet this nasty, disrespectful woman. Damn bitch.*

As if not having sex with Claudia or the prostitute wasn't bad enough, according to a light on his dashboard, his transmission oil was now leaking. He spotted a K-Mart and pulled over. He would have to buy oil, Stop Leak, and Handi Wipes.

In front of the store, a young girl with black hair, he guessed no older than eighteen, was trying to bum a ride to Portland. He told her he was heading in that direction, and he would be happy to take her there as long as she didn't mind waiting until he was done shopping. "I can drop you off anywhere," he assured her.

As soon as he exited the store, she followed him to his car, which was parked about a hundred feet away. She watched as he popped the hood and checked the dipstick, wiping it clean. After he finished pouring in the oil, she plopped into the seat next to him.

Before they took off, he showed her his navy check, implying he would be willing to pay her if she was willing to do more than just accept the ride. She didn't even hesitate to accept his offer.

After driving for a few miles, he pulled off and found a desolate area along the highway where they had sex. For the rest of the ride to Portland, they stopped a handful of times, having sex again and again. By morning, they arrived at Denny's, where they had breakfast. He figured he should also check on the transmission oil, so he handed her ten dollars and told her to pay for the bill while he went back to the car. But as he happened to turn around, he saw her pocket the money.

When she got back to the car, shaking his head, he said, "We have to get the hell out of here." But she didn't seem fazed at all.

Back on the road, since she had been wearing the same clothes for a couple days, she decided to change her outfit. She climbed into the back seat, rummaged through her bag, and yanked out a dress. Stripping down to her bra and then pulling the dress over her head, he glanced at her from the rearview mirror. She climbed over the seat, making sure she was close enough to his face for him to realize she wasn't wearing any underwear. Even though he wanted to keep driving farther away in case anyone from Denny's had called the police on them, he was too turned on to not pull over and have sex with her again.

Afterward, he barely stopped at all except for gas and "a few quickies." When he was too tired to drive anymore, he parked in a lot behind a motel, where they slept for a few hours. By morning, they were on the road again, but this time only for a short while. He decided to drop her off south of Portland without giving her a dime. As far as he was concerned, they had both fulfilled their obligations to each other. He got to have a lot of sex—the honeymoon he had been anticipating for days—and she got a ride to where she needed to go.

With about two hundred miles left to Seattle, he didn't want what he considered his honeymoon to end. It didn't matter if he was with his actual wife or a prostitute. It was all the same to him. He just wanted a woman to have sex with for the rest of the way.

As soon as he dropped off the last girl, he was already in search of another one in Portland. He circled the blocks around the city, but found no one. But he wasn't about to give up. He remembered Lloyd Center, a shopping mall, was only a couple miles away. He cruised by and noticed a girl, a "nice sixteen-year-old," as he described her to me, standing outside, trying to hitch a ride. He stopped to talk with her and learned she wanted to go to a town in Pierce County, Washington. She was in luck.

Along the way, they chatted about various things, and she revealed she had never seen the ocean. He wondered if she was from Timbuktu or some other remote place. He couldn't fathom anyone not seeing the ocean, so he offered to take her. He figured that would also be a great place to have sex.

In Washington, he stopped at Ocean City State Park in Hoquiam, where there was a beach. They walked on the sand and laid down a blanket, where they had sex and spent the night with the waves crashing in the distance. In the morning, they ate Campbell's chicken noodle soup straight out of the can with pieces of cardboard he turned into makeshift spoons. For a summer morning, the beach was still empty, so they were able to have sex again before leaving. *Everyone must be at church*, he thought and laughed to himself.

After passing through Aberdeen, he continued toward Seattle, leaving her somewhere in Pierce County as promised. Just like the previous girl, he didn't give her any money. He took off and didn't think about her at all; she had fulfilled her purpose.

He recounted this story to me in great detail, claiming he had never told it to anyone else before—not Claudia, not the Green River Task Force, not a friend, no one. Like most things Gary did, it was hard to understand his motive. Telling me one of his secrets could have been another ploy to gain my trust, and to keep me invested to ensure I always answered the phone when he called. Or it could have been pure and utter bullshit, another lie to tell just because he could. If he really did pick up those young women, I wondered if when he said he "dropped" them off, if he had actually killed them and left their bodies to decompose in places only he knew.

Fictious or not, there was some undeniable truth: he had never been faithful to any woman, despite his belief that having sex with prostitutes did not constitute cheating. Until the day he was arrested, he continued this behavior.

* * *

When he returned to Seattle, within a few days, he managed to find a decent apartment just south of the airport. Unsure what to do about Claudia, he tried not to think about it. He began his job at Kenworth that had been waiting for him since he graduated from high school, and he waited for the situation to resolve itself.

The following week he was neither surprised nor was he expecting to find Claudia at his doorstep. But there she was. The prospect of resuming married life, something he thoroughly enjoyed, made him feel hopeful she had followed him home to stay. That night, he tried to have sex with her, but she refused. She only wanted to talk. But to him, the conversation went nowhere.

It didn't occur to him to be honest with her that he had also made several mistakes by having sex with various women, some only days ago, and during the entire six months while he was overseas. What else was he supposed to do when he was lonely and without her? His sexual urges were simply too strong to ignore, stronger than everyone else's, he observed. What she had done, not giving him a proper honeymoon, putting him on the couch, and not coming home with him to Seattle were worse offenses. And now she was back and still didn't want to have sex with him. He couldn't figure it out.

They slept next to each other, but that was it. In the morning, she dropped him off at Kenworth and took the car for the rest of the day. She planned on visiting her parents and then later on she would pick him up.

Looking forward to being with her that night, a few hours later, he walked out of work into the parking lot, expecting to find her there waiting. He spotted his car, but she was nowhere to be found. Confused, he went back inside to see if anyone at the reception desk had seen her. The receptionist handed him his keys and a note that Claudia had left for him. She had decided to go back to San Diego.

He crumpled the letter and stormed out to the parking lot. He couldn't believe it. She had rejected him again, and this time it seemed permanent. And for what? His mind raced with possibilities, each more farfetched than the other. *She must be a prostitute*, he finally concluded. Although it was far from logical, to him it made sense. He was furious.

By the time he got home, he contemplated calling the airport and reporting that she had a bomb attached to her. Then they would have to either stop or divert the plane, and she would be arrested. Put through days of hell. As much as he wanted revenge, he knew this plan could backfire. So, he stewed instead, remembering his time with her.

He thought about all the opportunities they had to have sex on the drive down to San Diego after they were just married. But she never wanted to. They slept in rest areas for a couple nights, and that was it. Once they found an apartment, she was finally up for it, but even then, it didn't feel like there was much love between them. He didn't feel 100 percent "connected" to her like he thought he should.

As days passed, he knew she was not coming back, and he had no desire to go to San Diego to fight for her. He had been with her since 1967—four years—but now it felt like time wasted. He hated the idea of a divorce, but he had no choice. He flipped through the Yellow Pages and found a lawyer that would charge him $300. He thought it was too expensive, but he just wanted to get it over with. He mailed Claudia the paperwork, citing "cruelty" as the reason for filing for divorce. She didn't bother to challenge him, signed it, and sent it back shortly after. There were no assets to divide, no children to fight over. The whole process was quick and easy, like painting a room a different color. She seemed to erase him just the same. But to him, this was when "all shit broke loose" in his life.

In his mind, there would be no other option but for him to act on his rage one day. But first, he would wallow in it for a while, looking for any woman to replace what he had lost.

In his free time, he cruised around looking for prospective girlfriends, and he was successful. Within a month after his separation from Claudia, he met a woman named Cheryl. For a couple months, they dated and even traveled to Canada for a couple days before they both lost interest and the relationship fizzled.

Soon after, he joined a dating service where he met a woman named Camille, and within a month they moved in together, first in his place and then later in an apartment in Capitol Hill. But after a couple months, she met someone else, a deaf man, and she began to dedicate all her time to learning sign language, distancing herself from Gary until finally she left him for good.

Most of his relationships seemed to follow the same pattern: what started as intense connections ended as flat, anticlimactic conclusions he could barely remember. But when he met his second wife, Marcia, in early 1972, the cycle of short-lived romances was temporarily broken. Only a few months after his divorce from Claudia, he met Marcia while driving the Renton loop one night on his way home from the supermarket. She and a friend were in a car in the next lane when he pretended to be a cop and pulled them over. His short hair and assertive tone convinced them of his authority, so they did what he asked, terrified that they would get in trouble for drinking while driving. Idling in his red pickup, he demanded that they step out of their car and walk over to talk with him. When Marcia asked to see his ID, he began laughing, finally admitting he was not a cop. It became obvious that he had used this ruse as a way to talk with them.

As they continued their conversation, she noticed the grocery bag on the seat beside him and offered to cook him dinner. "My place or yours?" he asked smoothly. She felt safer at her own place so invited him over, where she did in fact cook him dinner. After eating together, they watched TV, and he went home. Within a couple weeks, they were dating, and six months later she had moved into his apartment. The next year, in December 1973, they were married.

However, rather than telling me anything about their marriage, he focused on their separation and then their contentious divorce.

"My second wife, she was into country western singing, and her parents went out to sing. I'd come over Saturday nights, and [they'd] pick up the guitars and the banjo and sing all kinds of music. Then she got into the damn—we had one child . . . the tubes wrapped around him, and [she] had to have a C-section," he recalled.

As I listened to him, I noticed that he again interrupted himself the moment he remembered something he didn't want to. In this case, it was when Marcia joined a band, making her less available to him.

"She got a band together after my separation, and she would play all these clubs . . . like the Eagles," he continued, reluctant at first. "Then she started smoking, and I don't like a woman smoking. She was my wife," he said.

As he listed Marcia's faults, he never once pointed out any of his own. Just like Claudia, he blamed Marcia for all the problems in their marriage. As I expected him to continue with his litany of Marcia's mistakes, without warning, the thought of smoking prompted the opportune time for him to tell me the first of many dirty jokes.

"You ever heard the [joke] if you ask your wife why [she's] smoking?"

"No, why is she smoking?" I asked, curious.

"She said, 'I'm never licked between my legs.'"

He waited for my reaction before letting out even a chuckle. Once he heard me laugh at the punch line, he also joined in, becoming more at ease. It was obvious that he was seeking my reassurance that there really were no restrictions as to what he could say to me during our daily calls.

"That is the thing. It's kinda nice to break up the monotony and have somebody to joke with," he commented.

He had said something similar on a recent call, and I had ignored it, but that he was saying it again alarmed me. As much as I stupidly wished he was just being nice, he was a serial killer. All his interpersonal charm was fueled by a dark desire I never wanted to confront.

If he was starting to view me as a romantic interest rather than a writer, was there a way to stop him? Although I hoped he was telling me more about his past with the intention to help me understand his perspective, I knew he could have been mimicking the kind of conversation people would have on a third date. The thought terrified me. So, I avoided it. I was relieved when, possibly picking up on my apprehension, he redirected himself to continue telling me about his separation from Marcia.

"She was out to have a good time dancing. I'd get off of work at midnight, [and] I'd pick up my son because I [was] working night shift, and she wasn't home. So, one o'clock in the morning she'd drive in and get up to go to—she went to dental school to be a dentist assistant—and so I had him all day, took him over to my parents, but by seven o'clock at night she [was] supposed to pick him up, but a lot of times she didn't," he explained.

Without knowing his background, it'd be easy to believe that he was simply a hardworking man also trying to be a responsible father. Hearing only his version of the story, in which he accused his ex-wife of neglecting their son as she hung out in dingy bars until all hours of night, I began to feel sorry for him. The more he portrayed himself as the victim, the more he garnered sympathy from me, something he seemed to feed off, down to the bare bone.

"And this was after you worked all night? You would then have to get your son?" I asked, indulging him.

"Yeah, eight hours or ten hours, I'd go home, and I'd pick up my son," he said, responding to my pity. "He'd be wide awake at one o'clock in the morning, so we'd stop by the doughnut place, and [I'd get] a doughnut for him, and on the way home—it was a half hour drive—he'd pass out on the seat, so I'd take him and put him to bed," he finished, laughing in between his words, as if happy to be reliving the memory.

"He didn't get up [until] seven o'clock or eight o'clock in the morning," he continued. "[I'd] give him breakfast, and he wasn't in school, so I'd take him over to my parents at two o'clock, let them babysit until five, and then Marcia would come by and pick him up, but a lot of times she wouldn't, so they kept him until midnight. I had a key to the house, and I'd just pick him up off the couch and take him out the front door," Gary remembered.

As he relived this routine from 1979, it was clear he wanted me to understand the amount of pressure he was under.

"Then after a while, she split up from me," he added somberly. "It was on a holiday . . . a Monday. She decided to move out. I wondered why she [said], 'You better take [Matthew] over to IHOP.' We went over there and had breakfast . . . I took him home, and I snuck through the back way, and she was moving out. A guy came over with a van and helped her move out of the house."

As he spoke, I could hear the frustration and bitterness in his voice, as if he was standing in the yard, powerless, watching her leave him all over again.

"And she didn't tell you this? She just did it?" I asked.

"She didn't tell me anything about it."

"Wow, that's messed up," I sympathized.

However, I wondered if he had done something that prompted her to leave without warning. I knew that when a woman plans an escape from a man in secret, usually she does so to flee from an abusive situation, out of fear of how the man will react to the news of her departure. I was certain there were important parts of the story he was deliberately omitting. Later I would learn the truth of his violence toward her. I also knew that when his marriage to Marcia began to fall apart, he had sex with prostitutes, reasoning that since he wasn't getting it at home, he had no choice but to get it somewhere else.

"Yeah," he said and chuckled, glad that I seemed to be on his side. "You know how women are, and men are. She took half of me."

I assumed he was referring to his son, since Marcia left with Matthew along with all her belongings, but he could have also been referring to the $200 a month in child support he had to pay.

At the time of our conversation, I considered that he could have tried to do right by her, that maybe she did not want to be tied down by the responsibilities of being a full-time wife and mother, that her own independence meant more than anything a family with Gary could give her. However, I eventually learned that she had many reasons to leave, her own safety at the top of the list. But while we spoke, he made sure I remained unaware of his budding violence toward Marcia.

Although there could have been times when Marcia didn't "fulfill her obligations," he failed to mention that throughout most of their relationship, he was distant and uncommunicative. "There was no real relationship. I felt he just wanted somebody to keep up house, clean for him, and do the shopping and cooking, and he was always in the garage with his cars . . . all he wanted was food and sex, and that was it. There was no communication, and any time we did talk, it would end up in an argument," Marcia said.

The contrast between what he wanted me to believe and what actually happened was severe—but at the time, I had no idea of the degree of his manipulation. I simply listened with curiosity and an open mind. Since there were instances when he was honest to some extent, it was difficult to identify his lies.

Just like when his marriage to Claudia ended and he quickly began dating other women, when he separated from Marcia in 1981, it was no different. During our conversations, he told me about his time with Nancy, another failed relationship in which he portrayed himself as innocent of any wrongdoing.

They had both been members of Parents Without Partners (PWP), an organization that held dances, trips, and weekly meetings for single mothers and fathers. Although Gary was already dating a woman named Robin from PWP and had moved into her apartment in Auburn, when Nancy expressed interest in him during a camping event at Camp Casey during Fourth of July weekend, it did not stop him from beginning an affair with her.

"How can you turn down a beautiful woman?" he asked, trying to make me understand the dilemma he faced at the time. "You suffer for beauty," he said.

As Gary and Nancy separated from the group, they walked together to a concrete bunker, secluded in the woods, where they had sex. Two weeks later, he had ended his relationship with Robin and had moved in with Nancy in her house in West Seattle.

"I was going to place to place . . . living in an apartment for a couple months and all of a sudden for some reason I decided I needed a woman, so I dated. You know how Americans [are], you shack up with a woman because you think you're in love and you [meet] a woman you might want to marry, and all of a sudden she [meets] somebody else, so she leaves you, and you meet somebody else, and you move out on them. The grass always looks greener on the other side, which it isn't. You meet somebody and all of a sudden you figure out no wonder she's single, nobody wants her," he laughed.

The relationship with Nancy lasted about six months, and it revolved primarily around sex, sometimes as often as three times a day. In his interrogation, he admitted that Nancy was probably the only woman to ever fully satisfy his sexual needs, claiming that he had "fantastic sex" with her. Since she was more open to experimenting and less inhibited than other women, she would agree to many of his requests.

Since he had brought up Nancy more times than any other woman—even Judith—I wondered if the feelings he had for her were more genuine, or if he was simply remembering the best sex he ever had.

When Gary described Nancy as someone special to him, I was not surprised. "My treasure was a nice, beautiful woman, and everybody wanted to know her. She'd read the [gas] meters for a living, and every guy in town wanted to meet her, but I just [kept] her to myself and have her not meeting my friends." In that moment of raw honesty, it became apparent how insecure he was, that he feared another man would easily steal her away from him.

Although his concerns eventually came to fruition and she did break up with him, it was not because she met another man.

"She didn't want to help raise my son and be with him. I'd take him over there, and it was a burden," Gary reflected.

Since Nancy's daughter was already fifteen and practically old enough to be on her own, she was not eager to act as a mother to a seven-year-old boy. "His son didn't care for me, and I didn't really care for him," Nancy admitted in her witness statement. To combat this conflict, Gary would often leave his son with his parents. "They spent more time with him than I did," Gary acknowledged.

Although that was a reason as to why his relationship with Nancy ended, like the others, he left out other pertinent details that if he had told me, would force me to question any sympathy I might have had for him. Later, I'd learn Nancy's experience was similar to Marcia's in that Gary lacked the emotional element needed to truly bond with another person. She explained, "The relationship was starting to bother me because he wouldn't communicate . . . He wouldn't tell me any of his feelings. He never opened up . . . I know I made three or four attempts talking to him, 'Please say something.

Tell me what you feel, or if you care about me, let me know that.' He didn't [show affection] except for just sex. We didn't sit around cuddling or anything like that. That was it, just sex . . . he had never let me know that he loved me . . . he just never told me or didn't know how to let me know."

The relationships he had with women after Nancy were just as short-lived. Roxanne, Lorrie, and Sharon—he would date all three of them at the same time while also beginning to kill prostitutes regularly. But by the end of 1984, he began dating a woman named Jan, who he claimed was responsible for slowing down his kill rate. Since they spent a lot of time together, more so than the other women he dated prior to her, he did not have much opportunity to kill. However, after Christmas 1984, he discovered that she had started seeing somebody else, ending their relationship.

In February 1985, he met Judith Mawson at a PWP dance at the White Shutters, noticing her kindness first, which seemed to set her apart from other women. Within a few months, she had moved into his house, where he had killed at least thirty women. In 1988 they got married and would remain together until his arrest in 2001.

Since Judith depended on him more than any other woman ever had, especially financially, she was more inclined to remain loyal to him. "I had somebody who cared for me, somebody [who] lived there . . . and she was dependent on me," Gary told detectives, explaining what he believed was the recipe for a successful relationship. Due to back problems interfering with her ability to work, she needed him to take care of her. Rather than object to such a responsibility, Gary welcomed it and even preferred it that way. "I think I needed somebody depending on me," he reflected. Being in such a position granted him more control than he ever had in a relationship before. Most of the other women he dated were independent and would usually end up leaving him, but it seemed Judith would always stay because she needed him. As long as he came home every night after work, which he always did, what was there really to question?

Gary provided a stable, abundant life for Judith—a house, a car, regular camping trips and vacations—and that was all that seemed to matter to her.

* * *

In his interrogation, he admitted early on that during his entire marriage to Judith—with the exception of the first few months—he would frequently visit prostitutes. Since many missing women involved in prostitution still had never been found, it was impossible to know how many he killed during that time. Although he didn't murder every prostitute he had sex with, he never stopped killing completely. Eventually, in his interrogation, he admitted to hiding the bodies farther away so police wouldn't discover them. But there were several that he let live that became his regulars. A woman by the name of Jennifer, who lived in an apartment on Des Moines Way, was someone he had sex with multiple times through the 1980s and 1990s. Another regular he remembered was petite and would hide pot or crack in her vagina. For fifteen dollars, he had sex with her at least twenty times. Even though he didn't kill these women, becoming a regular didn't necessarily make them off-limits. Alma Smith, for instance, had also been considered a regular, having sex with him a few times at his house, but he still killed her in 1983.

In his address book, he'd disguise several women's names and phone numbers—more of his regulars—often penning a male's name alongside theirs, so if Judith looked, she'd believe the names belonged to a couple, a friend from work and his wife. Next to their names, he'd list a car part and a price to make Judith believe he was helping them fix their vehicle and was keeping track of the cost. However, the price was really so he'd remember how much each woman charged for sex.

Through most of his marriage to Judith, he would wake up two to three hours earlier for work so he could hunt for a woman to have sex with before his shift, and depending on his mood, kill her. But Judith never questioned him. She believed it took him longer than it actually did to get to work. She also believed he enjoyed going to Denny's for breakfast, stopping for coffee, and reading the newspaper before easing into his day at Kenworth, where he'd spend eight hours—or sometimes longer, depending on if he worked overtime—with a mask digging into his face to block out the fumes as he painted trucks. Sometimes he really would stop for breakfast, but on most mornings he'd use his few hours of freedom to hunt for women. PAC Highway, Rainier Avenue, Aurora Avenue, downtown Seattle, nowhere was off-limits.

Other times, after leaving work at three thirty, he would stop at his parents' house, where he would drink a cup of coffee. On the way home from there, he would sometimes squeeze in sex with a prostitute and still be able to walk through the door when Judith expected him at five. Meanwhile, if Judith happened to be out shopping around that time, she would rush home so she could be there when he opened the door, never guessing that he also was rushing home, but for reasons that had little to do with his desire to be with her, but rather to ensure she remained oblivious to him having sex with other women.

"I was always, constantly looking, always picking them up and dropping them off . . . and any woman I wanted to kill at that time . . . I [was] just paying more attention to not being seen, not being tailed, and [I] worried about where I was gonna go take her to kill her," he admitted to detectives. "I like sex every day and should have asked more of Judith, but I didn't. [So, I] went and seeked other women all the way up to I was arrested," he confessed. "I think I just had to have a woman on the side to have sex with and then to go out and kill prostitutes."

Whenever he could, he would have sex with prostitutes, women he described as "young and sexy" that he found "psychologically better" than the "heavyset" women he would often end up in relationships and marriages with, but he wouldn't always kill them.

Years later, after Gary's conviction, the media would embellish that the love Gary had for Judith had changed him from homicidal to a loving husband, which in turn prevented more women from dying at his hands. Judith seemed to go along with this narrative, reflecting that "he was the best, at least to me."

But she was deluding herself. His mood and how much time he had were often the main factors in Gary's decision to kill or not to kill. He would need a couple hours minimum to hunt for a woman, have sex with her, kill her, and then dump her body, all the while making sure Judith never became suspicious of his whereabouts. If he planned to kill a woman after a union meeting, for instance, and the meeting ran late, he would be forced to return home to Judith, defeated. His decision not to kill was not an act of love, like she seemed to believe. With Judith always waiting for him at home, he was forced to be more accountable, which aided him in controlling his impulses.

In contrast, at the height of his killing in the early to mid-1980s, he was engaged to Roxanne, but since she had not moved in with him, he had more time to see prostitutes and kill them. Since Judith had "moved in, I had a little bit of a restraint on the mass killing. I slowed down," he told detectives. But he never could stop killing entirely, explaining to Sheriff David Reichert that he'd "Slow down . . . and then maybe [kill] again . . . urges hit, you know."

During one of our conversations, he went on to tell me that if a man "goes off with the first woman he meets, that's bad [for] the woman he already had." I guessed that was an acknowledgment of all the times he cheated on his wives.

That was the thing I had come to learn about Gary. In his indirect confessions to me, he was always capable of distinguishing right from wrong, knowing that his choices had the potential to hurt anyone who loved him. But he didn't care. His decision-making aligned solely with his own desires. He even advised me that when I didn't feel like having sex with my future husband, I still should. Otherwise, I'd run the risk of him cheating on me or leaving me, "and you don't want that," Gary warned, drawing on his own experiences. When his wives or girlfriends didn't have sex with him as often as he preferred, he then felt justified to find a prostitute to satisfy him. In his mind, he was trying to prevent a man from doing the same thing to me. Meet a man's every demand for sex, and I would be rewarded with loyalty.

But, really, a woman's devotion to Gary didn't matter. Any chance he could, he would try to find another woman. For instance, one time while driving the motorhome he and Judith had just purchased, with one of their poodles in tow, he picked up a woman in the 7–11 parking lot in Federal Way. For twenty dollars—money he pocketed when skimming the top of the stack he and Judith earned during a swap meet or yard sale—she agreed to sex. He drove with her to Safeway, where they parked and went into the back of the RV. There, they had sex on the bed, which he described to detectives as "pretty good." He then went straight home to Judith, as if nothing had happened.

When he would find a prostitute before work, he would try to go to an area where Judith or her daughters never ventured. But really, it didn't matter. He knew he could always talk his way out of anything when it came to Judith.

In the late '90s or early 2000s, one morning before his shift, he had sex with a woman named Linda across the street from where one of Judith's daughters lived. Since Linda was drunk, she was a better date than he expected, prompting him to try to find her again for another one soon after. It didn't matter that she left her panties behind on the floor of his truck for Judith to find later that night. As she held them up, demanding to know where they came from, Gary said the first thing that came to mind. He found them in the driveway, and in an effort to clean up, threw them in his truck. "Well, get rid of them," Judith ordered, as if making them disappear would remove all her doubts and fears, rewriting the truth that he wasn't cheating on her. Just like always, she had believed him, or at least it seemed that way.

Even after being a main suspect in the Green River killings in 1987 and it was revealed that he had visited prostitutes throughout the 1980s, Gary still convinced Judith to marry him. It didn't matter that their home was ransacked by the police in an aggressive search for evidence against him. She believed, or rather deceived herself, that his days of seeking other women to have sex with were long behind him. He wanted to marry her, and that was all that mattered. She didn't even have to work anymore if that was what she chose, a decision he left up to her.

Although he usually had sex with prostitutes, other women were not off-limits. To him, it didn't matter what kind of woman he had sex with as long as his needs were met. Finding a woman to have sex with him for free would be too much trouble, so he never really tried. Often, he felt uncomfortable and nervous speaking with women, something I noticed during my first few calls with him. It took him some time to open up, and when he was in public it was no different. With prostitutes, he didn't have to worry about offending them, so he found it easy to talk with them.

But one morning in the 1990s, hours before he was expected at work, Gary had a rare experience. While cruising Rainier Avenue, he flagged down a woman he believed was a prostitute. She walked up to the window of his truck to speak with him, like most prostitutes would, but instead of negotiating what he wanted and a price, she began to unload on him all the problems she had been having with her husband. She had been cheated on, leaving her enraged and distressed.

"Well, would you like some companionship?" Gary asked, mindful of her vulnerable state and all the ways it could benefit him.

The woman agreed, but he would have to accompany her to the yellow cab she was supposed to be driving. She was on the clock. He parked his truck and followed her, climbing into the front seat. She drove down Rainier Avenue, and after a few minutes, he directed her to a secluded spot he had taken many women before. After she parked, they both got out and slid into the back seat, where they stripped naked and had sex. If nothing else, she wanted to at least feel she was getting revenge on her husband.

A "morning fling," Gary called it. And he didn't even have to pay for it.

Afterward, he drove to work, regretting that he had not learned the woman's name or phone number. He would have liked to have sex with her again, especially since it didn't cost him anything. He contemplated calling the cab company, but what would he say? "I just had sex with one of your cabbies, and I'd like to get in touch with her?" The last thing he'd want was to get her in trouble. Then she would never want to see him again. So, he let it go, resuming his regular morning activities: searching for prostitutes, having sex with them, and sometimes killing them.

Besides finding another woman's underwear, there was no other concrete proof that Gary was cheating on Judith. But in November 2001, two weeks before his final arrest, his infidelity screamed directly in Judith's face.

While driving down PAC Highway, his normal route, he couldn't resist the urge to pick up a woman. When he found a young one with a nice body, what appealed to him most, he waved to her, flashed money at her, and pulled over down the street in a parking lot. She walked over to him, and he got out of the car, meeting her at the back of the pickup, where he opened the tailgate to make it seem he was doing something else, something innocent. He had noticed some cops nearby, so after telling her what he wanted, he asked if she would meet him in the next parking lot. But as he was about to drive off, a cop car pulled up alongside him. He had been duped.

After he was carted off to jail in Kent, an officer called Judith, informing her that Gary had been arrested for soliciting a prostitute, something a lot of husbands do, he told her. If Gary really intended to cheat on her, she wondered what she had done wrong to make him do it. She considered Gary's infidelity, but the pain of imagining it was too great. He would never betray her like that, she convinced herself. "He's a friendly person, so he probably looked at somebody and smiled . . . even when you're walking by somebody in the store or you're shopping, he'll smile and say hello," she reassured herself.

While waiting for the opportunity to call her himself, he thought about what he would tell her. "I could always try to lie to her, that something happened in traffic." He was scared of her reaction but knew that "she had to find out." Off the top of his head, he couldn't remember anyone else's phone number. Besides, who else could he have called? He would never want anyone in his family or from Kenworth to know he had been trying to pick up a prostitute. "[Judith] was my last hope," Gary said. She always believed his lies, and he was confident it would be no different now. When he swore he didn't do anything, she seemed to believe him, even asking if he was okay.

He hated the idea of anyone he knew spotting him leaving the jail, so he instructed Judith to pick him up from the K-Mart parking lot nearby. Once he was free, he jogged to meet her. Nearly out of breath, he lied that he had pulled over to close the window in the back of his truck when a woman approached him, and he was arrested. He flashed Judith a smile, one that always worked in his favor, and he knew she believed he was innocent just like the hundreds of times before when she took him at his word that he was working overtime or attending a union meeting.

Her naivete coupled with her total dependence on him blinded her from ever becoming suspicious of him. She had placed him on a pedestal, and if he were to ever fall from the towering height of it, her entire universe would be obliterated. She lived as though even *the idea* of his absence would cause an apocalypse in her world, one that she could never see herself evolving past.

Judith was willfully blind to all his indiscretions over the span of their sixteen-year relationship, ignoring every sign. But as much as she tried to sweep all his lies under the rug, the fabric would wither to shreds, exposing years of dirt buried beneath it.

Until that happened, Judith remained a dutiful, trusting wife, never doubting Gary's word. After his arrest for solicitation, he even convinced her that it was in his best interest to plead guilty to the charges. Hiring a lawyer to prove his innocence would be too expensive, he persuaded her. Appealing to her frugalness, something they had in common, she followed his logic that pleading guilty and paying a fine would be the most cost-effective solution.

On top of that, Gary had been ordered by the court to take an HIV test or run the risk of getting fined an additional thousand dollars. Without question, Judith scheduled the test for him and then drew a map of a new route he could take from his mother's house to avoid driving down PAC Highway. Another part of his punishment was to stay out of the prostitution area, and Judith was determined to help him do that, not realizing how difficult it would be for him to not have sex with more women.

During a conversation with Sheriff Reichert, Gary once referred to himself as a "natural liar," something he did with ease and sometimes just for the hell of it. His entire life had been that way. But when it came to women, we were all pawns in a rigged game in which he was the perpetual winner, always prized with whatever he wanted from us: sex, acceptance, adoration—and in my case, sympathy, as I tried to understand him while he offered fragments of his life.

Soon after his final arrest he filed for divorce from Judith, telling her it was for her protection. The media would continue to hound her if she remained legally tied to him. He also wanted to ensure she would receive any money available in their savings and a full profit from selling whatever property they owned before he would be forced to pay unavoidable legal fees. Although he might have acted in her best interest, no matter how often he professed his innocence at the time, deep down, he knew he would either be put to death or spend the remainder of his life in prison. He would never return home to Judith, despite his feigned hope.

When reflecting on his divorce from Judith, unlike his other two exes, he took full accountability. "My last one was because of my sexual . . . anomaly I guess it was, that was—I had a problem with sex," he admitted, without telling me anything else, most likely because it would have been impossible to evoke sympathy from me, what he seemed to want more than anything. If I saw him as a person rather than a serial killer, then that meant hope was alive for him to feel accepted by a woman. An unrealistic dream, but it was one he ran toward anyway, with or without my consent.

CHAPTER SIX

Feelings for Me

My body jolted as though I had been struck by lightning. Sweat drenched my shirt, the thin cotton sticking to my back. I could barely catch my breath, like I had been smothered by the pillow at my side. The darkness hurt my eyes the same as the light; it was impossible to adjust to my surroundings, my own bedroom. Somewhere a siren wailed, and for a moment I wondered if the emergency was mine. Until the high-pitched discordant loop grew fainter, I sat alone with my panic. Down the block, a garbage truck squeaked its brakes and rumbled. A *dong* of the metal dumpster plopping back onto the ground followed, like a tribal drum calling for a ritual of silence to begin. I twirled a loose string from the blanket around my finger until it cut into my skin. I had to pee, but the bathroom seemed too far of a destination. Too dangerous. *Could someone else actually be here?* I contemplated my safety for what felt like hours. Cars whooshed by in short intervals, and eventually I was reminded of reality, and where I thought I was only minutes ago became a memory:

An enormous house with a flower-lined walkway and a wooden porch. I strolled to the front door, and my finger sunk into the bell. While I waited, I scanned the motley of flowers in wild rows—chrysanthemums, azaleas, and roses—all bobbing their heads in the breeze as if music possessed them.

A plain woman with blond stringy hair and thick-rimmed glasses invited me inside. Not a dab of makeup, not even lipstick, colored her face. *Just like a nun*, I thought.

It took a minute for me to recognize her, but then I knew. It was his wife, the one often shown in the newspapers. *Why was she still here?*

Curtains were drawn in each room, blurring the furniture, things that could have been his that I wanted to hold and study in my hands. But she rushed me through to the back of the house.

A kitchen. The polished linoleum—a perfect-teeth-white—dazzled under my feet. *Should I have taken my shoes off? I forgot to ask.* The pastel blue cabinets reminded me of a baby boy's bedroom. *Nothing bad could live here.*

The counter space, clutter-free and long, snaked around the entirety of a wall where a coffee pot brewed. Off by a window, a table booth, like the kind in a diner, was set with teacups instead of coffee mugs that rested on tweed placemats.

Off the kitchen, a door swung open to a dark bedroom. The light from the kitchen invaded the carpeted entryway. "Don't go in there," she warned. "Let's drink our coffee."

But I didn't listen. I had too many questions. I inched closer and closer until my eyes fell upon him. He sat at the edge of a bed, big enough for two people and neatly made up with a quilt and pillows leaned against the headboard. He wore jeans and a button-down shirt; there was nothing crude about him. He smiled and gestured for me, the way one excitedly calls a friend over to divulge a secret, to sit on the bed with him.

"Run! Hurry up," his wife pleaded. "You know what he is."

Somehow the door was starting to close as if he had secret powers and was willing it to lock. "I'm sorry. I'm afraid," I told him, expecting him to care, to stop.

His smile faded like he never meant it, like he was always stone.

I pushed through the door and bolted, my feet thumping through the house, rattling the glass knickknacks displayed on shelves. Then I was free, the flowers he might've planted crushing under my feet.

* * *

Just as Gary began occupying more space in my unconscious mind—a dream of him interrupting my sleep each night—the amount of time we spoke each day also increased. It became a regular occurrence for him to use his entire hour of "rec" to speak with me, prompting him to dial my number after each twenty-minute conversation ended, until he was directed to return to his cell for the night.

As if I had become the center of his world, what he looked forward to most all day, he was enraptured in some kind of honeymoon phase of a relationship, and he seemed to become addicted to me, or rather the idea of me. From a psychological perspective, it could be argued he was displaying classic narcissistic traits, love bombing, or showing excessive amounts of attention to a new source of supply, which happened to be me. And I couldn't have been more grateful.

To outsiders, I could understand why that might make me sound insane, crazy, out of my mind—any criticism would suffice. But being the center of his world meant he was inclined to spend as much time as he could talking with me, and those lengthy conversations gave me a new kind of access to him. A longer call made it feel as if we were sharing a drink at a bar, allowing extended intervals of his thoughts to unravel before me in real time. As a writer, I needed that to happen.

Right before we hung up for the second time, we had been discussing the process of dying, but a few seconds later when he called back, his mind had shifted somewhere else. Within minutes, he was advising that during sex I should also use a vibrator so I could climax at the same time as the man, certain that would put me in "high heaven." It was evident he was perusing through his extensive catalog of sexual encounters and speaking from experience. Later, I'd learn that he and Nancy would experiment with various sex toys, a vibrator being one of them. As he spoke, he seemed to be reliving this sexual experience while also including me in a present fantasy.

It was difficult to switch gears alongside him, and I was reluctant to do so, since in his mind, he was now putting me in a bed with a man, who he probably imagined as himself. Although it seemed I was a sexual object to him all along, he was never so blatantly obvious about it until now. His discretion was disappearing, and I couldn't bring myself to consider what would happen when it was all gone. Soon enough I could be pressed against the hard concrete of his desires, unshielded, and forced to feel those jagged edges against my skin, betraying all boundaries.

The thought of where he would try to lead these conversations unsettled me. I also couldn't ignore that he was sexualizing me immediately following a discussion about death. Leaping from death to sex with no segue revealed just how close they were placed in his mind, like two countries bordering each other. And I was caught somewhere in the middle, as a sex object and someone who desperately wanted to understand him, and on some level, someone he longed to understand him.

So, after ten months of communicating, when he rushed the words "love you" at the end of a call, hanging up immediately afterward to prohibit me from responding to avoid rejection, I should not have been too shocked. But I was.

As I stood paralyzed in my living room, I was grateful to hear the click that followed when he hung up, silencing his voice and leaving him with no option but to retreat to his cell where he would have to keep his thoughts of me to himself, at least for the night.

I had no idea what those words really meant to him. A year ago when I read the book about Judith's marriage to him, *She Married the*

Green River Killer: The Story of an Unsuspecting Housewife, she claimed that he never expressed his love for her if she didn't say it first. Part of the reason Nancy dumped him was because he never said those words to her at all. It seemed he learned over time that most women liked to hear they were loved. By saying those words, he assumed he would become more trustworthy, allowing him to get more out of the relationship. I still didn't know exactly what he wanted from me, but my theory seemed more logical than believing his feelings could be real.

As the rate of calls increased, letters from Gary began to arrive in my PO box at least once or twice a week. Much like his calls, I began to expect them. Considering the brutality he was capable of, it was hard to believe the gentleness of his hands that printed all his words in ink light enough it could pass for pencil. If I were to run my fingers over his small writing, there would be nothing to feel, no shapes carved into the page. In each envelope, multiple pages would be stuffed inside, different letters spanning the course of a few days, always picking up where our phone calls ended.

After he told me he loved me, I was hoping the subject would not resurface, but wishful thinking rarely works. In one letter, he broached the topic in classic Gary fashion, through Bible verses. "Maria, read Song of Solomon. It's a love story, girl and king. Love between man and woman," he wrote, a subtle reference to his supposed "feelings" for me.

Since nearly everything he did and said seemed to hold an underlying meaning, I read a couple of translations of the story, trying to make sense of the message he was sending me. Written as a collection of erotic love poems, it describes the love and passion that exists between a man and a woman with an emphasis on the beauty of the sex they have together as a married couple. Suddenly, his purpose became clear: discussing this story would be another way for him to talk about sex and gauge my reaction, something he seemed to enjoy.

I was not surprised. With all the time he claimed to spend reading the Bible, it seemed he was only scanning it for the parts about sex, his perversion hiding behind the sanctity of the scripture's intended message. By saying he loved me, he attached emotion to his desires, and the Bible verses he shared with me celebrated such feelings. I figured that since he couldn't physically have sex with anyone, the next best thing would be to speak with a woman he found attractive about the act. By using the Bible to initiate such conversations, he appeared harmless, genuinely curious about deciphering the meaning of God's word. The more I thought about it, the more I wondered if he was trying to soften his image so I would see him differently.

Soon after, he began to hint toward a romance that was confused in generalities. "If you got good communication and it's a friend also, it could be a start of a relationship," he said. I couldn't be sure if he was attempting to reveal more of his feelings or just making conversation for another reason only he knew.

Uncharacteristically, I disagreed with him, arguing that sometimes a friend remains just that throughout the duration of a lifetime. To make my point more valid, I used my friendship with Asher as an example, a man I had been friends with since kindergarten. But no matter what I said, Gary didn't believe that Asher and I had an entirely nonsexual relationship. He accused Asher of having feelings for me. "Did you ever ask him why? He's always around for you," he asserted, insisting that the only reason Asher, or any man, would stay in my life would be due to their romantic feelings for me or an ulterior motive driven by their sexual desires. "Make sure he's not being led on," he warned, as if I had been toying with Asher's heart, and possibly his own, all along.

His concern that I could hurt Asher seemed personal, as if he was fighting on behalf of himself and all men against selfish, insincere women. Since he started killing, he had been leading this battle, even admitting to a psychologist who helped law enforcement secure his confession in 2003, that in addition to the control he loved to possess, it pleased him to know that when he would "take away another woman" she wouldn't be able to "hurt anybody else," as though he were protecting the entire male species.

"You don't think a man and a woman can be friends? Just platonic friends?" I blurted out in disbelief.

"I think you can, but you got a mindset, too. You gotta communicate. He's gotta—if he's sitting there wanting to marry you, and you just want to have friends, that's not—" he said, stopping himself from saying anything else, out of what I surmised as annoyance at me and everything I claimed not to know, all the feelings men could harbor for me.

For a moment, I longed for something uncomplicated, where no one said, "I love you," or if it was said, no one expected you to say it back. But the truth was, it felt precarious, like this entire situation with Gary was built on unstable ground.

CHAPTER SEVEN

Blame

It became apparent to me that Gary hated all women and viewed them as nothing but sex objects. Because they sometimes rejected him, and he often felt controlled by his insatiable desire for sex—which they didn't always want to give him—over time, his hatred grew, and he adopted the belief that women purposefully teased and taunted him with their bodies. "[They're] causing hurt to other people, or to me, of having a vagina that I can't screw all the time . . . by seeing what pain it has on a man . . . cause everybody's out for your vagina and waiting in line . . . and here you flaunt that around, and here I'm in control," he once revealed to an FBI profiler.

It seemed his reasons to kill were endless. Ex-wives and ex-girlfriends that had hurt him, the control Marcia had over him when he gave her money for child support, the control all women, even prostitutes, had over him—after all, he needed them to fulfill his sexual urges—were all catalysts to his wrath that ended with a woman he thought no one would miss, that he described as "garbage." He admitted to detectives, he felt "pleasure" when "taking a woman's life. They're the cause of my problems, women. The divorces. The lies they told me. The hatred. When I killed her, at that time, my hate for myself was gone for that day. For that short length of time."

Deep down, he struggled with the idea that he was a man who frequently visited prostitutes, and he hated to think of anyone he knew finding out. If he killed them, then "she's dead and gone, she's disappeared. In my mind I know I killed them, but nobody else knows I went to a prostitute because they're all dead," he explained to a psychologist after his arrest.

In my conversations with him, he would sometimes describe his disappointment in the sexual experiences he had with many women he would pick up. Lying flat on their backs, leaving him no choice but to "do all the humping," they never even acted like they enjoyed having sex with him. No words or moans would escape from their mouths to indicate they were even the slightest bit turned on by him. Worse, some of them wouldn't even bend over for him, a position that would usually guarantee he'd ejaculate, and for that, he thought they should be punished. Since he was the customer, he felt they should ensure he was satisfied and do whatever he asked; otherwise, what was the point?

But instead, some of them would rush him along and end the encounter not caring if he came or not. In those instances, he reacted in anger, his hands at their throats or his arm wrapped around their necks in a chokehold. "Unplanned kills," he'd call them. In those cases, he didn't pick up the woman with the intention of killing her. But if something happened to set him off, he'd feel he'd have no choice but to end the woman's life. Other times, he would simply be in the mood to kill and drive around in search of any woman selling herself to fulfill that desire. Faking an orgasm, letting him finish, talking dirty to him, there was nothing the woman could do to change his mind. The truth was as long as he felt like it, he would kill any woman if given the opportunity.

But what could he really do with a streetwalker, he asked me. If he wanted to taste her, he couldn't. Unless he commanded her to get on top of him, she never would. And even then, she wouldn't move with the same unbridled enthusiasm as a girlfriend, a wife, or a regular one-night stand. To him, prostitutes "were worthless. To have a streetwalker out there with a beautiful body and you can't do anything with her. You [just] give her sperm samples, basically," he complained. The only remedy for his rage then was to feel his hands around her throat.

It didn't help that he also blamed them for transmitting venereal diseases to him rather than take responsibility for his own negligence to practice safe sex. He claimed if the women had not given him diseases over the years—chlamydia, gonorrhea, and warts, to be exact—then their lives would have been spared. It became a common subject, one he'd spend entire phone calls ranting about until he had no choice but to return to his cell for the night.

"A prostitute . . . they're full of disease. There's a big chance of them getting VD of some sort," he said, disgruntled.

Listening to him blame women for transmitting STDs while acting as though men had no part in the problem made it difficult for me to silence my own outrage. But I reminded myself that if I really wanted to know him, I had to listen without interrupting him; in those moments, he revealed the truth about himself, the principles that governed his life, especially his reasons to kill. Buried beneath his rhetoric, his general attitude about women was there, like mold proving a piece of fruit rotten. No matter how much he tried, the ugly parts of himself were impossible to conceal forever.

This conversation was nothing new. For months, he had been cycling through every way to blame his victims, and his letters to me were no different, containing the same line of reasoning: "As for prostitution, a woman's body has 3 holes. It's often men are in them all of the time or all at once. They pay women for sex. The women, teens are human sperm banks . . . VD is every woman and teen. Most areas, no doctors to cure them, so they pass VD to every man," he wrote, as if this should make me sympathize with his decision to murder women.

"So, when you were killing prostitutes, is that part of the reason, because of the diseases they carried or could potentially carry?" I asked during a phone call.

"You got to pay for it, a prostitute, and if the prostitute is not right . . ." he trailed off. If I scraped away most of his long-winded ramble, his point was clear: If you're paying for something, no matter what it is, it should work well and be free of any problems. Why should he have to pay for a damaged product? To him, a diseased woman was just that. The threat she posed to his own health meant she did not deserve to live. Why should a woman, especially a prostitute, exist, if he couldn't have sex with her, or if he did, he would end up suffering as a result?

Since Gary would have unprotected sex with prostitutes routinely for most of his life, he had good reason to obsess over contracting venereal diseases. When he married Judith, it became an even bigger priority. If he ever passed anything to her, it would be impossible to explain. He was quite skillful when lying to her, but he knew there were some things that even she would not be so naive to believe. So, throughout their marriage, he made a more conscious effort to use a condom whenever he had sex with another woman, but occasionally when he got caught up in the moment, he wouldn't bother.

Instead, he would resort to his next defense plan: drench his penis in cologne or alcohol, a practice he had the utmost faith in, to "kill any bacteria." However, scientifically, it has never been proven that cleaning the genitals with alcohol prevents the transmission of STDs. Although alcohol could kill any viruses such as herpes on the outside of the skin, once inside of the body, it would not be an effective solution. But he remained stubborn in his beliefs.

He brought up venereal diseases to me so often, you'd think it was a problem that still afflicted him, even though he had been barred from the prospect of having sex with anyone for the past twenty years. As time went on, it became clear that he still harbored resentment toward the women who infected him. If he hadn't already killed them, it seemed like if given the chance, he would still want to exact his revenge on them for committing such an unforgivable offense.

His obsession with contracting diseases—not just STDs—dated back to when he was sixteen and met a girl while stocking shelves at the Gov Mart Bazaar. She walked into the store one day, flirted with him, and invited him over to her house, requesting that he bring some beer. Paying two dollars to an older guy who worked with him, he was able to procure a six pack.

Later on, they shared the beers, sipping from the same bottles. But he never even got the chance to kiss her, never mind have sex with her like he wanted. Once they ran out of beer, he started to feel sick and went home.

The next day he woke up sweating from a high fever, sicker than he had ever been. When he went to the doctor, he learned that he had mono, the kissing disease. He assumed the girl he shared the beer with had given it to him, which enraged him. It was bad enough that he didn't get to have sex with her, and he would have to miss work, but he also never saw her again. "You start to get into a nice relationship with somebody, and somehow she disappears," he reflected, assuming she probably just used him for the beer he bought her.

The rest of his life would be the same way, believing most women were liars who only wanted to take advantage of him. To him, I was no different. But as long as he pretended I was a virgin, some kind of cherubic presence in his life, he would continue to speak with me.

When I made the mistake of telling him I also had mono as a teenager, he resisted hearing the story. "I don't want to ask you any questions," he said, hesitating. "How did you get it, from some kids at school?"

For an entire summer I made out with a boy who had run away from home and then dyed his hair sunburn red. Until I got mono and couldn't leave my house for two weeks.

"I don't know. I think sharing a drink with someone," I lied.

I listened to him breathe what sounded like a sigh of relief. My innocence was intact again. I knew I could never tell Gary the true story. I had to be who he wanted me to be, if I was ever going to get anywhere with him. What he once wrote to me stayed in the back of my mind: "Maybe God put you in my life for this reason, to listen to what the females [I killed] didn't accept." According to him, since these women didn't "accept God's gift of grace" when they were alive, they would be damned to burn in hell. "They made their bed, now they have to live or die with it," he said.

He recounted his experiences contracting venereal diseases, which dated back to when he was overseas in the navy and started having sex with prostitutes. As if he had just looked down his pants to discover a collection of bumps forming on his penis, these memories seemed just as antagonistic to this day, as he described sailors burning the warts off with matches or a hot iron.

"Sailors . . . they would go out and sleep with a woman and all of a sudden they got warts," he said.

During his interrogation, he admitted, "I caught three to four times different kinds. If we had a condom, we used it. If we didn't, we didn't use it . . . a lot of times I was a little bit drunk . . . the brain was a little impaired. . . . and horny and watching them dance and stuff like that. Come over and sit on your lap, rubbing me up. Turn you on," he reflected, trying to excuse his poor decisions.

However, while talking to me, he only discussed the aftermath of having sex with these women rather than the experience itself. He sounded bitter toward them for giving him diseases and then forcing him to deal with the unpleasant consequences.

"Burning if off, wouldn't that cause scarring and all sorts of—"

"Well, it would. It's gonna cause scarring and teaching guys not to have sex anymore. If she doesn't look that good to have sex with, don't do it," he said and laughed.

"Yeah, true," I said and laughed with him.

"If you got a guy that has VD, especially in the service, they don't give you a blood test. They take a sample of your . . . infected penis. Dip in—"

"What, with like a Q-tip?"

"A Q-tip, the penis gets the sample, and you look in a microscope, but your penis is, for a guy, [it's] how your penis is looking. And you got yellow stains on your underwear, so you know you got something, so you gotta go to the doctor, and you got some kind of disease, and he gives you pills for it," he recalled, making it sound like a lesser ordeal than how he actually felt about it. As Gary often did, he turned the subject around on me. In the same way he would size up a woman who got into his truck, trying to determine if she was "hard-core" or just starting out, he did the same with me when gauging my knowledge on any sexual topic he brought up. "You got the damn people, that they're rapists; a lot of times they got all kinds of venereal diseases. You ever hear of anybody having herpes, or not herpes, but vagina warts?"

"Not that I know of. I don't think I know anybody, personally," I said.

"You got a woman, and she gets—study up on that—it's called venereal warts," he directed—another homework assignment in addition to trying to figure out who else he could have killed. "Call a doctor up or look up venereal vagina," he instructed.

He can't be serious.

There was no telling what he could've asked of me next: describe to him the images littered over the internet of diseased vaginas, like helping the blind understand the magnitude of a house fire or a sunset or anything worth seeing. "Well, the wart is just like [the kind you get] on the hand and feet, but if you have a vagina wart, it's out and inside a woman. Outside of her, up to the uterus or, might even be past that," he explained. "It actually makes your vagina smaller with the warts on it . . . They're all inside of a woman, and one time it was you can't get rid of them. They'd give you medicine that doesn't work . . . once you got it for a woman, it's hell—I know a woman who had it, and she never remarried," he reflected, as if there was no other choice but to condemn her forever.

He made it sound like ending up in bed with diseased women was another misfortune he suffered in his life, one he blamed entirely on them. While reading the witness statements, I would learn I wasn't wrong. According to two ex-girlfriends, he had passed herpes to them but took no accountability.

One woman described that when she realized she had contracted the disease in 1982, she confronted Gary about it, but he denied giving it to her and even tried to gaslight her into believing that she had infected him.

He demanded to know, "Well, then where did I get it? How do you explain that we both broke out with it at the same time?"

"You had it from before. It takes twenty-one days to get it, anytime within twenty-one days," she argued.

But he never admitted that he passed it to her. Although she was angry with him that not only had he given her a disease, but he was clearly having sex with other women behind her back, she remained in a relationship with him for two more years, even planning to marry him in June 1984. She explained, "I felt real dirty, unclean . . . like nobody else would look at me ever again . . . I thought he would be the only one who would look at me."

As he recounted his version of the story to me, this woman remained unwanted forever, when in reality, she did in fact fall in love with another man, the reason she left Gary. I wondered if he was lying about what had happened as a way to salvage his ego that still seemed to be bruised all these years later. Back then, not only did he find this particular ex unattractive, but thanks to him, she also had herpes, and she still didn't want to be with him.

"She really never could get married?" I asked, challenging what I knew was a lie.

"Nobody wanted her anymore because she was—yeah, you can't have, I guess you can have sex with her, but you gotta make sure you take alcohol and wash off yourself—"

"I don't know if that would work—"

"Well, it might kill any warts, but the warts on a man isn't—one wart on a man—venereal warts get in a woman's vagina, and she gets it in her mouth and in her vagina, and then it just spreads like wildfire," he explained.

"What about wearing a condom?"

Irritated by the suggestion, he retorted, "A condom would, but what happens with a condom, it breaks." I wondered why he couldn't just say that he found sex more enjoyable without using protection.

"But nobody wanted to be with her because . . . being with a woman, you want to have sex with her. Well, you can't because you'll get warts on your penis," he said.

"Yeah, I can see that being a deal-breaker."

"Look at venereal warts on the internet," he insisted. "I knew a woman that's married who had it . . . she got it from her husband, but she went into hiding. There's no record of her. She couldn't have sex anymore," he explained. I had no idea who he was referring to, or if the people he described were even real, but I focused on the takeaway of his story. According to him, pleasing a man was a woman's only purpose. When she was no longer desirable, she had no choice but to erase herself from the world.

"Wow, but—"

"She went into hiding. There's no record of her anywhere anymore," he repeated, sensing I was about to ask who the woman was before he cut me off. "Maybe she did pass away . . . but it's all in front of you on the internet . . . So, look it up. You don't want to get that damn thing," he warned. Otherwise, I, too, would be rendered useless and marked for death, apparently.

"If a woman had venereal warts, she was killed by the pimp," he sermonized. "In the '40s and the '50s, they used to kill the women, the prostitutes." He had told me this before, but now he was filled with more passion, like he *really* wanted me to understand and agree that a woman afflicted with an STD deserves death. "She can infect . . . three hundred and sixty-five days a year of guys," he calculated. He seemed irritated by the number.

"They would kill them?"

"Yeah. They would take the women and kill them. I don't know what they did with the body. But, yeah, the pimp would kill them because it's gonna ruin his whole business." By telling me this, he seemed to justify his own reasons to kill. *I'm not the only one*, he seemed to be reminding me, as if this collective killing of women would make all his violence toward them acceptable.

"Any woman who has vagina warts is gonna give warts to the guy, and then the guy goes home and gives the warts to his wife, and she has babies, and she has a cesarian, and it's a cycle," he continued, defending his reasons why a diseased woman should be disposable. According to him, they were the true perpetrators. These women would infect men with a disease, and the men would then pass it on to their wives, unmasking their infidelity. By Gary's logic, men were the true victims, sometimes even losing their marriages, so strangling these women to death also became an act of retribution. "And it's painful, too, for a woman," he added, as if suggesting that killing them would put them out of their misery.

As long as Gary warned me of the horrors of genital warts—the worst kind of venereal disease, according to him—he would be trying to save me. If I remained pure and clean then I could fulfill my purpose as a woman, and he'd have one less reason to want to kill me.

For once, he was helping one of us survive, he seemed to be demonstrating. As if he was capable of good all along.

* * *

Adding to the offense of STDs was the way women would lie to him. If he asked any of the women he picked up from the street if they were clean, they would always tell him that they were, claiming that they were checked only a week ago. "But she had five guys in between [me] and when she got checked." Their lies were only fuel added to the rage burning inside him, always on the verge of spreading out of control.

"Is there any way of stopping [a] woman from going in and being a prostitute?" he asked, suggesting this would've saved them from dying by his hands. He considered the reasons why a woman would choose such a profession, firing off statistics that were not accurate. "Almost sixty percent of women that get raped go into prostitution," he said. If all it took was for men to stop raping women to decrease the number of prostitutes, why was he not blaming the rapists, then? But he would never consider such an idea. "Is there any way of stopping them?" he persisted.

According to his logic, if prostitutes didn't exist at all, then he wouldn't have had any women to target, preventing him from becoming a serial killer. I considered this possibility, but I believed he would have become a serial killer even if prostitutes didn't exist. He might've killed women more sparingly or targeted other vulnerable groups. But his desire to kill would never be dormant.

"It's not like their families tried to help them get off of the streets. They're why they [are] dead," he said, taking no accountability. "You got youth counselors. Maybe a rape counselor for six months will change them," he proposed.

In his mind, it was simple. If he didn't come across them, he wouldn't have killed them. But the reality was that even if they were not directly in his path, he would seek them out, driving around for hours until he found one.

* * *

The more he brought up what he perceived as offenses women made against him, I realized he would always see himself as the victim. Even as he recounted his version of what happened with a woman, Rebecca Garde Guay, who was able to escape from him, he tried to make her seem like the perpetrator.

"She wanted the twenty dollars, and then she bit me and took off with the money."

"She was the one that eventually went to the police, right?" I asked.

Although the incident had happened in 1982, Rebecca waited until late 1984 to file a report with the police. Since she was still involved in prostitution and did not want her name in the news, she feared coming forward. But when the Green River cases began to receive more publicity, she felt compelled to tell her story, believing the same man that had tried to kill her could be the one responsible for killing so many women in the area. After she provided a statement, she was able to pick Gary out of a photo lineup. She also remembered seeing his Kenworth work ID, giving police a direct lead.

He had already been on their radar after he was arrested for soliciting a prostitute in May 1982. In May 1984, he was even administered a polygraph, which he "passed with flying colors," he boasted to me. During the test he was asked if he ever caused the death of a prostitute, did he know anyone who ever killed a prostitute, and was he telling the police the truth. Based on his physiological emotional responses, it was determined the examination showed "no deception."

After Rebecca made her statement, Gary was brought in for questioning in February 1985, only two days after meeting Judith.

He didn't deny picking up Rebecca and paying her twenty dollars for a blow job. He didn't deny choking her, either. He told them the same story he told me: she bit his penis, forcing him to defend himself by choking her for a few seconds. He swore to them that he had no intention of killing her, and if she did happen to become unconscious, he was trained in CPR, so he could have saved her. Once both of their statements were on file, the detective asked Rebecca if she wished to press charges, and she decided not to. By the time he was arrested in 2001, the statute of limitations had expired, so he was never officially charged with her attempted murder.

However, Gary insisted she never pressed charges because the police believed him, not her. "I told them what the story was," he asserted. "Obviously, they see . . . so they saw that I had, ah, some marks on myself. And they believed me that she was the one that ripped me off."

I highly doubted that if she really bit him that the marks were still visible two years later when she gave her statement to the police. His lies were never-ending.

"But why did she bite you? Were you trying to kill her?"

"No. No. Damn," he said, irritated by my questions. "I was cheap, basically. Twenty dollars for a blow job, and the woman probably didn't—wasn't too good . . . you can't do anything because your damn pants are down or no pants on at all. But the idea is, they fight with you for money, and they go to a house, so you can't chase them," he said.

"How did that all happen? Isn't the price decided upon before?" I pressed.

"The price is decided on. And sometimes the woman changes her mind. They won't do sex."

"Oh, so that's what happened? She changed her mind?"

"No, she didn't change her mind. She just wanted to rip me off, basically, and go to a different city, so she won't have to see me again, basically. But that's it. Some women will do that because they got you down, because you got your pants down, and you can't chase them. And they go to a house, and they're protected."

When the police interviewed him after he was arrested in 2001, he told them that he and Rebecca had agreed on sex, but she changed her mind. "She wouldn't do sex. She just wanted to give me a blow job, and I never got a hard-on," he told them. I wondered which account was true. Did she actually bite him, had she changed her mind, or was he angry that he couldn't get an erection?

Later, he confessed to detectives that he sometimes had difficulty getting an erection with blow jobs, and that made him want to kill her. But he wouldn't dare admit anything about his sexual dysfunction to me.

"She took the twenty dollars. And the same thing with you, if you say, bite the guy, your best bet, to tell you the truth, your best bet is just give him a blow job," he advised. "Because if the guy is satisfied with the blow job, he's probably gonna walk away . . . If you fight him and bite him, maybe next time he's not gonna—he's just gonna kill you," he lectured, giving me advice as to what I should do if a man ever tried to force me to perform a sex act against my will. "You bite him, and you got a hell of a man out there that wants to get even with you," he said, hinting at what he wished he could have done to Rebecca.

"Did you ever cross paths with her again?"

"Never saw her again."

"But why would she bite you if she already had the money? I'm not understanding."

"I was holding on to my penis and trying to chase her with my pants down. And that's basically, ripping me off . . . I wouldn't have told anybody about it, but here I was being accused of why I was gonna chase her was because of that damn biting, and you can tell because they looked at it . . . and there was damage. But the idea is, a man's not gonna have more pride. You can't tell them I got a woman that ripped me off for twenty dollars for a blow job and she bit me. You're gonna get arrested for being with a prostitute, basically," he said.

As I listened, he seemed desperate for me to see him as the victim. She bit him, so he reacted. Wouldn't anyone do the same? She wanted to rip him off, so I should feel sorry for him. But his reasons to kill had everything to do with him and nothing to do with her—or any of the women—no matter how much he tried to persuade me they deserved it.

But he wanted my sympathy, so he continued to say anything he thought would promise it. As long as I continued to listen, there was always the chance I would believe him.

"But you got women that are—you have women that are prostitutes. You have dancers and barmaids and things like that. At that time, prostitution was just to make ends meet. . . . They want to buy birthday presents for their kids, well, they go out and have sex for twenty dollars . . . well, they were part-time, they're not professional prostitutes; they just do it because they need the money."

The hyperawareness he possessed of their backstories startled me. Was he recalling a specific woman, someone who had confided in him about her struggle and desperation for money that forced her to sell her body to him and other men, all for the sake of making her child happy? I imagined him listening to her with acute understanding, like a shrink nodding attentively, his eyes radiating warmth instead of judgment, as if to say, "You're in good hands." He'd appear sympathetic to her story of men abusing her and running out on her, leaving her with nothing but a screaming baby she loved anyway, loved enough to get in Gary's pickup and then his bed. Yet, what a relief to be with a "nice" guy. Even the position he wanted—from behind—seemed kind. It was better not to see the johns' faces sometimes. Until his arm wrapped around her throat, choking harder and harder, giving a new definition to what it meant to struggle.

No matter what stories they told him, he killed them anyway. But he seemed to recall these women as if they were friends from long ago who once trusted him with their sad life stories.

"At that time a prostitute is a girl, a teenager—it doesn't matter what year—she wants to go to the store and have somebody buy her a beer, and then she has sex for [it]. Somebody buys a beer for her . . . some guys will do that."

"So, buy them beer and they'd have sex?"

"They'll have sex for just a beer or two, and a woman at the store, women will have guys—a lot of time at the store I'll get a blow job or something, ya know, and half of the women out there, they're not prostitutes . . . Maybe a guy in the liquor store, somebody to buy them pot or something, and they'll have sex for some weed . . . It happens all the time . . . I did it for sex, basically," he admitted.

"And how much would a streetwalker typically cost?" I asked.

"Twenty dollars to fifty dollars for anybody on the street, basically. I remember there was a call girl, and she charged four hundred dollars for sex . . . [now], you look on Craig's List, you got prostitutes on there."

"I hear there's a lot of stuff on Craig's List like that, but they call themselves escorts," I said.

"I guess that's the truth. The law is pretty strict on escorts because they'll most likely go to a motel, and the woman meets you at a restaurant to get dinner and then you take the girl out for sex afterward," he said, describing it with unsurprising familiarity, this plot he had either acted out or fantasized about more times than anyone could count.

Much later, after watching hundreds of hours of his interrogation videos, I discovered that he regarded motel encounters differently. He swore he had never killed a woman in a motel—he'd be "asking for trouble" if he did. Yet, after those encounters it was not uncommon for him to be consumed with rage and unsatisfied, so much so, upon leaving the motel, he'd set out to find another prostitute, one willing to go to either his house or a remote location, with the sole intent to kill her. Other times, he would buy some of the girls a cheap meal at McDonald's or promise them one—an effort to gain their trust—and then hours later his arm would wrap around their necks in a chokehold, squeezing their last breaths from them.

"That's why it costs more, right? It's more high-end?"

"It's high-end, but most likely the women that are call girls are cleaner than a streetwalker, because a streetwalker, she don't care about giving somebody VD because [she feels] 'Some asshole gave it to me, I'm gonna give it to everybody else.' A street woman, she's gonna have all different kinds of VD because they're gonna get twenty dollars here and twenty dollars there," he said.

"What about when a guy takes out a girl and buys her dinner and she has sex with him, would you consider that a prostitute?" I asked. I wanted to know, how did he truly regard women?

"Okay, maybe in the case of them, money is not exchanged, but there's *value* exchanged, and that's what prostitution is. You read the law for prostitution . . . if you trade money for sex, it's called prostitution," he explained matter-of-factly.

According to his logic, I, too, was a prostitute in denial, then. How many dates have I had in which a man bought me dinner, and the date concluded with sex? In his mind, nearly *all* women were prostitutes, just some were more obvious about it than others.

But instead of arguing, I agreed with him. If I'd ever get anywhere with him, I figured it was in my best interest to spare him, of all people, a feminist lecture. It felt important to prove to him we were on common ground.

"I can see how that would be considered prostitution," I lied. "At the end of the day, if you're getting something in exchange for sex, that is prostitution," I said, paraphrasing his exact words to show my solidarity.

"Yeah. Well, that's the thing . . . a lot of times you got somebody exchange sex for—basically, prostitution because it's valuable to somebody . . . there's a lot of people that will exchange sex for anything, basically."

"It's the same thing as people who sleep their way to the top, people who will have sex with their boss for a promotion. That stuff happens. There's all sorts of exchanges," I added.

If I acted like I was on his side, I'd be one less woman for him to blame. In harmony, anyone becomes easier to talk to, and they will open up to unknown depths like a black hole before sucking you in and losing you forever. Why wouldn't it be the same with him?

CHAPTER EIGHT
Women as Objects

"My grandad used to say if you see a woman in a bra overweight . . . 'There's a lot of love in those hills,'" Gary said with a laugh. "With me, I used to say, 'You walk by an ugly kind of girl, and you look over, "Oh, look at that, there's dogface!"'" He laughed even harder before finally claiming as he often did that he was "just kidding."

Although I often cringed at his humor, I always managed a convincing laugh.

I wasn't entirely shocked to hear that he would revile women. During his interrogation, he had commented on how embarrassed he felt that his second wife, Marcia, was overweight. He also elaborated that he often felt that "all [he] could get [were] big people . . . that nobody wanted. I couldn't get a nice-looking woman," he lamented, which was part of the reason he enjoyed having sex with prostitutes.

However, Marcia claimed in her witness statements that Gary never made abusive remarks about her physical appearance. Whether he actually insulted women in passing, like he described to me, was hard to say.

What I did become sure of were his unsavory feelings toward women and his lack of empathy, some of the few things he was consistent about showing me. The women he killed, especially, he regarded as valueless objects to be used by him for his own purpose and pleasure. His words, unapologetic and cold, hammered into my heart a new kind of ache, different from any unrequited love or grief, but instead, sorrow, raw as a fresh wound, upon the realization that someone could exist with such indifference for the decades of pain they have inflicted. The more we spoke, the more I realized that if he could have gotten away with killing any woman, not just prostitutes, he probably would have.

Much like he used the Bible as a way to justify his actions, he also referenced misogynistic customs from other cultures. "You look at the Arab states . . . if you're married, [and] if a woman cheats on the husband, the husband has the right to kill the wife," he acknowledged.

"Yeah . . . in different cultures—"

"They cut off their sex organs, so a man keeps you from—keeps a woman basically for having babies. Basically, she won't run off because she don't need no feeling for sex," he continued, seeming to advocate for female genital mutilation. Since other cultures accepted this barbaric, prejudiced-fueled violation of women, normalizing his own violence became easier for him to do.

"And like I said, we have the right to kill you, too," he said.

For the first time, I felt actual fear while speaking to him, and it had nothing to do with losing the privilege to write a story. His ability to end my life and his "right" to do so became real in a way I couldn't imagine before.

For him, the urge to kill was difficult to control, like a cough or muscle spasm; he would give in to the impulse while other times he struggled to calm it. Even when it came to Judith. As much as he claimed to have cared about her and loved her, he still fought urges to kill her. He once admitted to a psychologist that evaluated him after his arrest, "I was having doggy-style sex, my favorite position, with Judith, and I had to refrain from killing her . . . It tapered off. [But] it was really strong at first . . . But more of me caring and helping her have sex . . . I always liked to try to get her to have a climax before . . . that took my mind off of it . . . if she didn't have one, at least I tried. And that took me away from wanting to kill her."

But when it came to his victims, nothing would stop his war against them. Since they were on the street and willing to get in his truck, in his mind, they were practically begging him for a punishment to be delivered. To him, they were not human—just a hole for him to fuck—so why should he behave as human in return?

If he was standing next to me, his hands would probably be at my throat until he succeeded in making me part of his past, then forgetting me like any other face in a crowd. Like most of his victims, he couldn't remember their faces, and I figured, if given the chance, I would be no different.

Yet, when it came to distant, unimportant memories, he would remember them as if they happened only five minutes ago. Although over twenty years had passed, he could remember the last camper he bought down to the last detail of the man who sold it to him. The motorhome was advertised on TV, and he wasted no time dialing the phone number that was listed. Before he knew it, he was handing thousands of dollars in cash to "an old guy with a mustache and a beard," who was "there with his wife," he told me.

He could describe the physical features of a random man who sold him a motorhome, but he could barely remember any of the faces of the women he killed. Many of the locations where he picked up his victims were also lost in his mind. Yet, the transaction of his RV remained clear in his thoughts, an occasion more notable than ending a life, according to him. It was hard to believe his memory was so selective, erasing each woman's existence so completely.

More valuable dead than alive, their bones became reminders of what he conquered, his possessions. In Gary's mind, the remains of his victims were his property, and whenever anyone took them away, they might as well have been breaking into his home and stealing valuable heirlooms. "She meant . . . a beautiful person that was my property, my . . . possession. Someone only I knew, and I missed when they were found or when I lost them," he confessed during his interrogation.

That was why after he killed Marcia Chapman (not to be confused with his wife Marcia) in August 1982, he pushed a large rock down the sloping bank of the Green River and used it to pin her body to the bottom of the water. Ten days later, he did the same thing to Cynthia Hinds. Like placing paperweights over loose pages, the women were kept in place, unable to float away from him, unlike Wendy Coffield and Debra Bonner, the first two victims he placed in the river in July 1982. Instead, they floated downstream, got snagged on debris, and were both discovered not even a month after they had gone missing. He was determined not to make the same mistakes again.

Later, as I retraced his steps, I tried to fathom the depths of his depravity. The Meeker Street Bridge with its rusted green beams stretched above the Green River like a belt. Across from it, I stood on the Peck Bridge, a short walking path that extends over the river. I pushed my body against the blue metal barrier, looking down at the murky water that slapped against rocks, where a shoreline formed. In July 1982, two kids riding their bikes did the same thing, but when they looked down they saw Wendy Coffield's body stuck on the rocks. With the exception of her shoes and socks, she was naked. Her hair danced with the flow of the water, and her hand seemed to be waving at them.

Gary had always referred to her as his first victim, although he was never entirely sure. He was certain he had choked her in the back of his truck, leaving her pants, shirt, and underwear noosed around her neck. He also recalled, after killing her, in a fit of lingering rage, he snapped her left upper arm out of the socket, breaking the bone. He drove to the Green River where it was dark and deserted, a perfect place to put a body, he figured. He stood at the edge of the river, where he dragged her body, and then launched it into the water. He watched her float away until it was too dark to keep track of where the water pulled her.

But after he killed Chapman and then Hinds, before he allowed the water to swallow them, he kept their bodies until the next day and continued to have sex with them. After he finished, before weighing them down in the water, he scanned the area, noticing smaller rocks strewn along the dirt and grass.

When his eyes fell on the rocks, he decided to slip one inside of Chapman, and then later, he did the same with Hinds. Although detectives tried to find a deeper meaning of this act, that he was trying to "plug" up the women, or he was "getting his rocks off", his reasons were more personal. By pushing a rock inside each woman, he thought that "nobody can screw her anymore." Since he felt that prostitutes were constantly "flaunting" their vaginas to men, he would take away their power by making what they were selling useless. The dominance it gave him over a woman's body and the turn-on he felt of experimenting with a woman's vagina was what mattered to him most. He also claimed that inserting rocks inside them was a way of trying to prevent himself from returning to have sex with their corpses again. Deep down, he knew returning to them was wrong, that he had become too twisted.

* * *

Depending on the angle of the sun, the water appeared either black or swampy green as it flowed beneath me. I tried to envision the early frenzy of his violence, the craft of it he experimented with until his methods were perfected. I walked the same path along the river he once did as he decided on the place where he would leave each victim. Boulders still walled the sides of the river. Kneeling down, I grazed my hands along the smooth, slimy surface of a rock that protruded from the water as if coming up for air.

Although he swore to detectives the women were dead when he defiled them, in his rushed meandering narration, he alluded to me that at least one of the women could have been alive as he shoved a rock inside her. "Somebody put a rock up a woman's vagina when she was still alive. Either she was passed out or whatever, and you wonder how in the hell it got in there, but you get into it. It's a lot harder getting it out." I remembered his words and winced, pressing my fingers along the jagged edges of a wide stone that rested on the bank.

During his confession, he was always adamant that he put rocks inside some of his victims *after* he had already killed them. He denied ever torturing anyone or hurting them in other ways besides choking them. But with me, his story changed. It was hard to believe he wasn't remembering his own experience when he brought up the rocks to me. He even included the detail of trying to remove the rock after it was inside the woman. Years prior, when he described it to police, he also recounted he tried to pluck out the rock, but it wouldn't budge. It was impossible to know what Gary might have done to each woman after he killed her; what really was the truth.

His fixation with inserting objects inside of women was nothing new. The idea of it had excited him since he was in the navy and stationed overseas. In the Philippines, he had witnessed barmaids insert beer bottles into their vaginas and serve them to the sailors that way; he had watched a show in Singapore in which two women stuck crimpers inside each other.

He had even tried to insert a beer bottle inside his wife Marcia when she was passed out drunk but stopped himself after a few minutes; and in 1981, a year prior to the start of his killing frenzy, he tied his girlfriend at the time, Nancy, to stakes in the woods and used a banana to have sex with her instead of his penis and then pushed grapes inside her only to pluck them out with his mouth.

On a two-week camping trip in which they remained naked the entire time, he had pounded four stakes into the ground and tied her to them with her nylon pantyhose. In Nancy's witness statement she described, "I was a little nervous, but that was just on my part. It wasn't that I didn't trust him, that I was worried he was going to do something to really hurt me or else I never would have laid down and let him do it . . . [the fruit], that was a surprise to me. The banana was just discarded afterward, but the grapes, he put them, one up at a time, and then tried to get them and eat them, and then he did . . . I know he put them in by his fingers and his mouth and his tongue, but I'm pretty sure that he went inside of me and then after that . . . he didn't climax or anything, but then he went back down to oral sex."

In my conversations with Gary, he seemed to reminisce of this experience. "Back in the Egyptian times, they show pictures of the women, [and] they're using grapes. I guess it was for the woman to get excited, so the guy can take them out. But that's been going on for years," he explained. "I got a joke about it. My husband hates vegetables, but he'll eat the ones that have been inside me . . . that's the only way he gets his vitamins," he said and laughed.

As the frequency of our calls increased, it had become a regular occurrence for Gary to expound on his fixation with the female body, specifically vaginas. The size of them, what could fit inside them, and how wide they could stretch were all topics of discussion. A lifelong obsession for Gary, after his arrest he even admitted to Sheriff Reichert that he would measure some of the women's vaginas with his fingers after he killed them and wished he would have returned to "every one of those sites and see how long their vagina was." By doing so, he hoped to determine how often the women masturbated, if at all, and learn about the muscles inside "that satisfy a guy."

But with me, he tried to broach the subject as casually as he could. So, he brought up cervical caps, a form of birth control that entails a doctor inserting a "flexible cup-shaped rubber device" over the cervix to prevent sperm from entering the uterus. If he spoke about something as commonplace as birth control, then he could ease into a discussion about inserting objects into a woman's vagina.

"Have you heard anything about a cervical cup?" he asked nonchalantly, calling it a "cup" rather than a "cap." In his mind, he seemed stuck on the design of it, the circumference as wide as a coffee mug, a drinking glass, or a decorative bathroom cup, he wasn't sure.

"I think it blocks off the woman from the man, to have sex, I think whatever it is," he explained. I couldn't tell if he was truly misinformed about what a cervical cap was, or if he just preferred the idea of pushing a large cup inside a woman. "You have to look up cervical cup," he instructed.

But to his disappointment, I didn't need to conduct any research. What woman didn't know most, if not all, types of birth control that were available to her?

"It's a form of birth control . . . it's not permanent . . . and you have to go to the doctor, and they insert it, and then it stays in there," I informed him.

"Yeah, whatever. But if it blocks the opening of the, the uterus—"

"So, the sperm—"

"So, you can't. Oh, so you can't get the penis in the woman—but I think that's what it's for," he refuted.

"No, it blocks the sperm from entering, not that the penis can't go in," I corrected him.

For a moment, he paused as if trying to envision what I was describing to him. "Yeah. Well, that would be a good thing," he conceded. "But it doesn't give the guy a chance to have—He's gonna . . . never mind," he said, still confused. It was as though he needed an instructional manual with pictures—the kind included with furniture, toys, or anything else that needed to be built by hand—to understand how such a device could function. The only knowledge he possessed even remotely similar was when he decided that he wanted to have sex with his victim's dead body again but wasn't able to due to the rock he jammed deep inside her. He believed a cervical cap was similar, leading only to abstinence.

It was hard to believe some of the misinformation that filled his mind. A lot of what he convinced himself about women had not been true, and he seemed resistant of the knowledge I tried to pass on to him, despite that he was always asking for it, picking and probing my brain as if he had elected me the spokesperson to speak on behalf of all women.

Beyond cervical caps, there were many objects he imagined inserting inside a woman, things he had been thinking about for the last fifty-two years since he returned from the Philippines.

A crowbar, a baseball bat, a ketchup bottle, a beer bottle (sometimes two), an umbrella, anything. He explained that for one to five dollars more, a prostitute would pose naked with said objects sticking out of her, while the john would snap Polaroids of her. Something to jerk off to later.

"This actually happened a few times," Gary admitted. "The thing is, you take pictures of her, and she does the posing, whatever she wants to do. She wants a baseball bat up her vagina, she'll do it," he said.

The whereabouts of these photos, I assumed, were as lost as many of the women whose bodies were reduced to skeletons by now somewhere in a wooded area. If he was ever going to tell me about these women, he would only do so if I *didn't* ask. I had learned my direct questions produced the vaguest answers. But if I allowed him total control of the conversation, sometimes he opened up and shared brief admissions he should have felt guilty about. I hoped this would be one of those times.

Instead of telling me anything about the women who were still missing, he was more preoccupied with coming up with ideas of what he could have done while also reminiscing about what he had already done and wished he could relive. Objects he could shove inside a woman simply because he wanted to.

The way he saw it, if he was paying for a woman, he owned her for that hour. Since she became his property, he could do whatever he wanted to her. The same way a person could cut down a tree in the backyard of a house they owned, Gary could instruct a woman to squat on a baseball bat to see how much of it could be swallowed inside her. "How many golf balls can you get in a vagina?" As long as he paid, he could find out, similar to a carnival game.

"And that is natural for a streetwalker to do. They probably do everything," he reflected.

Whether what he told me were fantasies or memories, I couldn't tell. But as he spoke, it seemed he still thought about shoving a bottle—or any object he wanted to see fit—inside a woman. When he hypothesized the measurement of my fists, telling me that together they would be comparable to the circumference of a baby's head if I ever gave birth, he was really guessing everything that could fit inside me. Without fail, he always reminded me how lucky I was to not be in a room alone with him, even if he only wanted to study the size of my hands.

* * *

Even though he was hundreds of miles away, locked behind a steel door, his energy seemed to linger at the river, a suffocating dark force that had the power to make the air feel unbreathable. Suddenly, I felt like I was standing in ruins. The weight of the air heavy with last breaths formed a silence like the sealed-up insides of a jar. I walked faster to my car with thoughts of everything he was capable of doing until I was sprinting, the soles of my shoes slapping hard against the ground, reverberating the only sound of life.

After driving for a few minutes, I stood in what was called Cottonwood Park, although it didn't resemble much of a park. It was simply a small plot of land along the banks of the Green River. Dead grass crunched beneath my feet as I followed what resembled a trail that was so overgrown with bushes and tall weeds it blocked out the river. After a few minutes, I was met with the same stifling feeling. Even if I had known nothing about Gary, the air would still feel heavy with the weight of everything he had done there.

In September 1983, after killing Tracy Winston, he left her body there at the base of a large tree. It would take almost three years before her remains, which by that time only consisted of a torso, were discovered by park employees.

"Cottonwood Park was a good place along the river, and it was a while after the other ones were found, so that's why I chose it," he confessed to detectives.

But the location was also familiar to him. Years prior, when he was married to Marcia, he brought her there to have sex. Then in the spring of 1983, while walking in the wooded area there with a girlfriend, Lorrie, he asked her for a quickie. In a witness statement, she recalled, he dropped his pants, and she took his shirt off to lay it on the ground. "He seemed to be aroused by the fact he might be caught," she remembered.

The emptiness of the park was enough to make me feel entirely removed from society. I surveyed the landscape around me, trying to find the tree where he left Tracy Winston, but all the trees seemed equal in height. The farther I walked toward the bank, the more I wanted to turn back. The car, which I had parked on the side of the road, was no longer in sight as I stood encircled by brush taller than me and trees that canopied the sky. At any moment someone could come up behind me and snuff me out, as simple as ending the flicker of a candle, and no one would ever know. I suddenly felt compelled to lift a rock the size of an infant and carry it in my arms, just in case I needed a weapon. If I had to bash in someone's skull, would I be able to? I imagined him walking the same steps, never thinking twice.

By the time I returned to the car, my arms were tired and dusty with dirt. I wanted nothing more than to keep driving farther and farther away, but everywhere I turned, he was there, reminding me of the worst things that could happen—what he made sure of—the only promise he could ever keep.

CHAPTER NINE

The Survivors

With only half an hour of daylight left, headlights from the passing cars had started to suffuse the oncoming darkness. Rain began to fall, glittering in the white brightness as traffic halted, and pedestrians crossed the street. Rebecca Garde Guay had just finished her shift at Quality Carpet Cleaners and wanted nothing more than to go home. She walked to the bus stop on 200th and Pacific Highway South and stared down as far as she could. Not one bus in sight. *I'll get home faster if I hitch a ride,* she thought.

The rain began to fall harder, so she stood at the curb and held out her thumb. Not even a minute later, a maroon Dodge pickup stopped alongside her. The man—which a few years later she would learn was Gary Ridgway—rolled down the window and seemed to study her face. He gave her a strange look—he neither smiled nor grimaced, but something about his gaze unsettled her.

She shrugged it off and asked, "Are you going to Burien?"

He nodded, not saying anything.

She opened the door and climbed into the passenger seat. "Are you sure you're not police?" she asked. The Green River cases had led to a bigger police presence, especially on PAC Highway, and she worried she was getting set up.

He reached into his pocket for his wallet and opened it to his Kenworth ID card. He held it out long enough for her to match the face in the picture to the man in front of her and to learn that he lived in Kent. She was satisfied.

As he drove down the highway, he began to complain to her about the terrible day he had been having. Earlier that morning he attended a court hearing and was prosecuted for soliciting a prostitute that was really an undercover cop working vice. On top of that, in a separate legal battle, the court decided his ex-wife would retain full custody of his son, allowing him to only have visits on some weekends.

Although he was telling her about his misfortunes, it didn't feel like he was talking to her. He seemed to just be talking, not caring whether he received a response. Finally she interrupted him: "Do you date?"

"Yeah, sometimes," he said.

"Well, a blow job's twenty dollars," she propositioned.

"Okay," he said, agreeing to the price.

"I know a spot we can go to down the road."

He turned down 204th toward the place she had in mind. He drove through a vacant lot behind some mobile homes and continued farther into the woods. She never went with anyone that far from the street.

He told her he didn't want to stay in the car, that it would be more private if they got out and walked into the woods behind the bushes. There would be less of a chance of getting caught there. She didn't like the idea of being so isolated, but she really needed the money. He handed her a twenty that she stuffed into her purse.

He walked at a fast pace in front of her as if he was in a hurry and wanted to get it over with more than she did. She could barely keep up as she followed him down the darkened path. Whatever daylight was left seemed to be snuffed out by the trees towering over them. The rain subsided into a soft drizzle, dampening the dirt below her feet.

When she got there, his shorts were already down at his ankles. She didn't bother to remove any of her clothes, and he didn't ask.

He barely looked at her at all. She set her purse beside her and kneeled down onto the wet grass in front of him. She held his penis, which was limp, and began gliding her mouth over it. He didn't paw at her breasts or try to caress any part of her body. He placed his hands on her head but didn't pull her hair like most men would. As she continued to bob her head up and down, she noticed he still was not hard.

Then out of nowhere, he pulled his penis out of her mouth. "You bitch," he scolded. "You bit my cock."

"No, I didn't. I never did that before. You don't know what you're talking about," she argued, caught off guard.

Without saying anything else, he pushed her to the ground, got behind her, and wrapped his arm around her neck the way a police officer would when trying to restrain someone. Tighter and tighter he tugged while shoving her face in the dirt. Since his shorts were still down at his ankles, he couldn't bind his legs around her to stop her from moving, what he would normally do to his victims. She continued to thrash beneath him, kicking as hard as she could, until they had rolled over. He was now on top of her with both hands around her neck, squeezing her throat as if he was wringing out a wet rag.

His face grew white as if he was becoming ill, and his hands felt cold and clammy as they clutched her throat. She considered screaming, but who would hear her? She was too far away from the mobile homes. She couldn't breathe at all but continued to struggle with him anyway. She kicked and moved her feet, not even sure if she was reaching him. Then somehow she moved from under him and broke free from his grip.

Trying to catch her breath, she asked, "What are you trying to do this to me for? I'll give you back your twenty dollars. I don't really need the money. I don't even know why I did this. All I have is my mother, my brother, and myself. If you kill me, they won't even know where I am," she rambled, climbing to her feet.

He stood there as if in a daze. She wasn't sure if he was listening to her, and she didn't bother to find out. If she stayed any longer, she knew he would try to choke her again. She grabbed her purse and began running as fast as she could. When she looked back, she saw him putting on his clothes. She ran even faster toward the mobile homes. Afraid he might chase her, she knocked frantically on the first door she passed. Hysterical and shaking with red marks visible on her neck, she explained that she had just been assaulted, and she was invited inside.

Down the road, tires rolled over the ground, getting closer and closer. She held her breath at the thought of him; she was sure he would have killed her and still would.

But she was safe now, she reminded herself.

From the window, she watched the maroon pickup speed past her, returning to the night.

* * *

Years later, when Gary was arrested, he would describe this encounter with Rebecca as an unplanned attempt to kill her, meaning that when he picked her up he had no intention of harming her. When he was interviewed by police in 2003, he claimed, "If I planned to kill her, I would had my shorts off." Through the years, he would tell many versions of this story: she bit him, and he was acting in self-defense; she had initially agreed to have sex with him but then only gave him a blow job that didn't satisfy him; the thundering racket of the airplanes overhead irritated him; when he couldn't get an erection, that prompted him to want to choke her, which was what most likely happened.

Since he wasn't in "the killing mood" and the "rage" he had was not "a hundred percent"—what it would normally take for him to end a life—and she began talking to him, staring at him directly in the face, he decided to let her go. Later, he described this decision as "beyond what I ever done before."

As he watched her run away from him, he stood there, pleading with himself, *Why didn't I kill her? Why didn't I kill her?* He knew it was only a matter of time before she'd report him to the police. Even though it took her two years, once she did, he became an official person of interest and would remain on the police's radar until he was finally arrested in 2001.

Similar to Rebecca, during the 1980s, there were two other women who fought him off, forcing him to let them go. But that was rare. Most of the time, when a woman entered his truck, he would remain in control, deciding whether she would live or die. The criteria that made a woman worthy of life were far from consistent and tailored according to his mood and capricious reasoning. Women who were part-time prostitutes trying to make extra cash on the side, he spared more than others. He recalled a teacher, bartender, college student, a senator's daughter, and a King County Health Department employee, all of whom he didn't kill because they were also "workers," and more valuable to society in his eyes.

During my conversations with him, he recalled having sex with dancers who worked at strip clubs and letting them live. After a night of watching women take off their clothes and twirl and grind their bodies against a pole greased with their own sweat, Gary, like a lot of men in the audience, would try to leave the club with one of them. That's if the price wasn't outrageous—sixty-five dollars or more. On a slow night, sometimes he'd get lucky and find someone willing to give him a bargain.

The way he saw it, most of the topless dancers were "worked up after showing their boobs off" all night. As long as he wasn't competing against any other men, money wasn't really a concern. A woman like that would *want* to leave with him and would be just as excited as he was at the prospect of a night of sex.

On these rare occasions, he would bring her home or accompany her to her place. But then there were nights he would go with her to a boat that would float around Lake Washington where they would stay until the sun came up. He was convinced that "women love boats," that the serene, romantic ambience would keep them hostage in bed next to him until morning. As the boat left trails of soft waves undulating behind them, they drifted farther away from the dock. For the next few hours it seemed they were the only ones to exist except for the moon's ghostly face glowing a pale light and the stars stapled over the black nothingness as if holding the entire night together.

In the deck below, the dancer would be topless, but now only for him rather than a large audience. Wanting him as much as he wanted her, she wouldn't just lie there like stone beneath him, something most prostitutes would do. In sync with his body, she would move to his rhythm, pulling him closer so he could taste her skin. "Making love to her . . . not just slamming her," he made the distinction. As long as it resembled love, as long as she wouldn't leave in the middle of the night or right after like the streetwalkers did, then she didn't deserve to die. Another distinction he made. But I wasn't sure how much I believed him.

"So why go to prostitutes, then?"

He could only offer a half-assed explanation. The topless dancers were disappearing from Seattle, starting new lives somewhere else, he guessed. "Maybe she's from New York, and she lives in Staten Island, and she's a teacher now because she was at a bar topless over in Seattle." In everything he remembered, he made an example of me, as if he really believed in the history he invented, that I was a woman that had gotten away from him.

The truth was he couldn't kill women that worked as dancers with the same ease as prostitutes. And killing mattered to him more than having sex. As much as he pretended to be a man that would have chosen a dancer over a prostitute if more of them were available, as if killing wasn't important to him, it would never be the truth. True fulfillment of his desires required having sex with a woman he could kill. But that didn't mean he didn't enjoy a one-night stand.

Afterward, he'd fall asleep with the woman in his arms, what he classified as the main reason for wanting to "make love to somebody." The confirmation of feeling wanted for an entire night as opposed to the thirty minutes to an hour a streetwalker would allot him was enough to subside his anger, even for a short while. "The last thing you see is a woman in your arms instead of like a prostitute, getting up . . . Getting up after having sex and then when you go back to bed you don't have that intimacy. You turn around and go to sleep or where if you fall asleep with a woman in your arms that's the last thing you see," he lamented during an interview with a psychologist after his arrest.

Going home with a dancer meant he would be with a woman who wanted him all night and wanted "the kiss" afterward. A woman that had sex with him like she was his wife and wanted "to hop on top of him and work her tail off to try to have a climax . . . humping him as much as [he was] gonna be humping her . . . like [he was] her man now." As opposed to picking up a prostitute who would never even smile at him and only "wanted money and wanted to leave."

During my conversations with him, he claimed that dancers were not the only women he thought worthy enough to live. Throughout the 1980s, while he was actively murdering women, he alleged he took on another mission: he tried to save some of them. He counted at least ten that were pregnant. Instead of driving them to a secluded area in the woods or to his house to kill them, he drove them to a bus station or to their parents' homes. "They swore they were never gonna go back, and I was pretty gullible. Everybody wanted to get out, so I helped them out," he explained. "I didn't want to meet the parents because they might think I'm having sex with their pregnant daughter. But I waited, and I saw them get picked up by their parents."

He recalled some of their names and where they were originally from, details if true, stunned me. When it came to most of his victims, he always claimed he didn't remember much about them, but these women, the ones he spared, were imprinted in his mind. For instance, in a letter he recounted, "Linda lived in Yakima with baby. No coat in the rain. Pimp kicked her out. I bought coat. Mom picked her up at Space Needle . . . Helen lived in Olympia. Pregnant. Parents came to SeaTac Red Lion to pick her up . . . Tony lived in Portland, Oregon. Pregnant. Dropped her off at the Tacoma train station. Parent took her home . . ." and the list went on.

Although I was skeptical, it was not unheard of that he let some women live. In 1983, he picked up a woman named Pamela from 15th and Commerce in Tacoma. In her witness statement, she recalled getting into his truck and having to put her feet on paint cans that cluttered most of the floor of the passenger seat. Gary always made sure to leave a tire, cans, or any other large object(s) in the front so he would have an excuse to have sex with the woman in the back. The front seat was not an ideal place to kill. The woman would be able to grab the steering wheel and honk the horn, and they would be more visible to anyone passing by. This time, his plan was no different. Once he parked, he would lure her into the back.

As he drove, he began to tell her about his day, that he had been working such long hours and didn't even know why he was out because he was exhausted, but then he decided he wanted some company, and that was when he found her. Somehow they began talking about her family and then religion—similar to conversations he'd have with me—never even discussing the details of their date. He made a comment, alluding that prostitutes were bad people. Although she wasn't religious, she argued that "God never condemned a prostitute." She went on to tell him that "[God] let a prostitute in His house, and I know He doesn't agree with it, but He still loves you if you're a prostitute." Gary stared at her, as though he was really listening to what she had to say. "God loves me," she said.

Before she knew it, they were all the way down South Tacoma Way, too far from where she wanted to be, and she started to get nervous. She asked him where they were going, but he didn't say anything. He turned a sharp right and then looked at her and said, "I'm going to tell you something you're not going to like."

"What?"

"I brought you out here to kill you."

"You did?" she asked, her heart racing.

"But you're different. You're different from all the others. I can't do it to you," he said. "You're special. There's something I like about you."

"Really?" she asked, trying to keep her composure.

"Yeah. Why are you out here?"

"Drugs . . . I don't know why I'm out here."

He started to head back to where he picked her up, not saying anything else.

"If there's something I can help you with, why would you want to do that to me or anybody," she said, breaking the brick-heavy silence.

"Never mind. It's nothing I want to talk about."

Fearful he would change his mind, she kept quiet the rest of the way. When he pulled over on 15th and Commerce, just as she was about to hop out, he said, "Good luck in your life. You shouldn't be out here." He then drove away, leaving her to breathe the cool night air.

Since he let her live, I wondered if there was any truth to all the others he claimed to spare. And what were his reasons? Simply to play God? Or by letting some of them live, did that help him kill more of them later on? When he let a woman live, other women would see her exiting his car unscathed. If they didn't see it, they would hear about it—women talked. The next time he was looking for a date, they wouldn't second-guess going to his house or a secluded area outside with him.

Although he had let Pamela live, I still couldn't rule out the possibility that he was telling me a lie. In his letter, he made it sound like he had felt sorry for any pregnant woman working the streets, but during his interrogation, he admitted in 1983 he had picked up a pregnant woman in Georgetown with the intention of killing her. He only decided not to when they couldn't find a place where she felt comfortable enough to date him. I knew he had also murdered Mary Meehan, who was eight months pregnant at the time, and then buried her in a shallow grave near Tyee Golf Course. He swore he didn't realize she was pregnant—it was dark, and she had only given him a blow job. Since he didn't have sex with her, he had not really touched her body.

The more we spoke, the more I noticed he seemed to care about the opinion others had of him. Killing a pregnant woman was one of the lowest things a person could do. The last thing he wanted was to have that information floating around the prison, so he vehemently denied knowing she was pregnant. And now, he seemed determined to prove to me he had a shred of humanity after all. He might've killed one pregnant woman, but he saved ten. Unless one of these women came forward, the truth would never be known. Even then, it would be difficult to corroborate.

If he did, in fact, spare them, it seemed like he regretted his decision to let any of them go. At the time, he thought he was giving them a second chance, and since they were pregnant, they would be more inclined to start over. But he learned that their own babies didn't matter to most of them. Oftentimes, they would give birth, hand over the baby to their mothers, and return to the street. Then, there was the issue of who they were going home to, since oftentimes girls ended up on the street to escape their father, grandfather, or brother who had been raping them. "You think you're doing good, but you're just giving them right back to the rapist," Gary lamented.

"Ninety percent of them go back into it . . . You don't like giving blow jobs to guys. It's not that," he said. They go back into it because "they're full of venereal disease. They don't have any money to go to a doctor. They're broke or they spend the money on drugs." It was impossible to really save them, he concluded, seeming to regret ever trying. "Are they the throw- away females?" he asked. He seemed to think so, no matter what I said.

"Active streetwalkers will go to hell. [They're] not saved by Christ," he reflected in a letter. Even after they were dead, it wouldn't be possible to save them, according to Gary's logic.

In the same letter, he also wrote, "Yes, two hot curling irons get the truth out. Where it hurt better. Jane Doe."

I had no idea what he meant. I wondered if he was remembering something horrific he had done to a woman that he had never told anyone about before, if he was fantasizing, or if he was recalling someone else's atrocities—he was in prison surrounded by other murderers. Of course, he wouldn't tell me, making me even more suspicious and doubtful that he had saved any of the women he claimed to.

How many women was he responsible for killing that had never been proven? I thought about the list I compiled early on in my correspondence with him. Their bodies were still out there, bones by now, in places he might've put them. I wondered if the police even cared to find them at this point, if they were ever priorities. Would their names remain fodder in a database, their lives unremembered with each passing year?

When Gary made statements hinting at unspeakable acts of violence and continued to tell me he had killed close to a hundred women, it was hard to believe he could spare anyone, releasing them into the night, without them ever knowing they were caged.

MOTIVATIONS AND PSYCHOLOGY

CHAPTER TEN

Sex and Pleasure

Standing on the glass floor inside the Space Needle made everything below seem in danger of being crushed beneath my heel like a cigarette. I stood there for a long while, rotating as the floor crawled along the same as earth. How could I not imagine myself falling? Glass shattering, some freak accident. A quick descent, but maybe for a moment, a conscious thought of knowing what it felt like to fly. Before gravity misshaped me, a blob of a body, contorted bones. A front-page tragedy. Would Gary recognize my face if it flashed across Fox News? Who would he call in place of me?

Before this anxiety completely consumed me, I snapped a picture of my feet standing on the glass with the city hundreds of feet below. When I returned to New York, I printed this photo and sent it to Gary, proof I had been there. I always felt I needed to convince him what I said was true, to silence his doubt I constantly suspected. If he believed everything I said, then maybe he would tell me something I wanted to know. At any moment, it seemed he could walk away without giving me any information or a second thought, the last thing I wanted to happen.

I didn't think much of the photo as I shut it inside a greeting card. My bare calves didn't seem enticing enough to prompt a reaction, nor did the Converse on my feet. It's not like I was in five-inch strappy stilettos, the length of my entire legs exposed. Not like it would have made a difference at that point. He was already telling me he loved me, calling me a trophy wife, acting jealous about my time spent with Asher, and making flirtatious comments.

That can of worms was open, their gooey, sticky bodies squirming toward me. There was no escape. They would touch me no matter what, slithering over me. Whenever Gary called, I tried to get out of those lines of conversation, but I had no choice. He had too much control and too much to say.

It didn't matter that I was wearing shorts, not a dress like he had daydreamed. When he got that photo and stared at it for over a month, all he saw were my bare legs and got carried away. "Did you see the guy down there looking up as you [were] going up there because you [were] wearing a dress with the tennis shoes on?" he asked. "Guys will make it up, I bet there's one woman not wearing underwear. I don't see panty lines. So, they look under and see if she's not wearing any underwear. Oh, men are voyeurs," he explained, as if making an excuse for his fantasy, what he had probably spent the last month jerking off to. How many times had he imagined this scene before growing bored?

It was only a matter of time before he imagined something else. "A honeymoon motel," he called it. On the second level, in each room—bedroom, restaurant, it didn't matter—a glass floor extended wall to wall.

At first, I thought he was describing one of those fancy hotels on a tropical island. In those rooms, you could walk over a square of the ocean. He laughed at the idea that something pretty could be cased under a glass floor. Gary was imagining something more elaborate and went on to describe a detailed fantasy of watching a couple on a date from below.

The more Gary described this, everything inside me recoiled, like twisting a rubber band, until I thought I would snap and break apart. It reminded me of the feeling I got when I was a teenager and a fat middle-aged man sitting across from me on the Q train pulled out his dick and began jerking off. I ran into the next car and wanted to hurl. Even though he didn't touch me (thank God), every inch of my skin felt contaminated with an invisible layer of grime. It was no different now, listening to Gary fantasize. To think his fantasy was born from a picture I thought was the furthest thing from sexual or alluring. I felt betrayed by my own intuition, naive as a schoolgirl.

"You know how guys are," he said, as if excusing his behavior.

How you *are*, I thought.

Since I couldn't run away, all I could do was resort to laughter and jokes, what I always did whenever I was uncomfortable or nervous. It was rather comical in an absurd way—a motel with a glass floor with random men craning their necks to watch people have sex.

I already knew that he enjoyed having sex outdoors with his wives, girlfriends, and many of the women he killed. Later, I would learn that he had welcomed spectators, even as a teenager, when he first started having sex. After dating a girl he met from high school for about a week, he had invited her over to have sex. When one of his friends in the neighborhood found out about this plan, he insisted that he hide in the bedroom closet and watch. Gary didn't object, nor did he tell the girl they had an audience. After he took off her clothes, she laid naked on his bed as he tried to push his penis inside her. But he couldn't force himself inside her without causing her pain, something he was not inclined to do at that point, to hurt a woman. So, he stopped, and the girl went home, never knowing that anyone else was in the room to witness her almost lose her virginity.

Whether it was a girlfriend, wife, or prostitute he led into the woods, the back seat or front seat of his car that idled in a parking lot, day or night, outdoor sex thrilled him. Just like his ex-girlfriend Nancy recalled, while they had sex on a bluff of a river during a camping trip, some people went by on a raft. For a second he stopped, startled by the audience, but then he continued, not caring who watched.

But what he really desired more than any other sexual experience was to conclude with killing.

For nearly all his victims, he'd follow the same routine: choking from behind until they were unconscious. If he wasn't certain a victim was dead, or his arm grew tired, he used his knee or stood on their throat. Other times, he'd use a ligature: an extension cord, pantyhose, a belt from a robe, a towel, a curtain tieback—anything near him. He'd then leave their naked bodies in remote locations—in clusters, so he'd remember where he put them—disposing their clothes in a nearby ditch, a Goodwill drop-off, or alongside the road. Sometimes he'd bury their jewelry or leave it in the women's restroom at Kenworth for his coworkers to find. One time he even gave a pair of earrings he removed from one of his victim's ears as a Christmas or birthday gift—he couldn't recall—to Roxanne's daughter.

When detectives asked him to describe each murder one by one, he couldn't; they were all the same to him. "I don't have that information to access to exactly each person cause they didn't mean anything to me. They meant less than a dog did," he told them.

However, when it came to his wives and girlfriends, the way he regarded sex almost sounded normal. In many of my conversations with him, he loved to describe scenarios in which he forced me to imagine what sex would be like with him. "You get a vibrator, and you get your wife, you do it right for your wife, and you turn her on, and you get all, she gets all hot and bothered, and she has an orgasm, and you have sex with her."

The specific woman was irrelevant, unnamed. "And then the penetration of the man can make her have a climax," he described, as if trying to seduce me, but all he had were his words and they were never going to work.

Years ago, during his interrogation, he said that he wanted to "drive" a woman "wild with sex." He went on to describe to a psychologist the intense satisfaction he derived specifically from tying up a woman, his love for absolute dominance, recalling his experiences with Marcia and Nancy. "I could take it and make them loud. Use the vibrator on them . . . it was pretty hot," he reminisced.

"The wife has an orgasm, the guy's gonna have an orgasm, too," he said, reveling in the idea of a woman's performance all for the sake of his satisfaction. Even if she faked it, it wouldn't matter to him. He expected a show. If he was paying for it, and the woman remained stiff and quiet under him, he'd kill her for adding another bruise to his battered ego.

But when it came to a woman using a vibrator on her own rather than an act of foreplay, Gary railed against this idea, preaching that "it wouldn't be right with God" and that a vibrator should only be used to help achieve an orgasm with a man.

Not right with God? His hypocrisy astounded me. In his mind, it seemed more acceptable for him to kill a woman rather than a woman masturbate alone.

"They have vibrators out there that has one part that goes inside the woman, and one side goes outside, and she can have an excellent orgasm without a man," he rambled, "[but it] should work to get you up to," he said, inserting me in the fantasy and then quickly correcting himself—"a *woman* up to orgasm, and then the man goes inside the woman," he elaborated. "It's not right to have a woman have a vibrator by herself because why would she want a man if she had a vibrator?"

"What about a woman who can have multiple orgasms? Wouldn't it be better if she could get off on a vibrator and also through sex with a man?" I asked.

He seemed perplexed, as if he had no idea of all the capabilities of a woman's body. "I've never heard of a woman or a man having multiple orgasms," he admitted.

"No, that happens. Women—I think it's like fifteen percent of women, they experience it," I said, but he still seemed bewildered. "Say if you have oral sex, right? And then a woman has an orgasm through that and then maybe ten minutes later you have regular sex with penetration, and then they have another orgasm after that. That would be considered multiple orgasms, whereas for a guy they need more time usually in between," I explained.

"You have a prostitute, that would be, a prostitute could have multiple orgasms with the guys," he said, elated to think of how multiple orgasms might be beneficial to a man. And he really believed that prostitutes should enjoy having sex with him. By that time, I wanted to bang my head against the wall until my brain ceased to think anymore. I didn't think he was a stupid person at all, but when it came to women—what they wanted and needed and how their bodies worked—he lacked all consideration.

"But do prostitutes have orgasms? You know what I'm saying?" I asked, nearly outraged.

"I don't know, but maybe," he said, hopeful. "I read the dictionary, and the female clitoris is like the penis. It gets hard just like the man does."

"But are you concerned about the prostitute [in that way]? It's different if you're with a partner. I would imagine if you have a wife or a girlfriend," I challenged.

But later on, I would learn that a woman's pleasure, for the most part, didn't matter to him, no matter how much he tried to convince me that it did. "Marcia said she faked a lot of her orgasms, so I figured maybe if Claudia did maybe it was just all my satisfaction. Maybe she didn't get no satisfaction. I don't know," he admitted during his interrogation. He explained that although he would have sex with Marcia twice a day throughout most of their marriage, he didn't think she enjoyed it. "It probably wore her out . . . foreplay more on her probably would have helped a lot more but . . . my dick controlled my mind, basically. I just wanted sex . . . I was more into sex for myself, not thinking much about her," he reflected.

By the time he and I started talking, he seemed to have formed solid opinions about the female body. He expected that most women faked orgasms simply because they were incapable of having any. It didn't have anything to do with the man's abilities; instead, he blamed the women for what he believed were their own shortcomings.

"Maybe you might have [an orgasm]—if it's hit by a vibrator, you might—because I only heard five percent of women have orgasms. Most of the women don't, I guess."

"Most women you said don't have orgasms?" I was appalled by his logic.

"Yeah, that's what one doctor said. Most women don't have orgasms . . . I don't know. You might want to check . . . call the kind of girl, a nurse or something like that. Maybe she can help," he said, fumbling his words. In his mind, it seemed he wanted to pretend I was a virgin without firsthand information. I couldn't help but laugh at his absurdity.

"The thing is, the woman does like a guy to have sex with her and just like a man does too," he rationalized. "And if it can cause them to have an orgasm, that's fine, and if it doesn't, well, maybe use—"

"But you know what it is, too? Women, they need more of an emotional—it's not just physical. I can't speak for all women, but I think for a lot of women, because we are more emotional, that we also need an emotional connection as well as a physical one," I explained, but it seemed impossible for him to grasp. Trying to make a psychopath understand human emotions was like expecting a blind person to appreciate a sunset.

"Uh-huh. That might be true, but I know it's true that they don't—for instance, a lot of times when you're having a woman, she usually pulls you away before, she gets controlled by it too, like twenty minutes of . . . working on a woman, she'll just pull your head away from the area because it's just, she's too sore to have any more work. Basically more than twenty minutes to have an orgasm for a woman," he recollected as if remembering a specific experience he had giving oral sex.

Finally, he concluded, "You gotta be a woman to give a woman an orgasm. I don't know if that's true or not. But it's sensible. She knows what to do with a woman, and because she's a woman herself."

"But that's not true. A guy can give a woman an orgasm."

"I don't know. I know they can with a vibrator," he contemplated.

As he consulted his memories, some of which were older than I was, they still appeared to be fresh in his mind. But all that mattered was what he wanted to believe, as if his conviction could make anything true.

His hypocrisy was more alarming, the way he would manipulate religion for his own benefit. When it came to sex, he considered God's word, but when it came to committing murder, he invented his own moral code. As he often did, he would dictate or summarize passages from the Bible, a selective process, to support his opinions.

In this case, the story of Onan from the book of Genesis worked as Gary's introduction to share with me his thoughts on coming inside a woman. First, he told me of Onan's experience. In the story, Onan's older brother had died, leaving behind his wife, Tamar. Commanded by his father, Judah, Onan married Tamar, expected to follow the rules of a levirate marriage. Once they consummated their marriage, rather than fulfilling his purpose to impregnate her, he "spilled his seed on the ground whenever he went in" to avoid creating a child that would truly be regarded as his brother's rather than his own. Displeased by Onan's actions, God put him to death.

As Gary explained the explicit details to me, he lingered on the idea of masturbation, believing the popular misconception that this story serves as a warning against it, when in reality, it only describes the outcome of not fulfilling the obligations within a levirate marriage.

"It is a sin to ejaculate and have your sperm go on the ground, basically," Gary confirmed.

"Why? Because it should go inside a woman?"

"Okay. It should go inside of a woman. Ejaculate and go on the ground, your seed is not going into the woman. You're wasting it, and it's against the males and God . . . it's a rejection [of the brother's wife] and it's also a rejection of the semen," he described.

"So, basically every time that people have sex, it should be to produce children?" I inquired, already knowing the answer. There was no way he could believe such a thing. He had sex with hundreds of women, and I doubted he wanted children with most of them, if any of them.

"Well, that is the—in the Bible, that's—we compromise," he finally said, stumbling on his words.

In previous conversations, he would pretend as though he was not guilty of having a ridiculous number of sexual partners or lusting after women without pause. Now, he'd have no choice but to be honest, to explain the convoluted agreements he made with God that were probably just as excessive as his number of sexual partners.

But he began on a smaller scale. If the woman "has a headache or she's on her wrong time of the month, well, he has to ask for a blow job. So, a lot of the times, the wife gives him a blow job just because it's a compromise. They compromise with God's word and . . . you do that," he justified.

But as he argued his point, he revealed much more than his manipulation of his supposed religious beliefs. He seemed to believe that no matter what, it was a woman's duty to satisfy him. So what if she was ill or in the unrelenting throes of a migraine? His dick came first.

"We are heathens. We compromise, and to get our, man's satisfaction, the wife gives a blow job. Well, that's not in the Bible, but you—it's a compromise. And you get the satisfaction, and she gets a—some women," he chuckled, "some women get nice jewelry for giving out blow jobs to their husbands."

As he defended his answer, I saw him more clearly. Not only should a woman always try to satisfy him, but depending on how she did it, it was simply another transaction in his everyday life. Like paying the electricity bill to keep the house filled with light, a woman sucking his dick was also a service requiring remittance.

"And the Bible accepts [blow jobs], or it's just one of those things?" I asked, calling him out on what I knew was mostly a farce. He tended to only abide by the stipulations of his faith when it suited him.

"Well, it's one of the compromises of the—I'm not gonna masturbate on the ground. I'll have my wife give me a blow job, a suck job . . . [but] everything is supposed to go in the vagina instead of in the mouth," he reiterated.

"Do you think people would really go to hell for that, though?" I asked.

"I think they do it because they want satisfaction . . . They do a lot of things in the Bible that they shouldn't, and well, it's okay."

In his mind, he was under the impression that he could be forgiven of anything. As long as he believed in the existence of God, he would have a free pass to sin. He could use women in any way he wanted, whether he let them live or die, and it was all acceptable. His satisfaction would always come first, and righting his wrongs would follow later as he worried over his own death, the unknown ending out of his hands no matter how much he tried to control it.

CHAPTER ELEVEN
Pedophilia/Age of Victims

No matter who Gary spoke to—psychologists, detectives, or me—one part of the story he told remained consistent: the sex he had with those he killed was always consensual. When he was first arrested, those interviewing him would question if he had ever raped any of his victims, but he would fiercely deny it. During our conversations, it was no different.

Rape was one of his favorite subjects to discuss with me, and he saw the threat of it forever looming over my head like a predetermined destiny I would never be able to escape. But he would act as though the men who committed such violence were separate from him. Since what he did to each victim could never be fully known, all that was left was *his* truth, but he was a pathological liar.

He had admitted to touching his cousin inappropriately and then later on fingering a girl against her will, but when it came to those he killed, he refused to consider himself a rapist. It didn't matter to him that killing the women instead of paying them the money he promised them technically made him a rapist—what woman would ever consent to have sex with him if they knew his true intentions? It also didn't matter to him that many of his victims were under the age of sixteen, which under Washington state law made him a statutory rapist, regardless of consent. The only label he would ever accept was that he was a serial killer, and he wore the title of the Green River Killer like a badge of honor.

"They [were] young . . . but that's what . . . serial killers do . . . they kill people. And I was a serial killer and . . . I didn't care," he told detectives.

Nearly twenty years later, when talking to me, the comments he made about the ages of his victims remained the same. "Somebody asked me, 'How old were the women?' . . . I didn't know! When I'm with a woman, unless you ask her how old [she] is—" he chuckled, "You know, a woman doesn't like to talk about her age," he said, trying to appear ignorant, which I knew he wasn't.

To him, a prostitute's age was irrelevant. Since he didn't regard them as actual human beings, that most of them were young enough to be his daughter meant nothing. "They were prostitutes, and they satisfied my needs at the time," he had no problem confessing to police.

I recalled a phone call I had with him shortly after Wendy Stephens, his youngest victim, had finally been identified in 2021 after being referred to as "Jane Doe Bones 10" for nearly forty years. I expected him to bring her up, but he never did.

Years later, I stood behind the Highline Baseball Field in SeaTac, where he left her, the dead brown grass that seemed to be pulled like a sheet to fit the earth, stretching out of sight and shining under the sun like a fresh penny. I craned my neck to a plane flying low overhead, its vacuuming breath dragging behind it, reminding me what he once admitted to police: "I used that noise for advantage for one thing, you know, cut down any, ah, noise in case she screamed." I wondered if Wendy Stephens tried to scream. Or did she realize it would not matter, that he would never have a change of heart even if he knew her age?

While we spoke, there was no acknowledgment of taking such a young life or the wrongness in using a child for sex. The only issue he seemed to consider when having sex with an underage girl was the trouble it could get him into later if anyone found out.

"And [then] you get a prostitute to say, 'Well, I had sex with him, and I was twelve years old,' and all of a sudden you got the guy losing his job as a manager, and then they want to blackmail him . . . You lose your family. You lose your credibility, and you're sleeping with a sixteen-year-old, [but she tells you] she's twenty years old, and [you] find out later they got pictures of you having sex with her," he rambled.

I listened in horror with quiet sympathy for all the girls too young to know any better and their excruciating last moments at his hands, while the only losses he seemed to care about were his own.

The only bearing their age had on him was their level of sexual experience, for he would find that the younger ones were more "innocent" and less "hard-core" and often did not know what they were doing while having sex with him. On one end, he preferred innocence over experience, regarding his younger victims as some of the most "special." Not only did he recount to police that the girls who had just become teenagers were "tighter," which made sex more enjoyable for him, they were often more vulnerable, so it was easier to control and manipulate them. They also didn't bother him with "woe-is-me" details of their lives like those who had been on the street for years. "She was happy to get the twenty dollars, and she wasn't telling me about any problems that she had . . . A lot of them like to tell you bad stories. 'I need the money because my kids,' and then you see marks on their arm, they're a drug addict. So you know they're lying to you," he explained to detectives. However, with the younger ones, there was less hassle, nothing he had to listen to that he didn't want to hear. "The young petite ones were the nonfighters, usually," he added, making them easy kills.

In my conversations with him, he often obsessed over my small stature, even encouraging me that I should invest in an inversion table to stretch my spine to try to become taller. According to his logic, if I became bigger, then I would no longer classify as a perfect victim for a man he was sure existed who wanted to rape and kill me. But the reality was he was most likely remembering his own unforgiving brutality and basking in how easy it was for him to overpower a woman my size, what he wished he could still do. If she happened to also be a virgin—something he decided I was in his fantasy—that would have been the ultimate prize.

"I guess they sell them [in Mexico]," he conjectured about young girls sold into sex slavery. "And if it's a virgin—a virgin's like a queen down there . . . you'll never see her again . . . you get a lot more for a virgin than you do for a regular woman . . . it's just the way people are. They want that virgin; they want to break her in."

I knew he was talking about his own fucked-up desires, and in that moment, I started to see him more clearly than ever before.

CHAPTER TWELVE

Jealousy and Fear of Rejection

As Gary and I continued to speak on a regular basis, from once a week to nearly every day, sometimes for hours if the officers allotted him extra time, I witnessed firsthand his struggles with making a real, authentic connection. In most healthy friendships and relationships, emotions anchor us to each other, and usually, this happens effortlessly through shared experiences or long conversations about our lives. Gary didn't know how to do this. When he tried, he came off awkward, like he was reading from a script, trying to play a role he didn't quite understand.

As much as he tried to conceal his true nature by feigning interest in my life, if our dialogue was different from what he envisioned—for instance, if I said something that interfered with the idea he had constructed of me in his mind—in those moments, his desire for control would surface like a splinter, his words swelling with bitterness until he felt he regained power over me. I could only conclude that his fear of rejection propelled him to act this way.

On a few rare occasions when he took accountability, he admitted that during most of his relationships with women, he had exerted too much control over them, forcing them to eventually leave him, with Judith being the only exception. Even though he knew the right words to say to appear self-aware, his actions revealed he was still the same person he had always been. He might've been almost three thousand miles away and confined in a cell for twenty-three hours a day, but that didn't stop him from trying to insert himself into my life with a dominance that reminded me of a possessive boyfriend.

If I ever deviated from my normal schedule, he would panic. When I forgot to tell him I would be teaching an evening college class, which prevented me from answering the phone, he called repeatedly, not giving up until he finally heard my voice. Although he expressed concern over my safety, thinking I had been raped and killed, I wasn't convinced of his genuineness. He seemed to *need* to know where I was at all times.

It was obvious that he would think of questions to ask me throughout the day and night and jot them down, as if *he* was writing a book about *me*. When he'd call, I could tell he was reading from what I imagined was a notecard like the kind a talk show host holds. I couldn't figure out how I went from trying to help solve potential cold cases to now experiencing what felt like either a job interview or a first date.

Questions such as the motive behind my website, Beyond the Crime, and what I hoped to accomplish with it, were standard if we were going to work on a book together. But the more I answered his questions, the more personal they became.

"I just want to know," he asserted. "You're over in New York. Why are you talking to a serial killer—a person," he corrected himself, "in Washington State?"

Hadn't we already gone over this several times? It felt like he was seeking some kind of validation from me. I explained, just as I had done before, that I always found his case interesting, and cared about learning more about whatever he wanted to share.

"Okay," he said, as if unsatisfied with my answer. "Am I the only one you picked out, or you got other people you talk to?" It felt like I was being interrogated by a boyfriend who suspected I had been unfaithful.

"In Washington, you're the only one I talk to," I answered truthfully.

"Okay," he said, void of any acknowledgment. "What do you do for a job? Ya know, you gotta pay for your website and things, so what do you have for a job?"

"I'm a teacher." Since he didn't say anything, I wondered if he was even listening. I added, "I teach high school, and I teach college."

"Uh-huh."

"And I also write. I write for *The Crime Report* as well."

"How many hours long, ya know, the teaching job—wherever your school is, is it six hours or eight hours, whatever it is? Is that your day job and then you got this as a night job?"

Although he was a serial killer, he also worked at Kenworth painting trucks for over thirty years, and often he'd work overtime. I figured he'd appreciate my work ethic, and that it might create more of a common ground with him. Finding some kind of mutuality felt essential.

"Pretty much. I have, in total, three jobs," I told him. But he gave no reaction. Instead, he moved on to the next question on his list, like he had to fulfill a certain quota by the end of the call.

"But what is—what—are you married or are you going to get married?" he asked, his words clumsy.

For a moment, I was stunned by his forwardness. Why did he want to know this? I began to suspect he had some romantic interest in me beyond his daily flirtations and rushed "I love you" at the end of each call. The idea frightened me. Part of me wanted to explain the importance of boundaries and that he was violating mine, but I knew that would probably cost me the entire story. Chances were he'd never call again if I criticized him. I had to play along to try to get more information about other cases, or at the very least, learn something about the inner workings of his mind that no other writer had access to. As I considered his invasive question, I felt like I was on a roller coaster hovering over the tracks right before a steep drop. Yet, I had to know the outcome, even if it meant derailment.

"No, I'm not married. Nope." I laughed nervously.

"Okay. It's just a question," he said, clearly picking up on how uncomfortable he had made me.

He resumed bombarding me with a litany of questions, but none of them were as personal. He seemed to know he had gone too far.

But his respect of my boundaries only lasted so long. A few weeks after that conversation, I began receiving letters from him.

When I retrieved the first letter from my PO box, it seemed unbelievable. There, in my hands, I read "Gary L. Ridgway" and the address of the prison in his small, neat print. Although our phone calls had grown more frequent, and he had started to talk more about his past—indicators of his growing comfort with me—I still couldn't quite believe what I was holding.

I remembered standing there in the same spot seven months ago, feeling defeated as I stared at the typed, generic letter his religious handlers sent out on his behalf. For him, to write a personal letter was a sign of trust; for me, it was a sign of progress. Many times after talking with him on the phone, I'd feel like I wasn't getting anywhere. But maybe I would be able to uncover some part of his truth, after all.

I held the same edges of the paper that his hands had touched and began reading. Right away I noticed the chaos of his thoughts. There was barely any organization at all—he jumped from one topic to the next—religion, politics, and then, my relationship with my longtime male friend I had mentioned to him, Asher.

In response to my most recent letter, he admitted, "My mind doesn't think as good as it should, so it went in one ear and out the other." I wondered if this was confirmation of what I had previously believed: his memory was becoming insufficient, or he was informing me of the difficulties he had with reading due to his dyslexia, reassuring me not to be offended by his forgetfulness. All he could seem to remember about anything I had said was that I planned on having a male friend accompany me to Seattle—at this point, I hadn't yet made any trips out there. Within the letter, he continued where he left off on the phone, inquiring if my male friend was a romantic interest. The questions he posed imitated the interrogation of a jealous boyfriend:

"Maria, are you standoffish with your male friend? Have you asked him why he's still around? Do you have a fence around yourself? Don't let him in. Does he offer you assistance, comfort, defense? Does he show love to you? Strong affection? Warm attachment? Unselfish, loyal to you? Is that also what you feel about him? Or are you just like brother and sister? Do you let him into your heart? Does he let you into his heart and life? Do you go on dates? Are you a couple or friends? Maria, best is to have one motel room, two single beds."

The only reason I could surmise for his litany of questions, which pushed way beyond the boundaries of general curiosity, was what I had started to fear: he was harboring a romantic interest in me. It was also possible he worried I would have less time to dedicate to him if I had to also fit a boyfriend into my schedule. If I had feelings for my friend, where would that leave Gary? Through his flirtations and declarations of love on the phone, he had already hinted at his attraction toward me, but now it had become more blatant. As much as it disturbed me, I tried to strategize a logical solution.

No way could I address it directly. What would I say? *Sorry Gary, but not only are you a serial killer, but you're old enough to be my father. No thank you.*

From what I knew, rejection fueled so much of his rage.

So, calling him out on his "feelings" and rebuffing his advances didn't seem like the best approach. The only logical solution would be to ignore it. I'd continue what I had been doing—laughing at his jokes, showing him kindness, feeding his ego—and if he believed I was returning his flirtations, then so be it.

Every relationship to him was transactional, it seemed, so why would I be any different? But determining what he expected out of the transaction was the hard part because he was rarely up-front about anything. I knew he didn't want money for commissary (due to his classification as an ultra-max inmate, he was only allowed to spend thirty five dollars a month, which his brother already provided). He couldn't have contact visits, so anything he wished to happen was impossible. He had already confessed and was sentenced, so there was no hope of a better outcome of his future. Subtle flirtations seemed to be all I could possibly give him. If that was his price in exchange for the truth, then I would live with it. There was no other way. Despite the invasiveness and disregard for any boundaries, I would respond to each question, reassuring him that Asher and I were in fact like brother and sister.

But Gary refused to believe it. A month later, when I visited Seattle and returned to New York, I expected him to call me right away. Since he had spent so much time providing me with suggestions of what I should do and see, even proposing I move there, I thought he'd want to know about my experience. But when I returned, more than two weeks went by with no contact.

I replayed our last conversation a few times, looking for any signs of animosity, but found nothing. The last words he said to me were, "I love you." Not that those words held much weight or could ever predict his actions, but I regarded them as proof of our affinity.

After dissecting our last phone call, the only thing I could think of was that for weeks before my trip, he seemed bothered that I'd be traveling with Asher and sharing a hotel room with him. But would he really cut off contact with me because he hated the idea of me coexisting with another man?

It seemed silly, but he was also a serial killer with a rage that had sustained him for decades. Fragments of his derangement had surfaced in the form of frenzied fantasies during our conversations, so I knew that rage was still set ablaze, thrashing inside him. Since he couldn't actually kill me, silence would be the next best way to punish me, I figured. Treat me as if I'm dead, as if his hands did choke me.

As much as I hated my research and story hanging in limbo, deep down, my intuition told me this pause was not permanent. He would bring me back to life, even if his only desire was to kill me again and again in his mind. I suspected he was having too much fun not to continue speaking to me.

Almost three weeks later, while I was at L & B Spumoni Gardens, he called. As I often did whenever his name flashed on my phone while I was in public, I ran to my car to talk to him, this time leaving a half-eaten slice of pizza in my wake. He offered no apology for taking so long to call, but I wasn't surprised. In the year we had been communicating, I only heard him say "I'm sorry" once, when he thought he had to return to his cell and interrupted me with a sudden and awkward goodbye. After rushing me off the phone, a few minutes later, he called back to tell me he misinterpreted the officer's directions, leaving him more time to talk. He then said, "I'm sorry I dropped you" and actually sounded sincere. But this time he didn't even try to explain his weeks of silence.

He also didn't ask me anything about my time in Seattle. If I had not brought it up, I doubt he would have even acknowledged I had gone there. It was as though he wanted to erase any thoughts he had of me visiting all the places he advised me to go. Pike Place Market, the Space Needle, Underground Seattle, all of it was to be wiped from my memory as well. Instead, he wanted to warn me of the likelihood of my rape without letting me say anything in response. Nothing new.

"You don't want to hear about my trip?" I finally interrupted, talking over him for a change. But I was met with a sigh. "I went to Seattle," I reminded him. "It's a beautiful city, but there's so much homelessness," I said.

After scolding me, in an "I told you so" kind of way that he had warned me it was not a safe city, he spiraled into a lecture on the lifelong hell of venereal diseases. It was not on his agenda to hear about my trip, especially anything I did with Asher. If I even spoke his name, I got the feeling I could be banished from Gary's world forever. So, I did what I had learned to do, what I had become an expert at: I let him be in total control. Otherwise, I would be another woman dead to him.

* * *

The control I gave him kept him calling nearly every day for months, even in the early hours of dawn, when he never wanted to talk before. On one October morning in particular, the sunlight burned my eyes as I struggled to open them. Squinting, I scanned my surroundings, which felt the same as trying to see underwater in a pool full of chlorine. I reached for my phone, which was vibrating on the pillow beside me. *Who the fuck could be calling me so early on a Saturday morning?* Rubbing my eyes, Gary's name came into focus on the phone screen along with the time. 8:45 AM, which meant 5:45 AM his time. *He never calls this early in the morning. What the fuck?* I feared there was some emergency situation unfolding, a fight in the prison, an inmate had tried to attack him, or someone he knew had died. I took a deep breath and answered, awaiting the terrible news.

I dug my elbows into the mattress and turned my head toward the pillow to try to block out the light bleeding in between the blinds. Gary's voice sounded hoarse, as if he had just woken up, too, or he was exhausted from having not slept at all. I wondered if he had been awake all night pacing his cell, his obsessive thoughts keeping him in constant motion until his door unlocked and he was able to call me.

The pleasantries we exchanged were faster than usual. No questions about the weather, how my day was going, or what my plans were for the weekend. There were other things on his mind that were more urgent.

He asked how I would define a virgin, as if that was the most important question he'd ever asked. My uncaffeinated brain tried to keep up and make sense of him, something that was difficult to do even after drinking an entire pot of coffee. We both knew the typical definition of a virgin was someone who has never engaged in sexual activity involving the penetration of a man's penis. It had to be a trick question.

My silence extended seconds longer than he could bear. If I wasn't going to tell him what a virgin was, he would do the honor, which I suspected he wanted all along. "No sex, unmarried, girl or a woman, free from sin, pure, chastity, modest, fresh, unspoiled, no human contact, officially no first man . . ." he read from a list I figured he had written during the night.

Did he not think it was possible for a man to be a virgin? But in typical Gary fashion, he left no window for a follow-up question. "Is that what you believe you are? Are you? Do you have that much of a fear? If you lost it, would you mind losing it?"

For months he had waffled between two fantasies of me: whore and virgin. I was back to being his pristine virgin. Immaculate Maria. One of his favorite fantasies of me. But it was way too early in the morning to play this game.

No matter how many times I had tried to set him straight that I wasn't a virgin, he either interrupted me or ignored me, reciting multiple "uh-huhs," which he always did whenever he wasn't really invested in the conversation. He did the same exact thing when the police interviewed him.

"You're asking me if I'm a virgin? Is that what you're asking me?"

"Yeah, I'm asking you. Somebody popped . . . your hymen, or inside, took your cherry, basically. That's what they say. Would it mean that much to you?"

"Gary, look. I mean, I'm thirty-six years old. I've been in a lot of relationships. Long- term relationships. I've been in a few, so I guess you can put that together," I said, killing his fantasy as gently as I could.

Even though I had never lied to him, I felt like I had. I hated the idea of sharing my sexual history with him, so there was a lot he didn't know. But why should he? He was someone I was interviewing for a book I often second-guessed I was even writing. He was not the type of acquaintance, or dare I say, friend, that I would share such personal details with, and he certainly was not my boyfriend, no matter how many times he told me he loved me. Yet, I felt guilty, as if I had led him on to think something that wasn't true, even though he had refused to listen to me whenever I tried to correct him.

"Yeah, well, okay." He seemed to accept my truth for once. "Has any man ever finger fucked you?"

If I had been drinking a cup of coffee, I would have spit it out. Granted, many of our conversations had become overly explicit, and in some instances, depraved, depending on how much violence was on his mind that day. But he never asked me such a direct question, nor did I ever hear him use the word "fuck" before. "Bullshit," "hell," and "asshole" were occasionally dropped into conversations. But sex was always just "sex." When referencing the female and male anatomy, he always used the technical terms as if he was reading from a textbook.

I debated sharing some experiences I had with men and decided against it. The idea of telling *him* made me queasy, especially when I considered the sexual gratification it could give him. Perhaps letting him think I was a virgin would have been easier.

He hated even a second of silence; it didn't matter if my quiet contemplation would lead to an answer. If I wasn't going to discuss finger fucking, he would, but as usual, he quickly moved on to the topic of rape, reminiscing when he fingered a girl against her will when he was a teenager, and then the fantastical story on repeat in his mind of my own rape.

"Is it worth for your boyfriend or husband . . . to be killed for . . . saving you from getting raped?" By the tone of his voice, I knew he thought no man should ever risk his life to save me from any kind of danger. If I wasn't a virgin then it was pointless. The guy saving me would then be just "another notch in the wall." Unimportant. So, why should I matter to any man, then?

"I would imagine he'd be fighting more for my life than anything," I said.

But Gary didn't seem to agree. If I wasn't a virgin, I decreased in worth as a person, the same way a car depreciates and loses value the more it's driven. "When you deflower a woman, it's a trophy for a guy," he said.

"Why is that a trophy?"

"Why?" He seemed outraged by my feigned ignorance. "Well, because a woman values her vagina so much, she wants to keep it clean, so why give it to everybody out there?"

"But—"

"You give it out on your first date or second date, then there's twenty dates, and you give it out to the guy, well, the next thing to do, he's gone. All he wants is a vagina, virginity, and [to] take it away from you."

"I don't know if that's all. If you're in a long-term relationship with someone, most of the time they're not gonna just dump you after that," I tried to reason.

"Well, that's . . . maybe it's just your opinion, but if you want to keep your virginity for your first man, and you're not really a hundred percent sure of the guy, you're not gonna give it out," he repeated.

"But how old do people usually lose their virginity? Most of the time it's like eighteen. How old were you?"

Bothered by my question, he hesitated. "Probably eighteen."

"Yeah. I think that's the normal."

"Well, okay, you're not willing to step on this," he griped, annoyed that I had been disagreeable. "You have a beautiful wisdom and mind and everything, but maybe it's misdirected. This will be the last leg of the call because I want you to get out of America," he said.

"What?" I tried to follow his logic, but I was lost. I didn't agree with him that most men immediately dumped a woman after having sex with her, but why did I now have to leave the country?

"I'm not gonna call you because I want you to get out of damn America—"

"You're not gonna call me?"

"No."

"Why aren't you gonna call me?"

"Because I don't want to have you stuck in damn America and only go four hundred miles. You got a four hundred mile car, okay, and now you gotta charge it—"

The automated woman's voice interrupting the conversation to remind us we only had sixty seconds left couldn't have come at a worse time. I started to panic. If he was serious, I only had sixty seconds to convince him otherwise. I suddenly felt like I was actually fighting for my life. I had invested over a year researching what could be a potential book. I had spoken to him almost every day, even when it meant abandoning a shopping cart filled to the brim in the middle of the supermarket just to take his call.

Could he detach from me so easily and treat me as if I was dead? Yes, he did that with all the women he killed, but he also didn't have long conversations with them nearly every day for over a year. That had to mean something, I scrambled to convince myself. But in the back of my mind, I doubted if I mattered to him at all. I remembered how easy it was for him to punish me with weeks of silence when I returned from Seattle, all because I had traveled with a friend who also happened to be a man.

Maybe he could really dispose of me like yesterday's trash and never look back. Whatever faith I had in his humanity was waning like a moon swallowed more each night by a black sky. Soon there would be nothing left of him to believe in.

"No charging stations, right?" he said smugly, interrupting my flustered thoughts.

His paranoia was nothing new. For months he had been under the impression that all Americans would be forced to purchase an electric car, and there wouldn't be enough charging stations to accommodate everyone. I would then end up stuck in New York forever, where he was certain I would be raped and killed. If I wasn't killed by my rapist, then he was positive I would become a prostitute.

"But what does that have to do with you calling me? I'm confused."

"Well, I want you to get out of America."

The clock was ticking. Only thirty seconds remained, and I wasn't sure if we would ever speak again.

"But I can't just up and leave. I have a job—"

"Well, you can because if you don't you're stuck in New York, and you can't go anywhere. You can't go across the country."

"Why not?"

"Maybe next summer you can, but after this, what are you gonna do?"

The line disconnected, and I wondered if he had already started to walk back to his cell. Or was he punching in my phone number again, like he always did whenever the call ended? I was fully awake now, out of bed, and pacing my bedroom floor. I stared at the black screen of my phone. *Could that really be it?*

Then the vibration from the incoming call tingled my hands. I exhaled a sigh of relief, as if I had dodged a car wreck at the last second.

"You got all those guys and all they want to do is they want to rip you off . . . how many guys have you gone out with who haven't wanted to have sex with you? You got a mind, but . . . you're not steady on your own there, your own life there. You're gonna settle for some sloppy guy, and maybe he has a job and he's making ten bucks an hour, but you're stuck with him for five years until you divorce him," he spiraled.

"I'm so confused. What does that have to do with you talking to me?"

"Because to talk to you doesn't give you any chance of you getting out of America."

"That's not true."

"How are you gonna get out?"

"But what does that have to do with you talking?"

"Well, I'm not calling you because one thing is I want you to get out, and okay—you got forty percent of the women that get raped in America. They go into prostitution, right?"

"But if you didn't call me anymore, honestly, I would be hurt. I would feel hurt by that."

"You'll be hurt, but it's the best thing for you," he said, not caring at all.

"This isn't gonna happen overnight, and I don't know, you saying you're not gonna talk to me, that's just hurtful to me."

"That is hurtful, but it's the best thing for you," he repeated. I sensed that he was getting some kind of satisfaction hearing me grovel. He knew how invested I was in writing a book about him. Threatening to abandon the project in the middle of it only reminded him of his power over me, a punishment for stepping out of line. Because I wasn't a virgin and I told him so, because I wouldn't tell him about the men who fingered me, because I would become a prostitute and because I wouldn't become a prostitute, because I would marry a man that wasn't him, because he loved me and wanted to kill me and wanted to fuck me and wanted to make love to me and wanted to choke me until any memory of me was gone and wanted to hold me, all at once.

"But you don't have to stop talking to me because of this. That's extreme."

"Well, we'll talk more about that this week," he said. Pleased by my relentlessness and that he was able to evoke such a strong emotional reaction from me, he repaid me with some hope that our communication was not over.

It was clear he felt he was back in full control. I never returned any of his "I love yous," but my frantic reaction at the thought of him walking away from over a year's worth of work confirmed that I cared a lot whether I heard from him again. It was easy to take out of context. My worry mimicked that of a desperate girl willing to tolerate anything from a man who treated her horribly. But it was more than that. It had nothing to do with romantic love but rather the love of hearing and telling an important story, one that needed a lot more dissection and understanding than it ever had been given. It had taken over my life, so I couldn't fathom the idea of not finishing it. I was awake before noon on a Saturday. If that wasn't proof of my dedication, then what was?

As if he didn't just threaten to cut off all communication with me, he resumed asking me all the questions he had on his mind: what I preferred my vagina to be called—"pussy" or "vagina." The last thing he'd ever want to do was offend me like he did Judith. He recalled when he was talking dirty to her and used the word "cunt." She became hysterical, enraged by his disrespect. *If she only knew the half of it*, I thought. She never questioned him about anything, and she rarely got mad at him. But this time it was different. She drew the line at "cunt."

"Well, if you're calling her a cunt, that would be a different story," I said and laughed. But he didn't appreciate my humor.

"Well, that's the thing, your vagina is a vagina. It's not a damn cunt," he exclaimed. Another decision he made for me. It didn't matter that I thought "vagina" sounded too formal every time he said it.

Once it was settled that he wouldn't use the word "cunt," he resumed telling me more of his fantasies. I listened as I always did, trying to walk around arm-in-arm with him in his mind, as if I was on a tour at a temporary pop-up exhibit and had to take in as much as possible before it disappeared. At any moment, I knew he could disappear just the same. All I'd have left would be what he had already given me, no matter how much I asked for more.

CHAPTER THIRTEEN
Power and Control

When Gary killed, he always did so to feel in control, knowing he would be the one to decide when a woman took her last breath. During his interrogation, he said, "Women had control over me, and I don't like being controlled. I had control when I killed the women."

Since he was in prison, he would have to find another way to duplicate those moments when he felt most powerful. He knew I sought specific information from him, but when it came to his secrets, he remained tight-lipped.

I wondered if it was a ploy to keep me invested. Any day he could call with a detail that could help solve a murder he had committed decades ago. He knew I was always anticipating it, and I learned early on it would be up to him when he decided the wait would be over, if that ever happened. In the meantime, I would have to engage in any conversation *he* wanted to have.

In the beginning of our correspondence, with his insistence, I conducted an internet search of women who had gone missing from Seattle in the 1980s until his final arrest in 2001. Seventy-one names populated a Microsoft Word document along with whatever details I could conjure up regarding their disappearances and whether their remains had ever been found. As I noted the date each woman went missing, I couldn't help but wonder what their lives had been like and what had happened on the last day anyone had seen them alive.

Did Gary pull up alongside each of them, asking for a date like any other guy desperate for sex? Nothing unordinary. Did they all get into his pickup truck, not realizing when the door closed and he started to drive away that they were seeing those streets for the last time, and by tomorrow their faces would only exist in memory?

That's if anyone remembered their faces. He certainly wouldn't.

The majority of the women on the list were teenagers or in their twenties, the prime ages when the contagion of invincibility destroys any common sense and good judgment. So many of these girls and women had followed the same path, as if it had been predestined like a clock's steady hand moving from one hour to the next: they would run away from home and end up on the street working as prostitutes, many with a drug addiction to feed. Despite my attempts, I could not find what had led these particular women on this trajectory to such a cruel fate—the internet only provides so much backstory. However, in each case, during the mid-'80s until the early 2000s—the years Gary was active—they all disappeared from various parts of Seattle.

As I stared at some of the photographs I had managed to find of their faces, many of which were smiling—out of pure happiness or just for the sake of the picture, it was hard to tell—I wondered if the last person they had seen, touched, and spoken their last words to—a possible pleading for help, for life, for mercy—could have been Gary. Would he remember anything? But more importantly, if he did, would he ever tell me the truth? What would I have to do to prod his memory and uncover his secrets? The journey I had embarked on felt long and tedious, impossible to navigate, but I continued typing the names of each woman into my Google search bar anyway.

In a few of the cases, their remains had been discovered along with a cause of death. The ones that had been strangled obviously stood out to me, even more so if they had been involved in prostitution in the areas Gary frequented.

Just as he instructed, I printed out a list of his forty-nine confirmed cases with the date each woman had gone missing along with the location. Then, I printed out the list of cold cases, including as much information as possible in the hopes that he would remember even a minor detail. I was confident that he would at least *want* to talk about some of them.

After stuffing the lists into an envelope, I made what was becoming a routine trip to the mailbox. Afterward, eagerness for his call consumed me.

* * *

I wasn't sure what I expected—a confession? An acknowledgment of my research? A confirmation that he had at least received the lists? But he never brought up any of the cases. Was it intentional, or had he genuinely forgotten?

Whenever I tried to ask about the unsolved cases, he barely let me get a word in, switching topics as swiftly as a toddler who becomes bored of a toy and throws it to the side only to find a new one. Politics (he was a Republican, he proudly shared with me as he praised Fox News for their uncensored coverage about the Democrats), his family (his brother was "a hundred and fifty percent Democrat," causing them to bicker), the Covid shot (should there really be one or two shots—he was undecided), the weather (it had snowed on his birthday and didn't stop for an entire week), and without fail, he seemed to always find a way to bring up sex ("Cuomo was having sex with one of [his] workers and playing strip poker on an airplane," or referencing *50 Shades of Grey*, informing me, "There's a building in Seattle . . . and there's a bunch about sex, and the guy ties up these women, and he has sex with them.")

He seemed willing to discuss anything but the list of unsolved cases I sent to him. Like always, I felt if I was ever going to get anywhere with him, I had to let him lead me there. So, I put the cases on the back burner, expecting he'd eventually bring them up.

But he never did. After a couple months passed, I finally asked, "So, did you get the other mail I sent you? I sent you all those cases that we spoke about a while ago."

He paused, exhaling a faint sigh. My heart thundered in my chest, as if I was awaiting news of my own mortality.

"I received that . . . but it didn't really matter to me. Nothing seemed to bother me. Nothing to interest me about it. Just some people's names," he said as if bored by my question.

His words felt like bullets barraging my entire body. I couldn't believe it.

"So none of those—you weren't responsible for any of them, then?" I asked, trying to hide my frustration, something I seemed to do frequently when speaking to him.

"Not on there—they had that one woman—look on the conviction list, there's a woman by the name of "Rise" or "Reese." One of the people that I killed somewhere in King County or Pierce County or Snohomish County could have been her sister or her daughter."

He was referring to Carrie Rois, a fifteen-year-old girl he had murdered in 1983. She'd become part of the Star Lake "cluster," and it wasn't until 1985 that her remains were found. When I researched her family line, there was no information about her having a sister or a daughter. Could he have mixed her up with another victim? He confused women quite often throughout his interrogation, so why would that change twenty years later?

The only victim I was able to find with a family member—a sister—who had also disappeared was Cheryl Lee Wims. In 1983, on her nineteenth birthday, Cheryl had gone missing from Seattle's Central District, and in 1984, her remains were found north of the SeaTac airport, not far from two other victims left in the same area. Similarly, in 1990, Cheryl's sister, Deborah, was last seen in the Safeway parking lot located on 216th South and Pacific Highway, the same intersection where several other victims had disappeared. To this day, her remains have still not been found.

Just like previous conversations, Gary had once again given me a half-assed confession. I couldn't help but feel he was toying with me, purposely giving me only so much information but not enough to hold him accountable or bring closure to anyone. It felt as though I was starving, and he was dangling a steak in front of me, only to pull it back when I got too close. To top it all off, in a single breath he had also admitted to killing in different counties outside of King County, a violation of the plea agreement he made with prosecutors in 2003. As long as he confessed to all the murders he committed and assisted law enforcement in the investigation as best as he could, he wouldn't face the death penalty. However, this plea agreement only protected him in King County, meaning if it was ever discovered that he had killed in different counties, he could face the death penalty.[1]

But without real evidence, such as DNA or Deborah Wims's remains, what consequences was he really in danger of facing? Instead, this confession, which maybe was a lie, would taunt me as long as I spoke with him. When he urged me to research the cold cases he could be responsible for, was that only a way to test me to see how much I was willing to do for him? Since he had not divulged anything useful, I began to believe he enjoyed watching me abide by his commands just like he loved to be in control when he killed.

In the meantime, I remained subjected to his invasive questions, in the hopes he might admit to a murder no one else knew about.

"Did your mother get you on birth control pills at sixteen years old?" he asked out of the blue, like many of his prying questions. I figured he was trying to ask when I had sex for the first time.

He continued, "A lot of women will get their daughters on birth control pills at sixteen years old. Did your mother do that?"

[1]The death penalty was officially abolished in Washington State in 2023, two years after this conversation with Ridgway took place.

"Not that young," I said. "Not at sixteen. I think probably at eighteen." The face of my first love flashed in my mind, his eyes the color of all the oceans that could drown me, his small apartment in Astoria shut in with our cigarette smoke, his entire room painted black, swallowing the sun as we stayed in bed all day.

"But a lot of women do that because they don't want to get raped by somebody and have the rapist's—ya know," he said. That was the thing about Gary. You could always rely on him to tarnish a seemingly normal discussion with all his violent thoughts.

"Wait, what?" I asked, alarmed.

"Because they're getting raped," he said. "I was just wondering . . . it saves you from getting raped by somebody and getting pregnant . . . Somebody told me it's easier to get raped in New York than it is to get robbed by somebody. Is that true?"

Although he tried to appear sincere, all his intentions were consumed by whatever violent scenario he was imagining. That seemed to take precedence, not my actual safety.

"That could be true. I mean, thank God that has never happened to me. But I could see why that could be more likely . . . the subways alone have become more dangerous," I said.

"Well, at least you're underground . . . Some guy in a trench coat, and he'd be pulling up your dress, and you have sex with him . . . on the subway," he said, excited by the idea.

He had recently asked me if women ever wore dresses on the subway, and now I understood what he had been thinking, the plot that was developing in his mind like bad porn.

"It's the way people are," he added, as if everyone at their core was the same as him, void of morals and capable of the same atrocities, as if all men on a crowded subway desired nothing else but to rape women.

Before I could even find the words to respond, he was already on another subject and proposing a new kind of game, either/or.

He began telling me a story about a couple in search of a place to have sex before going out on a date for the evening when they stumbled upon an area where rapes had occurred in the past. But somewhere in the middle, he had abandoned his characters, replacing them with him and me. "If we go in an area where there's a lot of rapes, why get raped by somebody else when I can have sex with you?" He laughed. But it didn't seem like he was joking.

"Wow," I exclaimed, unable to conceal my shock.

"It's just, ya know, in some ways you're better to have sex with somebody earlier than get raped by somebody . . . Better to be raped by—have sex with your friend than to have sex with a rapist," he argued, trying to make me understand his logic.

But I would never understand the place he was coming from. If I wanted to try to understand even a fraction of his wickedness, I would have to continue playing along and tell him what I thought it was he wanted to hear.

"Well, yeah. I would imagine that's better than getting raped," I agreed, considering the terrible choices he presented.

"If you get raped, what would you do? Would you go into prostitution?" It seemed it was his goal all along to discuss my potential rape, to imagine me as someone he would love to kill. It really was impossible for him to be any other way.

"No, I would hope not," I said.

"If you do it—okay. What is your reason?" he asked, pretending I had given the answer he wanted. "Prostitutes are raped all the time . . . They like sex in their rear end and then they gotta give a blow job to the guy. And isn't that more downgrading [than getting raped]?"

I tried to remind him that many women who ended up in that position were also feeding a drug addiction. But what I said didn't seem to matter. Just like he always wanted me to know that I could easily be killed, he also wanted me to know what life as a prostitute would be like, as if that was my new fate, out of my control.

Soon after, he expanded on his ideas that became more explicit. It was important that I knew all the options of pain he could inflict on me. In nearly ten pages, he outlined seven scenarios he insisted could happen to me and then lost count. I wondered which example he wanted to cross off most.

1. "Not wanting it . . . the women and men held her down and cut off her clitoris . . ."
2. One rape victim had bleach sprayed in her vagina to destroy DNA. 20–30 year old woman. Barely alive, taken to the hospital . . ."
3. "One rape victim was sprayed in the face with bleach. Lost her eye . . ."
4. "Woman taken, raped for two days by four men. Bleeding in the vagina by the table leg. Bleeding in the buttocks by table leg. Her mouth and face were beat and enlarged because she would not swallow their sperm. Then douched her vagina, buttocks hole out with cold water from a garden hose. Dumped her on a side street, passed out. People found her naked . . ."

In each scenario, it was impossible to know whether he weaved in details from news stories, relied on his own imagination, or recalled actual memories since there were hints of his crimes.

As his list grew, the woman he described was no longer faceless. He wrote me in as the victim. Demanding my reaction, he taunted, "If that was you, would you be embarrassed? With wood splinters in ass and vagina. Hair cut off and burnt on head." According to him, if I was ever raped and murdered, it would be my own fault, and I should be ashamed for the way he hurt me. Meanwhile, he remained blameless. It would always be the woman who got into his truck with him, and in my case, who answered the phone day after day to listen to him.

"These rapes can be to God's people? Or not? Raped because they deserved it? Maria, if you get raped, did you deserve it? Alive wishing she was dead," he wrote.

I wondered what he accused me of in his thoughts, and if I was really guilty of any of it. He hated my friendship with Asher, who had now been reduced to just "the chef" whenever Gary referenced him. He hated the few times I didn't answer the phone when he called. He hated that I didn't tell him I loved him whenever he said it to me, sometimes asking if I had anything to tell him after he said it. A frustrated silence followed when I told him I had nothing to say before the call disconnected and he had no choice but to walk back to his cell. It seemed there were a lot of reasons I deserved for him to rape me, to wish he'd kill me.

But I had advanced too far in his depravity to turn back.

"Teen raped by five men for one day. One man put a flat ball up her vagina. Then put air in it. Maybe broke bones in her vagina and ripped hole inside of her. Cut off all her hair. Hung her naked on the side of the road. With a baseball bat out of her vagina. People took photos of her before calling the police. You think you would be embarrassed."

Maybe he didn't participate in a gang rape, but nearly everything else he described was something he considered doing to his victims or atrocities he had already committed. He once told detectives that he "thought about putting in a football, and [pumping] it up."

Putting these thoughts on paper meant he never forgot them, and sharing them with me, forcing me to consider the outpouring of his rage, was the next best thing to actually doing it.

As far as I knew, he never drove a baseball bat inside a woman to kill her, although he confessed to wanting to do something similar. "I had a fantasy of putting a woman on a post . . . the post in her vagina, but I didn't do that," he told detectives. "I'd take her out to some remote area maybe gag her . . . have her clothes off and slip the pole up her and get the pole firmly in the ground and pole it up while she's still alive. Maybe have her hold on to something so she could . . . until she got tired, and she let go and she would die sooner."

As he described his fantasy to detectives, he thought about what would excite him most if he ever made it a reality. "If I did, it was arousal of watching her in pain, dying. You live by . . . having guys put dicks in you, now you have a pole up you and you're going to die that way. But I didn't do it."

As though he was ashamed to hear his own thoughts out loud, he began to cry. "I get the feeling that I was really sick. That's something only somebody's who sick would do. Watching somebody die that way," he lamented to the detectives.

In his letter, he lost count of the number of ways he could kill me. I wondered if everything he suggested would happen all in one night alone with him in a long session of violence.

"Why did the rapist put a bottle in her vagina? How hard would the rapist have to push to cause blood? I've heard she wanted to leave New York. Looks like that's not in her future. She was a beautiful woman once. Can't tell how she died. The animals ate all flesh. How old does the bones tell you. Someone said she's a teacher. The rapist tears her vagina with a knife . . ."

By the end of the letter, I was the only one he had in mind.

"To inflict all kinds of pain. Twisted thoughts . . . Why can't a rape be having sex with no pain?"

"Take photos of her body parts naked. Put things inside her. After sex and clean up. NO DNA. Glued her vagina. Steal her ID and stuff. I will be back. Or I will be watching you . . ."

"Have you always looking for him everywhere. Fear of the unknown . . . Let her know she's part of him. Ownership . . . nightmares . . ."

Since he began dialing my number, I had not gotten a full night's sleep without seeing his face.

KILLER CHARACTERISTICS

CHAPTER FOURTEEN
Planning Ahead

Five months into our correspondence, I broached the possibility of visiting Gary at the prison. I figured sitting across from him would help to strengthen whatever rapport we were building. I would become a real person in front of him rather than just a voice on the phone, words on a page. That could possibly influence him to tell me more, secrets he kept for the past thirty years that could help solve a case. However, my plans were quickly foiled by the draconian prison rules, which he expressed a slight resentment toward. "I don't have no choice . . . you have to be family," he explained.

There's exceptions to rules sometimes, I irrationally told myself. I wasn't willing to accept defeat just yet, so I resorted to research to determine whether there was a way around the strict regulations. To my surprise, I discovered something even better. In an effort to initiate rehabilitation over punishment, Washington policy makers were committed to modeling their prisons after the ones in Norway. One of the first changes would be to modify the rules as to who was allowed to visit those housed in the most secure unit of the facility, IMU, where Gary was located. I couldn't wait to tell Gary the news.

"Would you want to have a visit from me while I'm out there?" I asked the next time he called. Since he once claimed it was a hassle for him to even leave his cell to use the phone, I was half expecting him to say no.

"We're about three hours away from Seattle, [and] you have so much things to do in Seattle, you probably won't have time even to go anywhere," he said, trying to sound modest, like it would be too much trouble to fit a visit with him into the itinerary he was helping to create, with his endless lists of destinations for me to go to on my trip.

"No, I would make time. If I'm right over there, I'll come say hello . . . if you wanted me to," I said.

"Well, you can try. You can try, but there's a lot of things you want to see."

Did I hear him correctly?

"You're sure?"

"Well, you can try, but there's stuff you probably want to do and you're far away, but you can try," he said.

It was settled. I would fill out the necessary forms to gain clearance into the prison, and he would add me to his visitor's list. I would then schedule our meeting.

As I explained to him the next steps, he told me what to expect during the visit, acting like it would dissuade me from following through with it. I couldn't tell if this was due to his own apprehension of meeting me, if he really felt embarrassed by the uninviting conditions, or if it was a combination of both.

A glass partition would divide us, like the windows bank employees stand behind. There would be a phone on either side, which we would use to talk to each other, "just like we're talking now," he described. But we would be able to see each other, he emphasized.

"But that's all you can do," he said, almost despondent. "You can't touch."

Normally, I would be adverse to such inhumane conditions, but I was relieved to find out that all physical contact would be prohibited. He clearly longed for something different. Since his sentencing in 2004—nearly seventeen years ago—only when officers escorted him somewhere or when he visited a doctor had he experienced the feeling of a hand on his arm or fingers clasping cuffs around his wrists.

Guilt consumed me for feeling so insensitive, since I knew so much research had proven that human touch was beneficial for inmates, even improving their health. But the thought of his hands locking with mine, his body pressed against me in a hug, and what that sensation would do for him, made me thankful for the glass that would separate us.

On my laptop, I typed my answers into the electronic application form that Washington State Department of Corrections required all prospective visitors to complete. Address, birth date, Social Security number, any felony convictions; it was just like applying for a job. But then the questions demanded to know about my history with "the inmate" I was wishing to visit, how long had we known each other, what was our relationship, and had we ever committed any crimes together. "I was not even born at the time when he committed many of his crimes in the 1980s." *He'll appreciate that one*, I thought with a smirk.

Despite the new rules etched in black and white on the DOC website, I didn't fully believe they would honor their new "directives," and neither did Gary. The DOC had a way of muddling their rules, regardless of how straightforward they seemed. They could amend their words at any time for any reason, and rarely could their logic be challenged. Since I was asking to visit Washinton State's most notorious, and probably most hated inmate, I expected an immediate "no" to my request. Why would they grant him, of all people, extra leisure time out of his cell, and in this case, the opportunity to see a woman from the outside world?

A couple days later, quicker than I had expected, I received a response. For a few moments, I stared at the screen, hesitating to read the email. I was already disappointed by what it would say. But I had to know for sure. I took a deep breath and opened it.

"Holy shit. They actually approved me," I said to no one. I stared at the word "approved" as though it were an apparition before me. It was hard to believe the reality of what it meant, that in a few weeks I would be permitted to sit face-to-face with one of the worst serial killers to ever have walked the earth.

Later that night while I was at a restaurant celebrating a friend's birthday, Gary called. It had become habitual for me to run off from anyone I was with to answer his calls, and this time was no different. I jumped up from the table and walked toward the street corner, leaning into the doorway of a storefront to hear him better. I wasn't sure if he had already received notification of this new addition to his visiting list, but I couldn't wait to tell him.

"I got approved to be on your visiting list!"

I expected him to share my excitement, that the DOC had actually honored something they had said they would do, and without putting up any fight. But he simply said, "Okay," showing no emotion at all.

"They actually approved me," I said again, hoping to ignite a reaction from him. "So, all I have to do now is schedule the visit."

"Okay, do you know when you're going to be out here?"

"Well, there's an online form I have to fill out," I explained.

"Uh-huh." I noticed he always gave this response when he was either half listening or didn't seem to fully grasp what was being said to him.

"And they're going to give more time for visits. Right now it's just one hour, but I think they're going to give three hour visits. So, they said to just wait until August to schedule it . . . it will probably be I'm thinking either the fifteenth or sixteenth."

"Okay, that's good," he said, now seeming delighted by the news. "It's a Sunday, right? I don't know. I have to look to see when I have yard . . . but I would love to that week."

Besides the occasional visit from law enforcement and his lawyers, it had been seven years since he had seen anyone from the outside. In 2014, Senator Jenny Graham had gone to ask him about the murder of her sister, Deborah Estes, so it was far from a friendly meeting. As far as I knew, not since when his family still went to see him in King County Jail before his sentencing had he received a visit from anyone who was even remotely kind to him. No wonder it took him a few minutes to process the news and to consider the possibility of socializing with someone in a way that would be noncombative.

The more we talked about it, the more excited he grew about meeting me in person and began to plan the details of my trip to Walla Walla just as he had when he found out I'd be traveling to Seattle. "When you come over to Walla Walla you might want to just, you might want to—because it's about a three-to-four-hour drive to my place," he said, as if he was inviting me to his house rather than a maximum security prison. "So, you might just want to spend the night in Walla Walla someplace," he suggested.

As we discussed the technicalities of my visit down to the weather in August, the type of rental car I would drive, and the trunk space where I would keep my suitcase, I was reminded of his methodical nature whenever he planned to kill someone. He would drive around for hours hunting for the perfect victim: a woman alone, young, attractive, and trusting. As soon as he found one, he once described to detectives his common practice: "Show her money. Show her my penis . . . She asked for a cock. They all do . . . You always pull out and they always show their breasts or touch you or whatever." But he never appeared threatening, even during the encounter. It wasn't until she thought it was over when she realized her life was in danger and then close to ending. After she was dead, he would find somewhere that seemed "a good place to put a body."

But if picking up a woman didn't feel right to him—if there was a witness, a pimp nearby, or any bad feeling—he would abort his plans to kill her. Even if the woman was already in his truck, he would drop her off and find someone else to take her place. And she would never know her life had been spared. One hiccup in the plan, and he was out of there, never to be seen again. He was always planning ahead to ensure he would not be caught, and he did the same thing now, as he strategized my visit with him down to the last detail.

A few days later, the kitchen table vibrated from a notification that had gone off on my phone, signaling there was a new email in my inbox: a response from Washington State Penitentiary. My heart hammered in my chest as I stared at the subject line, "Visit Approved—August 14."

I read the email over and over, until the words began to make no sense. "Your request to visit Gary Ridgway, #866218 has been received and approved. You Maria DiLorenzo are scheduled to visit at 3:45 p.m. on Saturday, August 14, 2021. It is important that you arrive and are ready to be processed into the facility 15 minutes prior to your scheduled time . . ."

The thought of sitting face-to-face with a man who asked me if I would prefer to get raped missionary or doggy style was enough to force me to second-guess if I was making the best decision by going to see him. I anticipated that he could be even more vile in person, expanding on the fantasies he had shared with me. Sitting behind glass in a small airless room, I wouldn't be able to pace the floor as I often did whenever I talked with him on the phone as a way to calm my anxiety. I would have to stare straight into his eyes, which would also be watching me and probably imagining all the things he wished to do to me. That idea alone was unsettling.

However, I knew if I passed up this opportunity, I would always wonder what he might have told me about other women he killed that had never been verified. Although the purpose for talking with him seemed to have gone off the rails with nearly every call saturated with his perverted fantasies, I still had a small amount of hope that I could find out information about those unsolved cases. It was worth a shot. So what if I had nightmares for years to come.

I wondered if he had received a notice that I would be visiting and what his thoughts were about it. Although he had expressed excitement about meeting me in person, he had also communicated his fear of passing by other inmates in the facility, believing a riot could erupt as a result of anyone seeing us together.

It was hard to tell if he was exaggerating or if paranoia had made him irrational. But I knew it was best to take his concerns seriously, since he was the one that had to live in there, not me.

The next time he called, I shared the news that I hoped he would agree was good. But rather than forcing myself into his world, I relinquished control to him, letting him decide if he wanted me there. The more we communicated, it had become clear as the glass that would separate us that he wished to exert power over anything he still could.

"The visit, I scheduled it for Saturday, August fourteenth. I don't know if that's okay with you, but if you want to think about it, you can, and then just get back to me and let me know."

"I don't know if I'll be able to go, but I'll let you know by the end of the week." Like always, it was hard to gauge his reaction.

"Yeah, let me know, because they approved it and everything."

"Okay, my thoughts are I might not be able to go to it . . . is your friend still going to be there on August fourteenth?"

I wasn't sure if the idea of Asher driving with me to the prison would irritate him or relieve him. It seemed to bother him that I'd be sharing a hotel room with a man, but he also once berated me for traveling alone. "Yeah, he's going to be around," I said. The more vague I kept the details, the less he would have to criticize or get upset about, I reasoned.

"Is he going to be driving with you?"

"Yeah, he would be driving with me, and then he would just take the car. I don't know where he's gonna go, but he's fine on his own exploring," I assured him.

"Yeah, there's not much to do [here]. Maybe just go to the tavern and watch the football game or something," he suggested.

He didn't dare to invite Asher to the visit. It seemed Asher's purpose was to get me to Walla Walla safely, and that was it.

"He can always look at the houses in Walla Walla and see if there's an Italian restaurant . . . and [see] what might help him find a job over there," he continued, getting carried away with the idea.

"You never know," I lied. "So, think about it. If it's okay with you, then I'll come," I said, letting him decide what would happen next.

"I'll think about it more. I'll think about it when I get back to my room," he promised before telling me he loved me and hanging up.

A week later it was apparent he had thought about our upcoming visit, but he imagined everything that could go wrong. Covid had been running rampant in every prison across America for over a year, but he had rarely mentioned how it was affecting him until now. Since a couple of guys on his unit were in total isolation, only able to shower and go to the yard once a week, he predicted that a quarantine would terminate our visit. To avoid the hassle, he encouraged me to drive to Spokane instead, assuming I might want to move there rather than Seattle or Walla Walla. "Get out of New York because the devil will probably start coming out of the woodwork over there," he said and laughed. For whatever reason, Spokane would be a sanctuary for me, a place I could never be raped or killed.

I couldn't help but wonder if there was another reason that made him feel conflicted about meeting me. Prior knowledge of his case revealed that he had been afflicted with a lack of self-confidence, making him feel insecure at times. Although for most of his life he had been successful attracting women and was rarely without a girlfriend, he often lowered his standards and dated those who would be deemed unattractive or overweight. However, the prostitutes he picked up were often young and pretty, women he assumed would never had given him a second glance if he wasn't paying them.

Now, as a seventy-two-year-old wrinkled and balding man in prison who had nothing but his imagination to rely on when it came to his interactions with women aside from the prison staff, I wondered if he felt safer within his fantasies. In his mind, he could make anything happen, much like he did when he was free and able to pick up a woman and kill her. But sitting across from me, he would be shackled and chained, and glass would prevent his hands from trying to hold mine, never mind finding my throat. I would then see him as he was, an old man, entirely tamed and powerless, all his former good looks ruined by age and the poor conditions of years in prison. Perhaps he worried that I'd no longer like him enough to answer his calls.

As days passed and my trip got closer, he began to call less. Each time we did speak, he updated me on the looming lockdown in the prison. Covid precautions and mandates had become more excessive in his unit. Twice a day a nurse would check his vitals and stick a cotton swab up his nose to make sure he was not infected with the virus. The phone and shower schedule had become "screwed up," confining him to his cell for longer periods. Yet, the visit had not been canceled as he suspected it would.

With clothes strewn across my bedroom floor, I tried to decide on an acceptable prison outfit. All the undergarments in my drawers turned into a heap of assorted colors I searched through frantically for the only bra I owned without an underwire—my "prison bra," as I referred to it. The only bra I owned that didn't set off the metal detector. Just as I was making headway, folding a loose T-shirt and comfortable jeans into my suitcase, my phone dinged. I figured it was a message from Jet Blue, reminding me to check in, since my flight was twenty-four hours away.

But an email from Washington State Penitentiary flashed across the screen. "Visit Cancelled—IMU South on Quarantine Status."

I stood frozen, dreading to know what else it said. I held my breath as I stared at the words: "Your upcoming visit [with] Gary

Ridgway #866218 on 8/14/21 has been cancelled. Unfortunately, we are having to cancel due to IMU South currently being on quarantine status. At this time a date when the units will be able to come off quarantine status has not been established."

Unwilling to accept defeat just yet, I rummaged through papers on my desk for the contact information of some departments within the prison. The visiting room sergeant seemed like the best person to call first. As I pleaded with him that I was traveling all the way from New York and it was too late to cancel my flight or hotel, surprisingly, he sympathized with me and expressed regret over how he wished he could do something to make the visit happen as planned. I even contacted the prison headquarters in Olympia, but I was met with the same bad news. Although it seemed hopeless, I packed my prison bra and outfit anyway.

A lot could change in two days, I told myself. The quarantine could be lifted. I could still sit face-to-face with one of the worst serial killers to ever roam the earth. I still could get answers. But the prison would remain on lockdown until after I returned to New York.

* * *

Two years later, still in pursuit of answers, I would visit Seattle again. But instead of trying to see Gary, I would arrange a meeting with someone I thought could help fill in the holes that remained in the unfinished stories Gary had told me. Then maybe I could prove their validity.

Since Tom Jensen was part of the Green River Task Force when it formed in 1982 after countless women's bodies were discarded around King County, I thought he would be able to share a unique perspective. When the task force disbanded in the late eighties, he remained the sole investigator, and after he retired in 2012, he continued to volunteer as an investigator, even corresponding with Gary until 2019. I remembered even Gary once telling me, "King

County or—Snohomish County . . . and then you got Pierce County . . . So, there was a lot of women—well, [Tom Jensen] has a list of all the people, all of the women I killed." I figured meeting with him would help me decipher the truth from the lies.

The day we met, a veil of white fog hovered over Alki Beach, making the trees I had become accustomed to seeing from the rooftop of my Airbnb invisible. Mount Rainier would usually be to my left, swelling against the sky like a pregnant stomach, but it was also gone, erased by clouds. The cool air reminded me of the onset of autumn in New York, and I was not prepared for the abrupt change.

Blasting the heat in the rickety Subaru Forester I had rented, I drove one mile to Me-Kwa-Mooks Park, a grassy area the size of a backyard I'd expect to find in the suburbs of Long Island or New Jersey. Pushed back from the sidewalk and with trees towering in the back, the park felt tucked away and unassuming. As I parked my car in front, I understood why Tom had suggested we meet there. Due to the subject of our discussion—Gary—he had worried that there would be "too many ears" in a restaurant or coffee shop. With the exception of a Fed-Ex worker making a delivery to a house up the street, Me-Kwa-Mooks Park was completely abandoned.

A wooden picnic table appeared as an obtrusive ornament in the middle of the grassy expanse. Wearing a white bucket hat and holding a cane, Detective Jensen was at the table, facing his body sideways toward the street and Puget Sound in the distance. I introduced myself and joined him, taking the seat across from him. Aside from a few brief emails, we had never communicated before. But there was no point in exchanging pleasantries to ease into a conversation. We both had questions that were more important.

He wanted to know how I had gotten caught up with Gary Ridgway, a reasonable inquiry. However, his tone reminded me of a disapproving parent, as if he viewed me as a stupid adolescent girl suffering from the trauma of a bad relationship instead of a journalist who had been trying to seek answers to questions that had remained unresolved longer than I had been alive. I started to explain my history with Gary, but rather than looking at me directly, he remained sitting sideways, facing the water. I was far from an expert on body language, but his unfriendly stance seemed to translate into a guarded dominance and a dismissiveness I tried to understand.

He had already shared his reservations with me in his emails, so I suspected he still felt the need to be cautious and suspicious of me. He never wanted to be a party to giving Gary any extra attention, but since Gary's stories could never be trusted, he felt it was his duty to intervene to "help sort out" what I had heard. Otherwise, I'd "run the risk of publishing a shitload of lies that could be very hurtful to families and survivors of his victims." I respected his position, although I knew he had the wrong idea about me. It was not my goal to glorify Gary or cause harm to anyone.

No one knew what I was up against when I'd spend hours on end speaking with Gary—the truth wrapped in lies, the manipulation, the gaslighting, the unsteadiness, the nonchalant brutality. But Tom Jensen knew. He had spent six months interviewing Gary in 2003, listening to his confessions. I suspected he was probably one of the few people who could commiserate with the uphill battle of conversing with Gary. I thought that would make us allies or at least put us on common ground.

But as I explained the first letter that I sent off to Gary in 2020, I felt just as invisible as everything in the distance that was effaced by the fog. I told him about the daily phone calls and the rapport I was able to build with Gary, and he continued to stare toward the water, never turning his body toward me once. He listened with little reaction to everything I said, as if I was recounting a mundane memory, like a weekly trip to the grocery store, rather than nearly two years of discussions with one of the worst serial killers in America.

The cool ocean breeze picked up, adding to my discomfort. I pulled my cardigan closer to my body and leaned into the table, the wooden edge pushing against my chest. Neither of us said anything for a moment, forcing both of us to stare toward the gray nothingness, how I imagined Gary's soul to be, a clouded and murky terrain, a place we both had been lost in before and desperate to navigate, if only to recover a fragment of truth. *Wasn't that what was bringing us together?* I tried to interpret his long, standoffish gaze that seemed to hold an opinion of me, but I couldn't decide if it was adversarial or amicable.

"Gary was warned," he finally said.

Prior to going to prison, he and the other detectives had told Gary that he would receive letters from people like me interested in writing a book about him. He was advised that he shouldn't engage with anyone if he didn't want to end up in a book. Until I had come into the picture, he seemed to follow their advice.

Tom chalked up this change in Gary to loneliness and his deteriorating mental health. Gary had been incarcerated for over twenty years, and he was not the same man as before, according to Tom, so it only made sense that he would want to talk to someone. I was not entirely convinced. For years, Gary had been flooded with mail from podcasters and writers, so there had to be a more precise reason he chose to speak with me. I knew I was of no value to him, but I did show him sympathy. That had to count for something.

When Tom shared with me that the attorney general, Bob Ferguson, and a couple detectives from the King County Sheriff's Office had recently waltzed into the prison to question Gary about cold cases, I easily predicted the outcome. Gary would never disclose even a crumb of his secrets to anyone he didn't establish a rapport with. I *knew* my consistent, unwavering sympathy was one of the deciding factors when Gary dialed my number over and over again. During the six months Tom had spent questioning Gary, he had learned a similar lesson. Tom was not one to show him much sympathy, but he did try to consider his point of view when Gary described his motives to kill. We both agreed that a new detective—or anyone, for that matter—would never be able to sit down with Gary and expect to extract all the answers.

The sheriff's office had sent Tom the tape of their interview to review, and it was no surprise that Gary had told them nothing new. In fact, most of what he said did not make sense. Tom explained that Gary's memories appeared jumbled and chaotic, worse than ever before, and he was difficult to understand. Interpreting anything Gary said took skill—he mumbled, skipped topics erratically, and lied the same way he breathed air. No way could someone sit down with him once and expect to solve a whole case.

If more victims existed, which they probably did, Tom lacked hope in finding them. There had been too many changes to the landscape over the years. Parking lots had been built over sites Gary deemed were dump sites, and if the remains of victims had not been preserved, the chances of finding any of them intact would be slim. Tom also believed that if any more victims existed, chances were, Gary placed them farther away. Time and convenience were major factors when deciding where he would put a woman's body after killing her. For the ones he put close by in Seattle, it probably meant he had to work a shift at Kenworth, pick up Matthew, fulfill some other family obligation, or adhere to a routine to ensure Judith didn't become suspicious.

When I asked about the investigation, specifically why Gary was taken off surveillance in 2001, Tom explained that for that entire year they had been following Gary on and off, but he always seemed aware that they were watching him. On the way to work he would go dumpster diving in junk yards, and sometimes he'd pull over to take a shit in the woods. But he would never stop to pick up a woman. Even when they planted decoys, women pretending to be prostitutes, Gary never stopped to look at them. That was the thing about Gary: he was hyperaware of his surroundings. If he felt something wasn't right, he would trust his intuition.

I wondered what his gut feeling might be now, if he had one at all, about me returning to Seattle and not giving up, and the detectives who were still chasing him, even though he had been locked away for over twenty years. Both our pursuits were endless. And Gary probably derived satisfaction from knowing the deep commitments that had been made to him—the control he had over people like Tom and myself trying to understand even a portion of him. To unearth the secrets he seemed more inclined to die with than ever tell.

CHAPTER FIFTEEN
Unremarkable

From the window of the plane, I watched New York grow smaller and smaller until it resembled the bumpy terrain on one of those raised-relief maps often found in schools. The kind I used to run my fingers along when I was a kid, not caring what part of the world I was touching. Now, nothing mattered more than where I was going.

I closed my eyes, willing myself to sleep. When I awoke, Mount Rainier swelled from the earth below, white and rugged like old skin. A postcard Gary had sent me captured the same image, except the body of the mountain was hugged by the orange glow of a dying sun. He had wanted me to see at least one of the places he would spend nights sleeping under a sky needlepointed with light from constellations, stealing the darkness. If I could vividly picture the places he loved, in his mind, that would entice me to leave New York and live somewhere in Washington, closer to him.

Once the plane landed, I exited from the terminal into the airport. I thought of Gary decades earlier, in 1983, walking these same steps, like any other person coming or going. Except he was there for another purpose.

Clutched in his hands was Marie Malvar's ID. After he noosed his arm around her throat—killing her—he dragged her naked body from his bed through his house, rolled her up in a piece of carpet, and dumped her in the back of his truck. He planned to discard her in Mountain View Cemetery, but along the way, a wooded ravine in Auburn caught his eye. *A much better place*, he thought. He hauled her body about thirty feet down the steep, narrow path and decided she was far enough out of sight. Since she fought so hard, she wasn't deserving of any company, to be placed alongside other women who shared her fate. So, he left her there alone as a form of punishment, her body tossed to the ground like a piece of junk that was no longer of use to him.

Her ID was all that was left of her. A few days later he walked into the airport, dropped it on the floor, and continued on his way, forgetting her face for good. He hoped that someone would stumble upon it and it would somehow fall into the hands of the police. If his plan worked, they would draw the conclusion that she disappeared while trying to leave Seattle, increasing the probability that she could be anywhere. Then they would stop looking for her, and the Green River Killer would fall off their radar. This concoction of a scheme was a precaution he felt was necessary, since the day after he killed her an officer had showed up at his front door to question him about her disappearance.

When Gary picked up Marie near the corner of 216th and Pacific Highway South, her boyfriend followed them into a motel parking lot. He ended up losing them when Gary drove back onto Pacific Highway South and made an abrupt left turn down 216th. Three days later, when Marie did not return, her boyfriend reported her missing and told police that he had scoured the neighborhood where he last saw her for the pickup truck. After hours of driving around, he found the red Dodge parked in Gary's driveway on 32nd Place off Military Road.

The police officer who rang Gary's doorbell that day happened to be an old acquaintance from high school. Mostly everyone who knew Gary remembered him to be quiet, polite, and harmless, and that time was no different. At the sight of Gary's face, always calm and friendly, the officer was no longer suspicious. As a formality, he asked the generic routine questions, an exchange that lasted only a few minutes. Gary admitted to visiting prostitutes occasionally, but he denied ever meeting Marie. Satisfied, the officer left, not noticing that the entire time Gary had been leaning against the fence to hide an injury on his arm, bright red and obvious. As Gary choked Marie with the pantyhose she removed to have sex with him, in the fight for her life, she had clawed deep red scratches into his skin.

Although the officer paid no mind to his arm, Gary was still spooked by the close call. He would have to cover up the scratches somehow. After thinking for a while, a solution came to mind. He poured battery acid over the gashes to make them resemble a burn. That would be easier to explain if anyone asked. He could always say that he scorched himself while working on a car, which was exactly what he told Judith two years later.

In the airport, I scanned every inch of floor I could, wondering which spot he chose. A detail he probably didn't even remember. I imagined the small boxed photo of Marie's face pointed toward the ceiling, people trampling over her last piece of identity, before an airport worker finally picked it up, recognized the general value of an ID, and brought it to lost and found. Because of this discovery, mostly everyone, aside from her boyfriend, believed she had left Seattle and was still alive somewhere else. Gary's plan worked.

His plans for me were possibly just as deliberate. Concern for my safety seemed like a decoy for his true desire, to have some kind of control over my life.

But if he had not been in prison for killing nearly a hundred women, I might've been fooled into believing he was a sincere person, like the police officer who showed up at his door that day. There were times when his kindness appeared to be just as real as anyone else's who loved me. The mundane conversations he sometimes initiated about family trees, camping, and places to visit in Washington, for instance, were his attempts to make me feel safe enough to forget he was a serial killer. I had to constantly remind myself that he had been practicing the skill of fakery longer than I had been alive. Oftentimes, no one even noticed his presence to consider him suspicious of anything, let alone the murders of scores of women.

Sometime in the 1970s, Gary flew to Las Vegas, pretending to be his friend Louis Young. Free airfare, a free motel room, and a wedding party where he could meet women and take advantage of free drinks, food, and dessert. What could be better? So what if he didn't know any of the other guests?

He showed up to the airport with the ticket his friend had given to him and looked forward to a weekend away from Seattle. Back then, identities never had to be verified, so as far as anyone was concerned, he was Mr. Young. When he got to the motel, it was the same thing. The desk attendant checked him into his room with no questions asked.

At the wedding, he took his friend's name tag and sat in the back where no one would notice him. He observed the crowd, making sure he had not received any unwanted attention. When he felt confident that he had blended in well enough, he began to walk around the room, mingling with the other guests. After a couple of drinks, his shyness wore off and he was able to converse with any woman who was alone that he found attractive.

By ten o'clock, he had passed along his room information to a woman he was certain he would see later that night. Tired from dancing and bored of toasting the bride and groom, he decided to leave, even shaking hands with people on the way out, as if they were his lifelong friends. As he relaxed in the quiet confines of his room, he waited for the rest of his night to start, the real fun.

As he laid down on the bed, after a half hour, a knock on the door forced him to his feet. Just as he predicted, the woman from the wedding was there, wanting the same exact thing as he did. Sex with no attachment or commitment, a story that would stay in Vegas long after they had gone on with their lives, never to see each other again.

"We made a night of it," he recounted.

Seeing how easy it was to wander into a banquet room, he began to make a habit of it. Family reunions, high school graduations, retirement parties, no event was off-limits. He could pretend to be anyone, a friend of so and so, and no one would question it. They would accept his presence, the women especially, welcoming him with open arms. Gary learned that most of the time at any affair when a woman was there alone, she was often trying to forget her ex-boyfriend or get some kind of revenge on him by sleeping with someone else. These women were always looking to have sex with a man they could forget by Monday. Gary was the perfect candidate to help fulfill their mission.

As he divulged these stories to me, I couldn't help but laugh at first. Before becoming a serial killer, he was a serial wedding crasher. What a bizarre résumé. But the more I thought about it, the more I recognized the patterns in his behavior that seemed to be taking shape even back then, before he killed anyone.

He could blend into any room, any crowd, any neighborhood, and remain undetected. No one ever raised an eyebrow at him, even if he didn't belong. His unassuming demeanor, quiet and shy, instantly categorized him as harmless. The way he was able to joke with women and make them comfortable enough to leave with him and shack up in his motel room for a weekend said a lot about his skills as a charmer. Years later, women would get into his truck just the same and many would break the cardinal rule of prostitution and agree to accompany him to his house, never expecting to take their final breath there.

Until his arrest, no one—except the few officers who steadfastly believed Gary was guilty but couldn't prove it—believed he could be capable of such violence, the habitual strangling of women. In 1987, when the task force became more suspicious of him and even searched his house, nearly everyone who knew him overlooked that he could have been the Green River Killer. It wasn't until he confessed and pleaded guilty to 48 counts of aggravated first-degree murder in 2003 that those closest to him had no choice but to believe his guilt.

Fooling people and pretending to be kind was part of his expertise. With me, it was no different.

When he would ask me what I planned to eat for dinner because he was "always interested in learning stuff like that" about me, it was hard to believe it was all an act. It reminded me of a gesture that a father, boyfriend, or anyone who cared about another's well-being would make.

But then I remembered the faces of his victims, and that he would sometimes ask them if they had eaten dinner or if they were hungry. To convince them of his kindness and that they were in safe company, he would sometimes buy them a meal at McDonald's before having sex with them and strangling them to death. And now, he was using a similar tactic on me to gain my trust.

Spending hours listening to him act like a decent person while also knowing the extent of his cruelty was a struggle that never ceased. When he would say things to me like, "You're breaking the monotony," appreciative of the good conversation I provided to him in a place where he existed mostly alone with no one to really listen to him, it was hard to believe he was anything but sincere. How often was anyone willing to try to know him in a real way, without fishing for the gory details of his crimes? When he'd make jokes and say, "Just to get you to laugh," as his reason for trying to be funny in the first place, it was easy to think he really meant well. When the jokes were childish and borderline corny, it was even easier to see him in a nonthreatening light.

"Did you see that rain—dogs flying through the air . . . oh, there's a Siamese cat with blond hair! Those damn things. Those things hurt when they hit you!" he said and laughed, following a discussion we had one day about idioms.

He had even convinced himself that he was a good person. During one conversation, he expounded to me on the golden rule in the Bible, as if it were new to me—"Treat others how you would like to be treated," he said.

Although he could have been learning the concept of general kindness, I suspected he always knew it but chose not to apply it. Yet, there he was, actually saying to me that you should "treat others how you would like to be treated." His hypocrisy dumbfounded me to the same extent as all the senseless tragedies he had caused over and over again.

When he spoke about love and marriage he *almost* sounded authentic, like an actor giving an impressive performance in a movie. "When you get married—that is making love, not just having sex," he asserted.

But did he really know the difference? If someone was unfamiliar with his past and clueless to what he was capable of, he might seem well-versed in love.

"A friend can help you out of a ditch. They can help you up, and you can help the other person up, and at night, for instance, you and your husband—the husband and wife will keep warm because they're close together at night. Who can be warm when you're by yourself?" he asked, referring to the Bible passage in Ecclesiastes. By now, he had recited it to me several times and had partially transcribed it in a letter.

Gary often paraphrased or quoted scripture when he wanted to appear sincere. It was as though he was incapable of communicating his own feelings on subjects such as love or friendship. He had to plagiarize them instead. However, when it came to talking about sex, he didn't need any kind of supplemental material, I noticed. His own memories were enough.

But as much as he wanted to convince me he was capable of doing good, he seemed to also want to show me the monster within him.

CHAPTER SIXTEEN
True Intentions

On the top shelf of my closet, a collapsible canvas-lined box held a stack of scarves. Gray cashmere stitched with silver strands, burgundy sheer nylon, black silk printed with velvet roses, blue crocheted wool, heavy enough to make you sweat in a blizzard. When Gary asked me if I owned any scarves, I considered this collection that had been tucked away since March. His question was innocent enough, although odd, but that was nothing new. He often asked random, offbeat details about my life.

He stumbled over his words, until they finally made sense. He advised, "When you go to the Space Needle, make sure you bring a scarf for your head . . . You'll be there in the summer. It won't be cold, but it will be windy."

To further defend his case, he pointed out that in *Sleepless in Seattle*, Meg Ryan wore a scarf on her head as she stood peering over the city from five hundred feet in the air, and I should do the same.

For a moment, he appeared as any other thoughtful person would, expressing genuine concern for my well-being. I tried to determine the depth of his sincerity while remembering what I already knew about him. Before his arrest, throughout the course of a single day, he'd step into different characters: the considerate, doting husband or boyfriend, an innocent, lonely single father just looking for a good time, desperate for a date, then a violent killer incapable of showing the slightest bit of mercy to women who ended up unclothed and bent over in front of him.

The conversation veered off course countless times before he returned to his original question. However, this time it was more heavily contaminated, leaving me with an uncomfortable feeling.

"Did your mother tell you to carry a scarf with you all the time?"

"No, she never did." I contemplated why my mother would give me such advice, and all I could come up with was that sometimes the weather fluctuates without warning, so it would be good to be prepared.

"Oh," he murmured. It was clear he had been expecting a different response.

"Why? Was she supposed to?"

"Well, I guess it's better than a sock," he said. He seemed to be mulling an idea over in his mind, thinking through the steps of a long process.

"What does that mean?" I asked, baffled. Was he really that worried I wouldn't be warm enough at the top of the Space Needle?

He paused, as if considering what he should tell me, like I had caught him in a lie he was attempting to smooth over. I waited, listening to him inhale and exhale, the soft rhythm of his breath I had come to know as well as a neighborhood I had lived in, the night and day of its pulse.

Then, as if he had remembered a private joke, he laughed away the silence. "You laugh because you're a virgin, basically, and you put the scarf in your mouth so when you scream because of the sensation of getting your hymen broke," he clarified.

I was so perplexed by his explanation, all I could muster was a bewildered "oh" followed by a nervous giggle. In his mind, as he sometimes did, he had made me as innocent as possible. Somewhere I was with him—in a bed, the back of a truck, a motel, the middle of the woods—and he was forcing a scarf into my mouth, gagging me, to not hear me scream.

"You have to have that," he said and laughed, humored by the thought of hurting me. "Your mother should tell you [to] carry a scarf with you, put it in your mouth, so you don't have to take off your socks," he attempted to explain his reasoning. But it was too convoluted, too sick to ever make sense.

"I've never heard of that," I finally said. "Is that something from an older generation, maybe?" I prodded, trying to determine where such a sinister idea had originated. When he created such blackhearted plots, I wondered if each thought he had was original or plagiarized. It seemed an important detail to help measure his depravity.

"Might've been. Yeah, might've been," he agreed.

He continued to laugh at whatever he was imagining. "Yeah, because the woman has it—when the hymen breaks, it tears, I think, and the woman screams," he repeated.

"Well, I've never heard of that," I reiterated, hoping he would recognize his own absurdity and change the subject. But there was no budging him from his daydream, what would be a nightmare for me.

"Nobody tells you about that," he said as though I should be thanking him for passing on his wisdom. "You'll be keeping up the neighbors," he said and laughed. In his make-believe world, he considered another possibility. A scarf was no longer stuffed in my mouth. Instead, the piercing sound of my screams were loud enough for someone else to hear.

I waited for the moment when he would wrap the scarf around my throat. Pulling, pulling, pulling. There was no other way for him.

"Well, it doesn't matter," he concluded when I didn't say anything.

It's not like his thoughts could ever become reality. It's not like I could ever die by his hands, no matter how many times he imagined it.

CHAPTER SEVENTEEN
Manipulation and Gaslighting

In a park in King County, seven to eight inches underground, Gary had buried a box—or a safe, as he referred to it. He had buried it there decades ago, and now he urged me to try and find it.

He had just moved to Auburn with Judith into their dream house. If anyone were to assess his life then, it would've seemed perfect.

But had he already tempted fate too many times? How many times had he lied to her that he was leaving early for work to stop for breakfast or coming home late because he had to attend a union meeting? The last thing he wanted was for the perfect life he created for himself to crumble before him.

If Judith ever stumbled upon his box, she didn't have the key to unlock it, and she would never dare to drill it open, but he didn't want to add another lie to his daily repertoire of bullshit. He also never wanted the police to find it, so just as he had been doing for years whenever he moved to a new house, he dug it up and reburied it in a different location closer to him, making sure to never keep it in his possession for too long out of fear his property could be searched like in 1987.

One morning, he drove toward Kenworth, stopping at a park he knew would be empty. With the box wrapped in plastic and secured in a backpack he slung onto his shoulders, he made his way to the walking path with a shovel in hand. Once he was certain he was entirely alone, he started to dig. When he was satisfied with the depth of the hole, he removed the box from the backpack, crouched down, and lowered it into the earth.

He thought about what he was leaving behind, a silent funeral for some of his most cherished possessions: photos of some of the women he killed. But the life he had created for himself was worth more. As he dumped the last of the dirt onto the hole, he flattened the mound with the base of the shovel and combed his feet over it.

I admit, I was wary at first. But as I read the one-page letter over and over, I noticed that some of the details were so precise—too precise—that they could pass as true. As he recalled what he put inside the box, it seemed he was exhuming the contents, what he considered a sort of treasure, from the dirt himself with his bare hands.

If what he was entrusting me with was true, then I was on the brink of a breakthrough. For over a year I had been waiting for a moment like this, succumbing to all his games and fantasies, leaving myself an open target for whatever twisted ideas he came up with next. All the sleepless nights now seemed worth it.

* * *

I never doubted he could be responsible for killing more women, and beyond King County in Seattle. I often wondered if the vague stories of murders committed in other states he would sometimes speak of as if they were his own were really admissions of guilt. During the 1970s, a female school bus driver had been murdered somewhere west of Portland, Oregon, and her body was never found, Gary recalled in a letter. He had a way of including sparse details of old cases that seemed to haunt his memory, women killed decades ago that were probably forgotten by everyone else except people who loved them. I wondered why he had remembered them.

In another letter, he told me, "[In the] 1970s or 1980s streetwalkers [in] Las Vegas were missing. [The] brothel was never charged for killing them. Most were dead, buried where houses were being built.

No one was found to who the killer is." His memory of these murders and his investment would make anyone wonder if this was another vague confession. But to prove anything he told me was an entirely different undertaking, and I wasn't sure he would ever be obliged to help without turning it into a rigged game I could never win.

The details he shared about these cases were often too vague to research, and he would gloss over them, treating them more like cautionary tales he wanted me to remember. Asking him about any of the random cases he brought up would only get me a lecture on the danger I was in, never information about what had actually happened.

I began to realize that even the lies he spewed revealed truths about him. Like in this case, his Las Vegas murder story proved he was still preoccupied with killing prostitutes. Even if he wasn't the one responsible, he chased news of their deaths like a high. It also validated what I already knew: he was fond of toying with me to keep me in suspense. By doing so, he mimicked his old life, those moments when he was in full control of a woman's fate. Promising most of the women he'd let them go if they stopped fighting even though he continued to tighten his grip around their throats, they were left in a threshold of anxiety between life and death, guessing if he'd keep his word. With me, he kept letting me believe that if I didn't fight him for answers, he'd give them to me, but the answers never came, and I knew if I pushed too hard, he'd only cut me off. With bated breath, I waited on information from him that could lead to more cases being solved or that could never come at all.

Since the number of women Gary claimed he killed often fluctuated—sometimes eighty-one, sometimes ninety-one, and sometimes a ballpark in between this range—I often wondered if he really knew how many lives he took, or if these numbers were merely guesswork.

But something about this box seemed real.

He described it as a small metal safe, no bigger than a foot wide. Painted dark brown with a key lock on top, there was nothing extraordinary about it. Just a typical safe people use to store jewelry, passports, and other important documents.

Stuffed inside were photographs—twenty, to be exact—he'd taken of women he killed, although he said, "Let's just say I didn't kill them" when I asked. I figured an officer had to be in earshot, or he was still trying to make me see the good in him.

"You could see their hands moving in the photos," he persisted, trying to convince me he was telling the truth. I already knew he had admitted to detectives to taking pictures of some of the Green River victims *after* they were dead. But I knew it was no use to challenge him. He'd only lie more.

In each picture, they were posed naked on the ground however he wanted them. He recalled a tattoo that one of the woman had on her ankle, but since he "didn't give a crap about that" he couldn't remember the design of it. Wendy Coffield and Debra Bonner both had tattoos on their ankles, but there could have been others. I wondered if dragging a woman by the feet when discarding her body stayed vivid in his mind, and that's why he remembered this detail.

Four spiral notebooks in which he recorded "what they talked about before they passed away" could also be found in this box. He said this as though he had no responsibility for ending their lives, as if they just dropped dead in front of him from anything other than his own hands. Within those pages, he wrote "sugar names" of women, their addresses and phone numbers, their races, whether they were dancers or bar maids before becoming prostitutes, their experience in brothels, and any details he could recall; for instance, "one white with stretchmarks left Las Vegas." On the surface, these personal histories meant nothing. But transcriptions of their last words or any detail that could make them stand out as individuals rather than statistics, to me, was sacred and worthy of trying to find. For a family member of a missing person, those details might be enough to prove they'd been murdered by the Green River Killer.

Included in his inventory were room keys 21 and 22 from the Three Bears Motel, where several of his victims went missing, a blue baseball hat, and a Camaro emblem key ring, which he stole from Constance "Connie" Naon after killing her. At the time, he contemplated stealing her Camaro, but he decided it would be too risky. The key ring would have to do.

The more I read through his list, the more believable it was that these things existed. Many serial killers keep souvenirs or trophies from their kills, so it made sense that Gary would do the same. It also made sense that he would bury any evidence he had, since he was methodical about not getting caught, even going so far as to clip the women's fingernails if they scratched him to remove any of his DNA, or change his tires if he left marks at any of the scenes.

Later, when I read his entire interrogation, I would learn that the photographs he took were a popular topic of discussion with detectives. Like trying to extract a stubborn tooth, they pulled and pulled, hoping they would say the right thing to get him to confess where he hid the Polaroids. But he refused. He always stuck to the same story: he ripped them to pieces and threw them out the window while driving down a highway. It didn't matter that they challenged him, reminding him how difficult it would be to tear a Polaroid, that it wasn't like a sheet of paper. Perhaps they had taken too much from him, so many of the women's remains he regarded as his possessions. He'd be damned if they took anything else. As if this secret was the last dollar he had left, he held onto it, waiting for the right moment to spend it.

For whatever reason, that time was now.

His reasons for not telling me sooner, when I was actually in Seattle, made me question his motives. He could have been saying anything to lure me back there, in the hopes I'd end up moving there, which he had been talking about for months. Or it was another test to see how much control he had over me to determine what I was willing to do for him. He could've been playing a twisted game of *Send Maria, My Naive Trophy Wife*—how he perceived me at times—*All Over Washington* in search of something that only existed in his own mind. With him, anything was possible. But because there was always the chance he was telling the truth, I continued to push my doubts aside and listen to him. But as I did, I felt like prey walking into a trap.

He had kept the box a secret for decades, referring to it as his "get out of death penalty card," he boasted. "My lawyers already made a deal. I'll tell them about the number of victims and where they are and everything to get off the death penalty. But I had that there for my trump card," he explained. At this point, considering his age and the amount of time that had passed, he was confident he would never face such a punishment. The chances of them finding any more bones of his victims were slim, especially since no one seemed to be looking.

Since he was getting older, perhaps he didn't want his souvenirs, some of his most cherished possessions, to be lost forever when he died. It made sense he would want someone to find them. He even insisted that I use a metal detector when I searched for the box, and if I found it, he instructed me to use a half-inch drill bit to open it. He seemed serious. Sure, he was fucked up, but would he really lure me—one of the few people to ever show him any kindness within the last twenty years—almost three thousand miles away to go on a wild goose chase? There had to be an end to his depravity, a soft spot, something human. Or so I hoped.

But I knew better than to write him back with my litany of questions. He would never want an officer to know about this. I would have to wait until he called and brought it up, when he felt it was safe enough to talk about it on the phone. In the meantime, I would have to be satisfied with what he had shared.

That night, I searched King County parks on the internet, making a list of those that matched his description. A foot from a bank hill, "off to the right side of a paved walking trail," where there was enough brush to hide him as he buried it. A park that remained empty on weekdays, especially in the winter. I narrowed my search to about ten, but this number would grow the more I researched.

But could I really fly to Washington and start digging up random parks to try to find a serial killer's trophies? He would have to give me more information, something specific, I decided. His hints would not cut it if he wanted me to embark on such an undertaking.

By the time I reread his letter for probably the hundredth time, there was not a doubt in my mind that this box existed in the same way I did, and he did. I imagined my hands prying it from the ground, the faces of beautiful women falling at my feet, learning their names and memorizing their stories, retrieving everything that had been lost, casualties of his cruelty, and restoring it all to a brand-new peace. If only it would be that easy.

* * *

"But where is this park?" I asked Gary for at least the tenth time. In previous conversations, whenever I brought it up, he pretended not to hear the question, talking about something mundane like the weather instead. Or sometimes he'd run off a list of parks he considered "beautiful." Places he hoped I'd visit someday when I started my new life in Washington.

"It's just a nice place to walk around and get some air and have a beer or a cup of coffee or something . . . I don't know what the name of it is . . . I know what they call it, but it's hard to . . ." he rambled.

Why was he always so conflicted over telling the truth?

"You got the ones on the sound, which is South Park, Seward Park, Seahurst . . . Lincoln Park, and then you got Dash Point Park." As he rattled off random locations, I reminded him there were a lot of parks in Washington. Did he expect me to dig up the entire state?

But as long as I was asking, he wouldn't budge on giving me any more information. Until I pretended well enough that my curiosity was dormant, and I made it seem he never even confided in me about a box, that was when he would resurrect the idea of it. He had to be the one in control at all times. What was I thinking?

He swore he forgot the name of the park, and I half believed him. There were a lot of places in Brooklyn I would go to all my life, and I never knew their names. Sometimes a place becomes memorized, encrypted, like a smell from childhood or a song; no directions would ever be needed to return to it. So, I tried to give him the benefit of the doubt.

But he taunted me with his secrets, "maps about the treasure I'm probably going to send you." Since he considered his victims his prized possessions, some of their bones still resting in places only he knew, I figured they had to be part of the "treasure" he was referring to. Rather than expand on these details, he'd change his mind and write me letters scrawled with Bible verses and his philosophies on the state of the world. How could he share his secrets with me when officers were always reading his mail and eavesdropping on our calls? I had no choice but to tell him, "Don't worry, I understand."

When the mail was delayed, probably due to Covid, he would hear nothing of it. "The damn prison should send those letters to you," he protested, assuming his mail had been confiscated. "The thing is, I'm not sending any secret messages. Why in the hell aren't they sending those?"

His secrets were always in the background, orbiting each conversation, until he decided it was time to let me in on them. "In prison, officers want to look at your letters, and see if there's no code in there, and nothing about the treasure . . . definitely nothing about any secrets you have," he continued, tormenting me with everything he knew I wanted from him. "Sometimes my mail stops the building. I don't know why," he said, faking ignorance. "My letters got no secrets in there. I'm trying to teach in mail more about the Bible than I'm talking about the secrets," he swore like he was taking an oath not to deceive me while he was really doing the opposite.

If I wanted to obtain any of the secrets he hinted at, I'd have to be patient, just as I had been for months. There was no other way except to participate in his games. As long as I followed his lead, he would be sure of my investment, and I would remain in his world.

But he did tell me that from the last house he lived in before he was arrested in Auburn, he would pass this park on his way to work in Renton. Now, at least, I could narrow my search.

Despite my best efforts to pry more information from him, he told me what *he* wanted me to know. That was it. I would have to figure out the park on my own. How good of a journalist was I, really? He seemed to be inciting me to prove myself to him.

I didn't even have to formally agree to help him. He seemed to know I would try no matter what. I would either prove the existence of this box to be the truth or a lie. So, I jotted down his instructions, even though I told him *maybe* I would return to Seattle in the summer.

My task didn't end with just prying the box from the earth. He wanted me to bring it to the Christian Faith Center, a church located in the South End of Seattle. According to his plan, the pastors there would help me sift through the contents. Together, we could identify the women in the photos, even if that meant studying their nude bodies under a magnifying glass to search for any scars, birthmarks, tattoos, or stretch marks. "A scar on her shoulder" someone in her family would recognize because they'd remember if "she got pushed off a swing. You know how kids are," he said. Words that made me feel sick.

A lot of them were still kids when you killed them, I wanted to scream. But I listened without criticizing him, a skill that had become like an art.

Once I drilled through the box to unlock it and had the pictures in my hands, he instructed that I cover the women's breasts and vaginas with tiny stickers in the shape of stars, the kind teachers stamp on homework. That would prevent anyone who might see the photos from jerking off to them, *his* women. If I turned over the pictures to the police, I ran the risk of a lewd aftermath, something Gary opposed. A pastor would be more helpful and honest, he insisted, especially since he believed the police didn't really care about any of the women that were still missing.

To prove his point, he brought up a woman he had killed that was referred to as Jane Doe Bones 20. Since the 1980s, police had had not been able to identify her, and Gary assumed they probably never would. "The Kent-Des Moines woman . . . she was a nice-looking teenager," he said, remembering a face no one could put a name to. "I know she was missing on a Saturday afternoon . . . I put her there Saturday night. But they haven't found a head," he explained, as if he was describing an ornament that had gone missing from his front lawn. "And the idea is nobody kept up with her . . . they got half the body, but they don't have the head. The head was probably pushed into the ground because it was down in the mud," he said.

Later, he would be proven wrong. In January 2024, Bones 20 would be identified as sixteen-year-old Tammie Liles. But just like when Wendy Stephens, his youngest victim, was identified in 2021, I doubted he had much of a reaction. Just another name that meant nothing to him.

But at the time, he feigned concern, trying to prove to me his heart was in the right place. Giving closure to the families mattered to him, he told me. I wondered if his true desire was really to add more confirmed victims to his list. Then he would be lauded as the "best" American serial killer of all time.

But his intentions didn't matter to me. I was already concocting my own plan. I would wait until the summer and fly back there. First, I would visit him and demand more answers about where he buried this box. Face-to-face, I was sure I'd be able to retrieve more information. Then I would purchase a metal detector and a shovel and walk through all the parks along his work route, digging up any part of the earth I thought he could have touched.

I, too, could be relentless.

CHAPTER EIGHTEEN

Arthur

Somewhere in Montreal, a forty-one-year-old man had just finalized a few more business deals—savvy real estate investments—the last of the year. Finally, recognition was being given to his family name, similar to that of Rockefeller. But it was not always this way.

It took years of working at Microsoft and then as a card counter in a casino before reaching a level of wealth that allowed him to travel through America and Canada with ease. He inherited some apartment buildings from his parents after they died—the one good thing his father ever did for him. For most of his childhood, he was beaten so often he didn't even feel human. He expected the injuries would eventually kill him, but that day never came. His father ended up dying, instead, and then his mother followed a few years later.

The apartments he now owned became his source of income but also his burden. A lot of the tenants didn't pay their rent on time, if at all. One legal proceeding and eviction after another, he had to find another way to survive before he lost his will to live, or worse, turned into the same mean-spirited, ill-tempered man as his father. He decided to sell all the properties and invest his money in motels. At least then, it'd be easier to get rid of customers who tried to cheat him.

He began growing his empire in America, since his family moved him there when he was ten years old. First in New York and then in Seattle. But he was ready to expand even more. He had a fierce desire to not only make more money, but to return to his roots, where he took his first breath.

By Christmas, he wanted to relocate permanently to Vancouver, gifting himself the new beginning he felt he had earned. He had finally made something of himself, despite his father telling him he never would amount to anything, and he had restored their family name in the process.

Arthur sounded like the kind of man you would never scroll past on a dating app, the kind of man women fought over but never won. Smart, single, wealthy, and attractive.

Gary could not stop talking about him one day, conjuring him out of nowhere, like a new character penciled into a script at the last minute. I was expected to believe that Arthur had existed the entire time. "You know, the guy I told you about," Gary dropped into the conversation casually. If there was an award for gaslighting, he would have won by a landslide. I tried to remember a time when I had heard him even mention the name "Arthur," but I couldn't. I was so obsessed with learning Gary's story, I usually hung on to every word he said, often taking notes after our calls. How did I miss this?

According to him, Arthur was a lifelong friend he had met at the Christian Faith Center, a church he attended in Federal Way. *That means Arthur must have been a teenager or in his twenties when they met.* I found it bizarre that Gary had a friend back then that was so much younger, and for them to keep in touch all these years seemed stranger. He barely had many friends to begin with, and no one I had known to stand by him through his entire incarceration, except his older brother. I couldn't wrap my head around it.

Since they were such great friends, Gary had told Arthur about me, prompting Arthur to search for me on Instagram. I questioned the possibility of this. Beyond the Crime was a public page, but it didn't contain my name. The only other profile I had was private and excluded my last name. "He knows who you are," Gary insisted, claiming Arthur had, in fact, found me on social media. "He thought you were a nice-looking lady," Gary added, waiting for my reaction.

I still wasn't sold this so-called Arthur had seen me, but it was no use arguing. The last thing I wanted was to give Gary a reason to threaten to cut off communication with me again. After seeing my picture, Arthur asked Gary to pass a message to me. He wanted to meet me in Montreal before the year was over. He would be staying with his cousins in Grandville, New York, for the next week, but after that he would have all the time in the world to get to know me.

For a moment, I considered Arthur's existence. We would meet at a coffee shop, and he'd show up ten minutes late, nearly crushing my hope and then reviving it a second before I got up to leave. He'd make an excuse—he had to take a call about one of his motels—and I would say I had forgiven him, although deep down I'd begrudge him. He would be too handsome to tell the truth to, the kind of guy you try to put an act on for as long as possible. You do your hair and makeup flawlessly and actually care about touching it up in the bathroom. You wear cute, uncomfortable outfits that show off whatever you think he finds most attractive. You smile a lot and never really tell him how your day is going or how you're feeling, all for the sake of maintaining a good impression. His blue eyes would look into mine as I talked, believing everything. The more I considered his existence, it was like believing in a ghost that flickers the lights at two AM. I knew I would never see him, just like Gary had probably never seen him.

He swore that Arthur was going to call me soon and offer to pay my first month's rent if I moved to Montreal. We could date, and if it didn't work out, I would not be obligated to repay him. But if we did get along, he would continue to take care of my rent.

But what was even more important, Arthur needed my help. A couple weeks earlier, Gary had given him a detailed description of where he buried his box of trophies. At the same time, Gary had also written me a letter, urging me to look for the box, even giving me advice for when I would go on the expedition. "Tell a few what your plans are there. You will need help. Need a good metal detector. While one uses it, the other one digs and looks out for everyone. Maria, wear the proper clothes. Gloves, shovel, hat from sun or rain . . . Don't say what you're looking for. Just stuff. People will steal what's not locked down. Don't broadcast what you are looking for. You still will find treasure of some sort. Just pocket it and move on. Note, the bench may have been moved or stolen. So check where there is no bench too."

But now, Gary was saying that Arthur had found the box. He dug it up in a park that was under construction. Just like Gary instructed, he drilled the box open, finding twenty pictures of women Gary had killed along with the spiral notebooks where he had recorded details of the conversations he had with them.

My heart fluttered with intense rage at the thought. I knew it was unlikely that Arthur existed, let alone unearthed a box of a serial killer's treasure within only a few days. And if it were true, I was bothered that Gary could betray me with such ease and then also confide in me about it like it was no big deal. He seemed to be gunning for a reaction. But I refused to let him know I was bothered. I acted unfazed, just like how I imagined I would act on my imaginary date with Arthur. If I told Gary what I was really thinking, I feared we would argue, and he would never call me again. I had to remain calm, and more importantly, I had to unravel the lies he seemed to be weaving and get to the truth.

Apparently, Arthur wanted my opinion about trying to identify the women from the pictures. "I'm happy to help him," I said, hoping on some level that I would be proven wrong and that a Canadian phone number would flash across my screen. That would mean Gary was telling the truth, restoring the small amount of decency I still tried to believe he had. But I knew the chances of that happening were slim. Every time I spoke to Gary, he seemed to have moved further from reality to a place where only he and Arthur existed. I was only invited into this world on an as-needed basis. And sometimes there wasn't any room for me at all.

As I awaited what felt like an ensuing banishment from Gary's warped reality, he mentioned another person he never had before, despite making it seem like he did. Betty Ann, Arthur's sister. She was thirty-eight, attractive, and had a boyfriend. Like me, she had become obsessed with gathering details about Gary's life. He boasted that she had flown to Seattle and visited one of the first apartments he had ever rented, the one he lived in with Marcia when they first met. While there, Betty Ann flirted with the building manager, and he allowed her to snap pictures of Gary's exact apartment.

As he told me about Betty Ann's research, I wondered if it was a ploy to make me jealous or to prompt me to book a flight to Seattle as soon as possible. When I didn't react to that news, either, and instead asked questions about why she was there and what she was hoping to find, he tried harder, cutting me until there was a deep enough wound, only to then pour salt into it. Arthur and his sister had also been working with a reporter, who would write about whatever cases ended up being associated with the box.

It seemed he was willing to do anything to rattle me. He wanted me to compete for his attention and his story, even if my opponents weren't real. Even though I doubted anything involving Arthur was true, I pretended like I believed him.

A few weeks prior, I had practiced a similar tactic when he told me about Ana, a woman he went to high school with, who he claimed was still his friend. He had said that "she was like you . . . a really sexy top ten woman . . . I wanted to be her lover, be with her, but never did. It never happened that way." Lured by the prospect of becoming a Hollywood star, she left for California right after graduation. But her life did not go as planned. She would be coaxed into believing she would "get the part" in whatever movie she was auditioning for as long as she slept with the producer, director, or agent, or sometimes all three and whomever else felt like it. She would attend parties that became orgies, and she'd be passed around along with the joints everyone was smoking. Instead of becoming an actress, she became a prostitute. When she got pregnant, she gave the baby to her parents for them to raise. Eventually, the love she had for her child forced her back home to Seattle for good. She ended up becoming a school nurse and falling in love with a man she was still married to over forty years later.

Gary intended her story to scare me out of becoming a full-time writer, believing that the only way I would ever get a book deal would be if I slept with someone. "Everybody's going to be wanting a piece of you," he warned.

Later on, I would request his phone records from the prison and learn that Ana, Arthur, and Betty Ann were not real, just as I suspected. None of the numbers he ever dialed were linked to anyone by those names. In fact, he only ever dialed a few numbers, the same handful of people willing to talk to him consistently, and I was one of them. I wondered what he would come up with next.

The more I demanded to know about the whereabouts of the box, the more intricate the story became. Arthur had decided to hire private investigators from King County who were now helping to contact the parents of the victims, but a lot of them had died in the interim. He then brought the box to a lab in Canada to comb it for DNA, but there were too many different fingerprints on the photos to determine much of anything. One photo had been smudged with lipstick, so there was hope yet. He elaborated like a parent telling a child a bedtime story—no detail was too outlandish as long as both parties were committed to believing in the fantastic wonder of it.

I wondered where the story would end, but instead it only evolved. The work Arthur had put into trying to identify the women from the pictures had inspired him to become an advocate to help prostitutes change their lives. Since the writer Arthur hired to cover the story was doing a lousy job, he wanted me to salvage it and join him in his advocacy. Gary was certain my "wisdom" made me the best person for the job.

In his vision, Arthur would buy an apartment building in Canada that would be used as a rehabilitation center for prostitutes. There, they would have access to an all-female staff of teachers, mentors, counselors, doctors, and nurses. Similar to a prison or mental institution, the women would not be allowed to leave until they completed the program. They would spend their days receiving mental health treatment and attending school, where they would learn that "sex is not love" and that they "are not sperm banks." At the end of the day, they would be locked inside of windowless rooms to ensure they did not escape or kill themselves.

Since I possessed the most "wisdom," Arthur would put me in charge of managing the building. He would pay for my apartment to live there and also give me a car and a salary—the same I made as a teacher and writer or more—and he would add it all to his business's "expense account."

In exchange, I would help to deprogram women from wanting to be prostitutes. "We must choose doing good to all . . . how to change people to make them live right and have peace of mind and have integrity. A code of the right values," Gary said. "Do you want to do something for you or do something for the women that are getting raped every year or getting killed in prostitution?" he asked, trying to guilt me into an unrealistic endeavor of saving women who would have been his victims if he was still free. But it was more than that, the idea of me interacting with and living so close to women he would kill was a whole new kind of fantasy. He became fixated on this vision where I would round up all the prostitutes I could find, lead them from the streets, and put them under one roof. His pure virgin in union with his whores, the perfect habitat, even if only in his mind.

To appease him, I reassured him that I would help, and together, we would save all the women he dreamed of killing. As ridiculous as it was and despite how annoyed I had become by what seemed like his constant lying, I recognized the instability of his mind more than ever before. He seemed convinced that Arthur could show up to the prison at any moment and sit with him in his cell to talk about all the women from the photographs. At this point, the evidence he claimed to have buried was the only thing I still believed in.

Somewhere, I was certain a box of his trophies existed. But he was trying to dissuade me from ever attempting to find it. Cold feet, second thoughts. He no longer wanted to share any of his secrets, what he called his "treasure." He wanted to ensure that box always remained where he had left it in the earth, rotting with the dead and everything that still thirsted for rain.

CHAPTER NINETEEN

Robin

The dull chirping of machines, like the tired, nightlong melody of crickets, echoed through the hallway that seemed to stretch forever. Gary scanned the room numbers, looking for his friend. One of his best drinking buddies from work was recovering from surgery, so he thought the nice thing to do was to visit him. Walking in what felt like circles, he glanced inside each room and noticed a girl lying in bed with bandages on her hands and face. *Must've been in a terrible car accident*, Gary thought, slowing down to survey the extent of her injuries like she was an exhibit in a museum. She was alone and peering into the hall, as if begging for someone to stop for her.

As a nurse was about to make her rounds to check the girl's vitals, she noticed Gary standing there. She told him that the girl was only twenty years old and had been beaten by her pimp.

"Wow, that's terrible," he sympathized. He had killed dozens of women by that point, but he managed to sound concerned, unsettled even. He learned she had also been in a coma for a few days before ending up on that floor.

Gary visited with his friend but couldn't get the battered girl out of his mind. On the way out, he passed her room again, and she was still alone. He stood in the doorway, and the girl's eyes sparkled at the sight of him.

He introduced himself and asked if she had any relatives. All of her family lived in Florida and had no idea what happened to her. For all they knew, she was dead. They chatted until visiting hours were close to ending. Before he left, he asked what she liked to read, and she told him old Westerns by Louis L'Amour. He remembered reading some of those books while he was on the ship in the navy. He promised he would try to bring her some and left for the night.

The next day after visiting his friend again, he returned to the girl's room with a few books he had bought from Goodwill. They talked some more, and this time, she confided in him about what happened to her. She had been living on the street, in and out of motels, and had gotten into a fight with her pimp and another streetwalker. They both took turns beating her, breaking a few ribs, fingers, and some bones in her face. They also held her down and cut most of her hair off, leaving her with an uneven bob. It was a miracle she was still alive. While in the hospital, she had learned that she was two months pregnant, news she was not expecting, despite her promiscuous lifestyle.

Gary listened to her story and actually felt sorry for her. There was something about her he liked—her vulnerability, her strength, how happy she seemed to be in his presence. He couldn't really put his finger on it. He just felt drawn to her, compelled to know her. If he had crossed paths with her on PAC Highway, he probably would have wanted to kill her, but under these circumstances, it felt different. She was no Jane Doe, and he was not a john. In fact, he had learned her name and even remembered it. Robin.

The following day, he showed up again. This time, she asked him to help her call her family in Florida. He dialed the numbers and handed the phone to her. She struggled to explain what had happened to her, trying to talk through tears. She passed the phone to Gary, signaling for him to do the talking for her. He spoke to her brother, relaying everything that had happened along with the hospital and room number. Her parents, four brothers, and two sisters were all on their way.

When they arrived a few days later, her brothers were suspicious of Gary. For all they knew, he could have participated in her attack. To put them at ease, he brought one of her brothers to Kenworth on a Saturday when not many people were around. Then, to verify his identity, he showed him his locker, which consisted of some clothes and day-old doughnuts. Her brother was convinced. He no longer suspected Gary of harming anyone, never mind Robin. After drinking coffee from a machine, Gary brought him to Angle Lake and the Duwamish River, since her brother had asked about some places where he could go boating.

For the next four months, Gary would continue to visit Robin. By the time she was ready to be released, she was able to walk on her own and had no intention of returning to the streets. She planned to move back to Florida with her family and start a new life.

But before she left Seattle for good, her brothers tracked down both of her attackers. They beat both of them, raped the woman, and cut her hair off, exactly what was done to Robin. Robin couldn't help but smile when she saw the photos her brothers showed her, as if she had finally received a gift she had been waiting for her entire life. Before Robin was discharged, she had also told Gary that her brothers ambushed the owners of the motel where she was left for dead. They beat them and tortured them in violent sex acts, using hot curling irons. Afterward, her brothers and sisters robbed whatever they could—TVs, money, anything of value. Although he had not seen it, he believed it. Her brothers seemed like the type of guys that lived for revenge.

When he told me this story, I only half believed him. He had already invented Arthur, Betty Ann, and Ana, so why not add one more person to his imaginary friends list? The only thing that convinced me was how plausible it would be for him to put himself in the path of a vulnerable, broken-down woman. At the end of the day, he was a predator always on the hunt for new prey. What could be better than finding a woman that was entirely defenseless?

Although it was possible he found something he liked about her, something he couldn't explain, which prompted him to not only spare her life but help her to reclaim it, it was also possible, if she was real, he had killed her when she was released from the hospital. After visiting her multiple times during the week, she would have trusted him enough to leave with him.

The number of women he had killed seemed infinite, a black hole of secrets. Like always, he wanted to know what I was willing to believe.

When I spoke with Detective Tom Jensen, he had no recollection of Gary's story about Robin and believed Gary was trying to convince me he was a "good guy" to win me over. But at the same time, he also thought Gary was probably hoping I would be able to prove he had a higher number of kills. Even if I couldn't prove it, planting the seed in the public's mind would have satisfied him. The way Tom saw it, receiving recognition as the most prolific serial killer in America mattered more to Gary than he ever let anyone believe, more than winning me over. His image, the methods of how he killed, his MO, all mattered, even if he pretended it didn't.

I told Tom what Gary had said to me about the unsolved cases, that if a prostitute was found strangled to death in or near the vicinity of one of his dump sites, she was his victim. But Tom was skeptical. He believed that Gary loved to please people. Of course, Gary expected that I would want him to confess to more murders. As a writer, he figured, nothing would please me more.

Tom recalled that when he and the other detectives interviewed him in 2003, Gary would constantly admit to murders he was unsure if he committed, thinking it would please them to pin another murder on him. Each day they would show him pictures of murdered women and crime scenes, and at first he would deny it.

Then after a few days, months, or even years, he would claim he remembered killing the women from the photos they showed him. As a result, they would probe him for more information, such as where he killed them, a location he would guess wrong.

Before Gary was sent to Walla Walla, Dave Reichert, the sheriff at the time, had told Gary he suspected eighty-one to be his total number of kills, and Gary seemed to run with that estimation ever since. Tom and I both agreed that Gary probably didn't know for sure. There were just too many women to differentiate, and he never bothered to look at their faces long enough to remember them. Only if something unique occurred would he remember details.

I wondered if Robin could have been another example of his selective memory. For the rest of my life, I knew I would think of Robin, if her existence was impossible to verify because she was never real to begin with, or if her bones had been lost to the earth in a place only Gary knew about.

CHAPTER TWENTY
Faux Concern

A lot of people who have never been to New York City believe that no place on earth could be worse. They believe shootings and robberies occur on every corner, making the streets unsafe to walk during any time of day. The subways might as well be another version of an underworld where people, no matter their age, go missing, taken against their will.

These naysayers of New York fail to see the beauty that actually exists in the city, lights that burn all night, bridges that connect to different boroughs and states, pulling everyone closer and farther away, the coming and going, constant like a heartbeat, the unaffected faces of seeing too much and expecting nothing, oceans and rivers too dirty to swim in but still nice to look at, the city's own decorative knickknacks, brownstones sticking out their stoned chests to dirty sidewalks, and depending on the season, trees growing fat and then thin, their bare branches like bones.

Gary believed mostly anything he watched on Fox News, and that included its depiction of New York as a crime-infested hellhole. Early in our conversations, intrigue prompted him to ask questions to determine whether the city really lived up to its dangerous reputation. No matter what I said, he became convinced that I would end up the victim of a crime, although I had never been one in all my life while living there. But his mind was made up: I would end up having to run away from men who wanted to rob or "molest" me, and his beliefs only intensified as time passed. Even his letters were liable to his all-consuming paranoia. "Maria, what [does] your life mean to you? If you get robbed: They steal from you. Are you just living to get robbed? Your dignity. Your honor. Esteem. Loss of your being [and] worth," he scribbled.

At times, he actually appeared genuine in his concerns. Through most of our correspondence, I wondered if he could be capable of any real kindness that wasn't self-motivated. I grappled with the idea of whether anyone could be pure evil, their every word and action a supplement of their manipulation.

Later, I would learn that others who knew him vouched for his kindness during their witness statements, so maybe it did exist on some level, or else everyone who had known him had been gullible to a degree. A woman he dated in 1981, Sharon, described him as "real nice" and "fun." Roxanne, the woman he almost married in 1984, believed he was "a kind person." Despite cheating on her and passing genital warts to her, she claimed, "He never did me any harm truly, physically." Nancy remembered her relationship with him was "very easy. There were no problems, no arguments . . . I felt safe around him." It seemed that many people, especially women, who spent time with him had a similar experience.

He couldn't understand why I continued to live in a city, in what he believed was constant peril, and I often asked myself the same question for reasons that had nothing to do with fear but with a desire for change. For all its beauty and promise, New York had failed me in a lot of ways. It was hard not to imagine living in a place where I wouldn't have to work at least four jobs just to pay my rent and bills, a place where I would not be haunted by what felt like an army of ex-boyfriends and friends that had become just people.

"There's parts of the city you don't go into, [so] why in the heck do you live there?" Gary asked for what felt like the millionth time.

He wasn't wrong that there were parts of the city that I and many other New Yorkers avoided, but that was simply a way of life, something he couldn't quite grasp. However, his question stayed on my mind. In my attempts to explain there was no place like New York, that the convenience of living there would be hard to give up, and that there was always so much to do, I was still contemplating the possibility of a better life. He seemed to either detect my lack of conviction or sense my desire for change.

"Where is your treasure? Is your treasure there in New York? Is your dream there? Is where you always wanted to be in New York?" he asked. For a moment, I was silenced by the unusual depth of his questions. By the way he demanded these answers, it seemed like the outcome of my life mattered to him.

"I don't know. That's a good question. I'm not really sure. Dreams and what I want to do, I don't need to be in New York in order to [write]. I could be anywhere," I said. For the first time I was saying out loud what had been on my mind for a while, that I wasn't sure if I wanted to stay there, and I was telling a man who seemed, in that moment, to care what happened to me but who was also a serial killer and had expressed some vile fantasies about me. Although I was not held hostage and could hang up the phone whenever I wanted, it felt like I was experiencing some form of Stockholm syndrome in which I couldn't help but acknowledge his humanity.

Buried beneath his layer of kindness, which was thin as a sheet of tissue paper, there was a free-falling pit to his depravity, and I got sucked into it. On a daily basis, he taunted me with what he made seem was set in stone, always my rape and sometimes my murder. There were no other outcomes more inevitable, even though he imagined a perfect future for me: one filled with afternoons spent swimming in the clean, baptismal depths of a lake, walking a winding path until the sun set, and then "to sleep under the stars," he wrote.

"Now, Maria, what is your life worth when you get raped?" he jotted in a letter.

After that, he never stopped talking about it, my body up for grabs. He demanded to know at what age I realized I was a target for men like him, although he would never implicate himself directly. He would pretend as though he was not part of *that* group of men, that he was a separate entity. Sometimes he wanted to protect me from the harm he knew I could be susceptible to—everything he was capable of—while at the same time, he was excited by the idea of it. A tug-of-war of his conscience, he was conflicted by what he said he wanted for me versus what he wouldn't be able to stop himself from doing to me if ever given the chance.

I walked that line with him, dutifully almost. It was the only way to maintain full admission into his mind. It was all a game, and I was neck-deep in it, nearly above my head.

The idea of me getting killed became an obsession, causing him to lecture me that I shouldn't travel to Seattle alone. He reminded me nonstop that there were "posters all over the city for missing white women," and I could be next. Whether his concern was the slightest bit genuine, or my imagined disappearance was part of a fantasy he had, was hard to decipher. Either way, he seemed to enjoy instilling fear in me that whenever I was alone I was in constant danger of getting killed.

"How tall are you?" he asked.

"I'm five one," I told him, allowing him to construct a more precise visual of me.

"Oh, okay. You're a little thing. So, you *are* small," he said, as if confirming this with himself.

"Maybe your best bet is, your friend from, you went to school [with] since you were a kid. Maybe you can talk to him about going [with you to Seattle]," he suggested. In one of his recent letters, he expounded on this same concern, reminding me that "A lot of white teens and women are missing there in cities of Washington, Oregon, and California. Hundreds. Maybe dead. Sent overseas to a harem, a group of females to one man."

According to Gary, if Asher refused to accompany me then surely I would be raped, killed, or kidnapped. As he continued to envision this scenario, his voice grew in excitement. The images I knew he was concocting, a five-one damsel in distress at his mercy, his fairy tale as frightening as war flashbacks, as he probably thought of his body atop mine, in control of everything that happened.

After warning me that it was only a matter of time before I would be raped and killed, Gary began to give me advice on how I could defend myself. "You know in your heart you will . . . Your luck will run out on you," he predicted. "If you gamble, most of the time the house wins. Maria, the house is the New York area."

Pepper spray, an alarm, a dye pack were all things he recommended I carry in my purse. Better yet, he thought all three should be turned into a patented invention, something that would be almost foolproof to scare off a man. *Weapons for Women by the Green River Killer.* I chuckled at the thought.

"Push a button and all of a sudden the guy gets sprayed with pepper spray, he gets the dye pack sprayed on him, mixed up with the pepper spray, and the alarm going off. It's gonna scare him away. No chance of raping somebody," he boasted, proud of his idea.

But if that failed, then I should kick the guy in the throat and the balls. And if that didn't work, I should piss myself. A man might not want to have sex with a woman who urinated on herself, he hypothesized.

However, this wasn't true for him. Later, I learned he admitted to detectives that in the mid-90s he dated a woman about five times who had a "problem with her bladder" and urinated on him during sex, but he continued to have sex with her anyway, claiming it didn't make him angry. Yet when it came to me, he pretended such an act of defiance would dissuade a guy from trying to have sex altogether. Maybe he would be satisfied with just a blow job. Wouldn't that be better for me?

"Even if someone is forcing you to give a blow job, can't you just bite it and then run away?" I challenged, remembering what I assumed was a lie, that Rebecca Garde Guay had bitten him.

"Well, you can, but your best thing to do is just go through with it because you're probably gonna break your jaw," he advised.

Since I was bound to be victimized, he continued to come up with solutions he thought would improve the experience. I could wear a necklace with a notecard as a medallion that I could tuck inside my shirt. In bold letters, it would read, "I have AIDS. Please use a rubber."

"Maybe that will stop somebody from raping you," he said, his tone serious. "But you gotta remind yourself that it probably will only stop about five percent of the males because [they're] sick anyway. They already got VD. It doesn't matter to them, getting AIDS."

But the only thing I was reminded of was our previous conversations in which he alluded to his own experiences of contracting venereal diseases. The risk of getting an STD never stopped him from having sex with a woman in the past, and in his fantasies, it was no different.

"You think a guy would care? You think someone who has that mentality to rape somebody would be deterred?" I asked.

"Well, it would only stop about one percent," he said and laughed. "Sometimes they rape you anyway . . . but it's an idea so you don't get raped. But if you do, tell the person, 'I don't want to give you AIDS. Wear a rubber,' and that way you'll lose your hymen, but you won't have any sperm inside of you," he advised, still believing I was a virgin. "It's just an idea. It's something that you can think about . . . you don't have anybody, so you are precious in God's eyes."

As long as he made it seem that he was trying to enlighten me on the evil of the world, his fantasies were justifiable to him. Claiming to protect me was the perfect way to expound on all his fucked up-desires, but I saw right through it. Every word he spoke exhumed a toxic breath. Mouth to mouth that could never save me as long as he was giving it.

PERCEPTION OF GARY

CHAPTER TWENTY-ONE
Lots of Gary Ridgways Out There

"Morals are shot. You have Gary Ridgways out there everywhere," Gary declared one day as if his name belonged to another person.

Was he right? Were there more men like him roaming the earth, an entire army of Gary Ridgways? I ran through a list of men I had dated. Granted, a lot of them were assholes—selfish and manipulative just like him. But I wondered if any of them ever thought about killing me when they were behind me.

Gary seemed to think of ending my life all the time. Even when he was fawning over me. Even when he told me I should stand naked in front of a mirror after taking a shower. "See what the guy sees in you. You got nice legs, you got nice hips and a nice stomach that's flat, and that's what a guy wants. He wants a woman to be beautiful and beautiful on the inside. And so you got to look at the way a man looks at you . . . and what does a man like? He likes hips, big breasts . . . he likes the butt . . . and he likes the vagina . . . they love the woman's vagina, and they're always in it all the time," he said.

He seemed to have studied the picture I sent him months ago, taking note of his favorite parts of me. It didn't matter that I was wearing jeans and a T-shirt; he always found a way to make anything suggestive. If killing was the ultimate gratification, I wondered how often he looked at this photo, how many times a day I was the woman he stood behind. As he became more explicit, I feared he was on the brink of initiating phone sex, worse than the quasi version he had been subjecting me to.

"You love the woman's body for sex," he persisted.

That was all it ever was with him. Women were not real people to him. He no longer put in effort to hide his opinions, like when we first started talking and he wanted to convince me of his goodness.

Just like he acted as though it was logical and normal to believe that all men secretly wanted to kill women, in his warped mind, all men were bound to treat women in the same disparaging manner.

"On dating, for instance . . . if a guy's looking at a woman, and there's sex in his heart, that's adultery," he said, as if he were teaching a class. "A woman has a nice—nice breasts, and she has a nice, big rear and everything, and some guys will want to have sex with her just because of that thing you know, because it's . . . they want her."

I didn't know where this lesson was going, and I was sure I didn't want to find out, but I knew I had to.

"Well, a woman is—some guys, they don't care, basically, he said and laughed. "Anybody that looks good to them, they have sex with," he said, obviously speaking from experience but careful not to admit it. *Classic Gary*, I thought.

"They lust after her. Guys will take her out to get—pick her up and have sex with her on the first date, and you're not supposed to think about that. Either way, there's an old saying I think—I don't know, you probably heard it, too. 'Wine them and dine them,' you ever heard that?" he asked, gauging my reaction.

"'Wine them and dine them.' Yeah, of course I've heard—"

"You know, you take the woman out to a nice dinner and then you expect to have sex afterward," he elaborated, as though he were visualizing it. "So, yeah, well, that's it. If you're a woman—a lot of women are that way," he said and laughed. "Just on the first date—but, oh, but that's a different thing," he stopped himself.

Even though he wasn't speaking about me directly, whenever he said the word "woman," he might as well have been speaking my name. We were all the same to him.

Years later when I visited Seward Park, I recalled the way he objectified my body, as if it would lure any man to murder me. His advice replayed in my mind like some cautionary mantra. "Stay away from Seward Park, that's a . . . kind of rundown area. You don't want to be out there," he warned.

In reality, it was not an unsafe place and was even reported to have a low violent crime rate. So, his reasons for keeping me away from there felt personal.

Without saying it—he didn't have to—Seward Park, for him, was a landmark of his own violence. For whatever reason, he didn't want me to walk the same ground where he took a life.

But I did anyway.

I walked alone down a trail into a wooded area, where he led Mary West to her death in 1984. Just like the others, he put down a blanket onto the dirt, where they had sex. After he climaxed, he lied that he thought he saw a car coming, forcing her to lift her head. With her neck raised, he wrapped his arm around it, pulling as hard as his strength allowed.

Scratching at whatever parts of him she could, she tried to free herself. "If you stop fighting, I'll let you go," he promised, something he would say to nearly all the women who tried to break free of him. But as she tried to gasp the cold February air, his grip tightened. After about a minute, she fell limp, and he let go, dropping her on the ground. He got dressed, and when his shirt touched his skin, his back burned from the scratches, engravings of her will to live. He folded the blanket under his arm and then dragged her farther into the woods, away from the walking trail. Moments later, he walked back to his truck, returned with a shovel, and buried her there. In the fresh light of morning, he meandered along the path toward his truck as if she was never with him.

Following the same desolate trail, I was just as alone. As I walked into the dense woods, the sunlight was erased. Even though it was the middle of the afternoon, it could have been the empty hours of dawn. If I screamed, I doubted anyone would hear me.

He really knew what he was doing, I thought, fully grasping how calculated his decisions were. He told investigators that he thought Seward Park was "a good place to have a date and kill a woman." He wasn't wrong.

Along the dirt trail, a sign poked out from the ground. "You are entering a fragile ancient forest," it informed me. "Please stay on the trail. Leave no trace and do no harm."

I shuddered. Memories of things he said to me, questions he asked, barraged my mind: Would I want to look into my killer's eyes while he ended my life?

I had to get away.

As I made my way back onto the walking path, Lake Washington appeared, the water wrinkling in the distance like an unmade bed. People walked along the path behind me, some of them men with intentions I would never know. *Gary once blended in just the same*, I thought.

I remembered his years of lectures, that it was inevitable I would someday be raped and killed, that I should stay out of Seward Park, as though if he had the chance, this would be where he'd rob me of my last breath. Because he had these thoughts, every man must be guilty of the same, he hypothesized, and he was not the only Gary Ridgway in the world. I wanted to doubt his logic, but I began to trust every man I passed less and less. Every glance in my direction, every innocent smile I dissected, expecting to find traces of him.

CHAPTER TWENTY-TWO

Separating Himself from What He's Done

It didn't matter that Gary was convicted for killing forty-nine women; he acted as though the predators, rapists, murderers, and torturers who would inflict insufferable harm on me until I became another body to add to their growing list of casualties were part of a different species, one he observed from the distance while he acted like his only intention was to keep me safe. He'd make statements like, "If you murder somebody, of course, you're not supposed to do that," and move on from it quickly, as though he were only providing a fun fact rather than calling attention to his own guilt.

He narrated this story of unmerciful violence as if it was not his own, always speaking in third person about what "a man" would want to do to a woman.

There was never any reason for him to show remorse when women were to blame for ending up targets of a man's violence. In a letter, he harped on why prostitutes remained on the streets for years. "Why [did] streetwalkers stay for the beatings. Stay for the rapes. Stay for the shame, pain, and [embarrassment]. Go back for more pain. Till death do us depart. And he moves on to another streetwalker," he said, summing up his cycle of hunting and killing. He understood their vulnerability and the horrors they endured on a daily basis long before he killed them. As he hunted for them, he knew so many of them would be stuck in that life forever, so he'd never be without a victim. As soon as he took one away, there was always the promise of another.

He followed this same pattern with all people that entered his life—girlfriends, wives, whatever I was to him. No one was ever permanent; when people left his life, whether on their own or not, there was no mourning period. Instead, there was always a search underway for a replacement.

He never pointed out anything that needed to change when it came to him, yet his criticisms of society were endless, long-winded tirades. During one call he blamed the stimulus check for many Americans' poor work ethic. "They got it right now that you don't have to work. Why work when you get fourteen hundred dollars?" he asked. He didn't think those checks should have been issued to anyone, including himself and other prisoners.

"I can't get any blowup women dolls in prison. An inmate will never have a woman blowup doll," he joked. "You can't get out of a prison and go visit somebody. Yeah, I got fourteen hundred dollars, I can buy . . . a vacation to go on for you . . . Why [are] prisons giving a check to guys in prison? Fourteen hundred and fifty dollars. For what? We don't work," he ranted.

"Commissary?" I asked.

"You get commissary, but that commissary will last you for your forty years in prison," he scoffed.

As he watched TV, news stories that mentioned any kind of sex work would instantly grab his attention. The debate between lawmakers about the legalization of prostitution led to a concoction of theories to spiral in his mind and then into our conversations. "They want to have brothels in America, and brothels will screw up the country," he predicted. "The country will go to hell fast. Being a religious country, and [they] want to have brothels, but what do you do at brothels? Ah, they're gonna have sex, so maybe you'll pray before you buy sex," he mused.

As always, he acted as though he wished the world was a better place, as if he had no responsibility for once adding to its danger. "Maria, there should be people out there who care, not men who want cheap sex of a teen," he wrote in a letter as if he was not one of those men. "Shame, VD, sex, pain—physical and mental—lack of caring. They don't deserve it."

He penned the words he knew he should say—it seemed he'd been doing this his entire life. As much as I wished he believed in what he said, I knew he didn't. The women he killed didn't deserve to die—he always knew that—but he ended their lives anyway. Just knowing that something was wrong would never be enough to stop him.

He was right that people should care, but he would never be one of them. No matter what he said, he would always want to have sex with women, preferably half his age or even younger, and he would always have the urge to kill them. He wasn't fooling me. But I let him think he was, if only to see if there would ever be a conclusion beyond his duplicity that would let me see who he really was.

CHAPTER TWENTY-THREE

His Reputation

At four thirty in the morning, Gary slid out of bed, got ready for work, and left the house. If the sky had been clear, a full moon—November's Beaver Moon—would have punctured the darkness with its pale glow. Symbolically, such a moon represents the end of a cycle, completion, and transformation. But as Gary drove down the driveway sipping his tea, everything in his life appeared the same, as if it could have stayed that way, unchanging and smooth, forever.

He drove his typical route, hoping to find a woman to have sex with before his shift started. He cruised the section of the airport where planes landed, and then he headed in the direction of Renton to Kenworth.

Just like killing women had become a routine, this part of his life was just as methodical. He worked through the morning and was just about halfway through his day at eleven thirty when two detectives showed up asking to speak with him.

At first, he suspected they wanted to discuss his arrest for solicitation from a couple weeks prior, so he was not alarmed. He was simply annoyed that he had to pause his work and that some of his coworkers had seen the detectives arrive. The last thing he wanted was for his fellow employees to crack jokes about him the way they did when he was investigated in 1987, nicknaming him "Green

River Gary." He hated when anyone made fun of him, especially at work.

He met the detectives in a break room, and to his surprise, they questioned him about Carol Christensen, not about his most recent arrest. They showed him several pictures of her that all looked like a different woman as he stared at her face.

"Did you ever have sex with her?" one of the detectives asked.

He lied that he hadn't. But the truth was he did have sex with her and then strangled her to death in May 1983. Unlike any of his other victims, after killing her, to "throw off" the task force, he redressed her in her clothes and transported her to a wooded area in Maple Valley. He guzzled whatever was left of some wine he had in his refrigerator and rested the empty bottle across her stomach. He then placed two fish across her upper torso and sausage on her hands—uncooked food he found in his refrigerator—and covered her head with a bag. But he told the detectives none of this.

When they finally seemed satisfied with his responses, they left, and he returned to work, unfazed. Since 1985, they had considered him a suspect, but they never had any concrete evidence to pin a single murder on him, never mind the eighty or more he was responsible for. He figured this time would be no different.

Shortly after three PM he clocked out and walked through the parking lot to his truck, where two different detectives stood waiting for him. They told him he was under arrest, instructed him to put his hands behind his back, and clasped cuffs around his wrists. But he was not worried, believing he would be free within a few hours. He was just embarrassed that some people in the parking lot had witnessed the whole thing. He imagined the gossip that would follow in the days to come and hated facing such scrutiny.

But when the detectives brought him to an interrogation room, read him his Miranda rights, and told him that he was under arrest for the murders of Marcia Chapman, Opal Mills, Cynthia Hinds, and Carol Christensen, he still thought he would be released; it would just take longer. It never dawned on him that earlier that year in March, advancements in technology had made it possible to reexamine the evidence—sperm left behind and samples he had given of his saliva. Ligatures had been swabbed again, and this time he was positively connected to at least four murders, although he was suspected of more. But he remained confident, admitting to nothing. Eventually they would set him loose, he believed, and he would drive home and walk through the door to find Judith there waiting for him, like always.

* * *

The dirt and gravel crunched under the car's tires as I turned down South 348th Street, a private road. When I recognized the house he had lived in, his disguise of a normal life, I parked and stared at it as if it was a historical monument. I remembered reading that when Gary and Judith had resided there from 1998 to 2001, a decoration indicating that the "Ridgways" had lived there adorned a spot above the doorbell, a time when his name didn't make anyone think of murder or depravity.

I considered his final hours of freedom, his walk from the front door to the driveway, the last time he would ever really be alone and unwatched. I pictured him standing there on that day, the soft drizzle dabbing his face, unaware of his fate, the years of stone walls and locked doors, and then me somehow at the end of it. The way he looked forward to finding a woman each morning, he looked forward to hearing my voice at the other end of the phone line.

But that day in 2001, he never would have thought the future that awaited him was different from the one he anticipated. He expected to retire in a few years, sell the house, move to Seaside, Oregon, and drive from state to state in his RV. He never thought of telling anyone even a fragment of his secrets.

With the car windows rolled down, I breathed in the cool air, *his* air. I imagined him climbing into his truck that day, never suspecting that he wouldn't return home again once he left, his brake lights flickering at the corner before he turned, gone forever.

* * *

For a lot of people in solitary confinement, I knew from years of research that depression and other kinds of mental illness could wreak havoc on them. After a while, imprisonment in a single cell for roughly twenty-three hours a day could drive some people to madness—some cut up their arms with a makeshift weapon (maybe a piece of plastic broken from the ceiling light fixture), some beat their heads into the unforgiving brick walls, others smear feces onto their naked bodies like lotion, some sleep too much or too little, some turn pale as a tumor, some cut off their own testicles, a story Gary once shared with me about someone in his cellblock—the effects could be endless. But in my conversations with Gary, I noticed little of this horrific aftermath.

He rarely complained about anything, except sometimes that his TV was broken. For whatever reason, the screen remained black while he could still hear the sound, leaving him to imagine the characters of whatever show he watched. Aside from that, he seemed to accept his fate without much resistance. I wondered if this outlook was something he grew into over time, or if he had always resigned himself to the idea of never being free again.

One of the few effects I noted from his lengthy isolation was his extraordinarily white complexion in his most recent mugshot, in which he really looked the part of someone who had been deprived of sunlight for years. A deserved punishment, but still hard to imagine any of it as a real existence.

The only thing he mentioned that could pass as a real complaint was his difficulty sleeping. Most of the time he tossed and turned throughout the night, paced the same floor as if it were a path to an exit, stared at the blank walls and ceiling, knowing their boring design by heart.

I had insomnia as well, and I wondered how many of our reasons for it were the same. Most recently, I stayed awake tormented by everything he had done, visualizing his arm noosed around a woman's throat, her neck bending to his strength, until she stopped breathing. The sight of him, relieved. Thrilled. I would then try to reconcile his atrocities with him telling me he loved me each day as if he meant it.

Even though he repeated to me several times over those few months that he could barely sleep, he never sounded tired, unlike me. His voice was always eager and energetic, like he had been drinking coffee all day, although he claimed that he had cut out caffeine. Eventually, I gathered that his brain was just wired differently. He claimed that since the 1970s, he had only gotten one to five hours of sleep every night. And when he was most active as a serial killer, he would barely sleep at all.

During that time, most days, he'd work eight- to twelve-hour shifts at Kenworth, drink ten cups of coffee throughout the day, and hunt all night until he found a woman to have sex with and possibly kill. Then, on some nights he would spend time with whatever girlfriend he had, visit the tavern on Thursday nights, go dancing with Parents Without Partners on Friday nights, and pick up his son every other weekend. Once he was married to Judith, his routine became less hectic, but he always made time to hunt for women. I wondered if exhaustion would ever catch up to him like all his mistakes eventually had.

But he maintained a routine even in prison. Each morning, he woke up around the same time and drank an eight-ounce glass of water. Then, he'd start walking back and forth in his cell. From one wall to the other, he'd pace the same few steps, his mind wandering to thoughts only he knew, his only form of privacy. Two hundred and forty times, he'd count his laps.

As I thought more about his imprisonment, I couldn't help but notice the glaring irony. Though to a much lesser degree, he had become acquainted with the fear that all his victims probably felt as soon as they realized he was a threat. Just like he was afraid of the pimps getting their hands on him all those years ago, he considered what other inmates would do to him if they were ever in a room alone together. After his arrest, he said, "Those pimps out there, they don't give a shit. They'll kill you, they'll beat you up and do anything they want with you, and they'll get away with it."

He said that even if he walked free someday, "Someone will be waiting with a shotgun because through the years a lot of kids out there lost their money. They lost a nice woman to go out and service to a man. And [I'd have to] face them, having to pay for killing the girls."

When I had planned to visit him, he explained that even if the visit wasn't canceled due to a lockdown, it would have been difficult for him to get there. "Just an hour of going to the yard is hard enough," he explained. He complained that when the phones outside his cell were already in use, in order to call me, he sometimes had no choice but to climb the stairs to the second tier. Along the way, he was subjected to "gauntlets of ridicule," he said, by other inmates who noticed him, the infamous Green River Killer.

I wasn't shocked to hear that others taunted him—prison was unforgiving, especially to anyone high profile—but I wondered why it took him nearly a year to tell me about his experience. The optimist in me wanted to believe that him opening up about his vulnerability was a testament to the rapport we had built.

As he spoke, it seemed as though he really wanted me to understand what he was up against. Every time he called me, he was taking a risk and making a sacrifice. As he described the hecklers he faced each day, it was as if he was begging for more of my sympathy.

I'd be lying if I said his ploys to make me feel sympathy for him were unsuccessful, but it had little to do with me recognizing him as a victim or martyr and more to do with the stories he shared in which he appeared human, a regular man existing in the world who wanted the same things as anyone else: family, love, acceptance. Whenever he spoke about his son, it seemed genuine. Such moments made it difficult to wrap my head around him brutally murdering countless women.

When he described the gentle act of once carrying his son in his arms while he slept and putting him to bed, he appeared to be someone capable of caring, maybe even love.

But the man he was when he made his son wait in the car after picking up Gisele Lovvorn and then having sex with her and killing her in a wooded area, knowing he would have killed his son, too, if he witnessed anything, made it seem as though the Gary Ridgway he spoke about in third person really was another person.

His careless behavior when it came to his son's well-being didn't end there. In the spring of 1984, Gary had taken his son on a camping trip, packing his clothes and bike in the trunk beside a bag that held the partial remains of Denise Bush and almost the full remains of Shirley Sherrill—two women he killed in October 1982. While his son slept, Gary stopped the car to leave whatever parts of them he took—their skulls and other bones—in Tigard, Oregon, in an effort to throw off the task force. In another instance, after killing a woman in his house, he dumped out the contents of his son's toy trunk, stuffing it with her body and then transporting it to his truck. "There was some neighbors out maybe mowing the lawn . . . I pulled her out and nobody was looking, and I just bring the trunk back in the house. Cover her up . . . maybe wait until the neighbors went in and just drive off," Gary recalled during his interrogation. On another occasion, while driving home one night from a family gathering, with his son sleeping in the car, unable to control his urges, Gary pulled over alongside one of his dump sites to have sex with a woman he had killed earlier.

The way he wanted me to forget the murderous part of him, he seemed to expect his son to do the same. He chattered on about visits in the prison, repeating twice that his son "could visit, but he's in Montana," before explaining that there was more to their estrangement than the miles between them. He believed his son's wife was to blame. "She don't want to have anything to do with me or anything or my family," he said. "She just wanted to isolate [him] from me back in Montana . . . She don't want anything to do with me . . . there's a bad taste in her mouth, basically," he accused.

Could he really believe his daughter-in-law's low opinion of him was the sole reason that prevented his son from communicating with him all these years? I was astounded by his lack of awareness. Just as he pointed blame at the Green River Task Force for not keeping track of all the missing women and victims, he was now avoiding accountability again. How could it not occur to him that his own actions of killing close to a hundred women had caused the disaffection of his son?

"You know how it is with husband and wife, you gotta agree with your wife, otherwise you gotta sleep in the doghouse," he said and laughed.

Reconciling these two versions of him became taxing, and I began to understand how so many people were fooled into believing he was a decent person. He disguised the ugly, terrifying parts of himself well, making him a perfect counterfeit of a regular human being.

With me, he followed the same script. "Maria, yes I said, 'I love you' at the end of my calls . . . I pray God can protect you . . ." In a letter, these words were sandwiched between his rape and murder fantasies of me. But what really stunned me was how he could go from maniacal to declaring love and protection, like there really were two people inside him battling, and whoever won decided what he'd do next.

On some level, maybe he didn't want to think about killing me. But he couldn't help it. He was the same locked up as he was free. The intentions never changed, even if he couldn't act on them. I was sure of this now.

The truth was he didn't care much about anyone, and even he didn't know why he was wired that way or what could have possibly changed him. For a moment I felt sorry for him. I tried to imagine going through life numb, never growing attached to anyone. Hell, even heartache seemed worthwhile when I thought about the emptiness that must have always pervaded through him. *What a sad, lonely existence*, I thought.

Yet, he seemed to cling to the idea that he could have changed if only he had learned how to value a life other than his own. In a hospital room, where a woman screamed her throat raw, sweating through a gown that clung to her body like a wet bathing suit and digging nails into any hand that would hold hers, Gary imagined himself there. Beside her or in the back of the room. It didn't matter. Just as long as he witnessed her push and push and push until she questioned her own strength, that moment when her womb emptied. If he could behold her pain, study it like a diagram that illustrated the anatomy of her suffering, if he could feel the heavy weight of it enclosed in a room, her cries deafening him—would he still have become a serial killer?

He wanted to know if I had the answer—if he saw a baby emerge from a woman and breathe the same air as him for the very first time, would that have made any difference in his life?

He contemplated this other fate as if he could go back in time and change every decision he ever made, as long as I said what he wanted to hear. But I didn't. I joined him in his contemplation, as always, trying to understand his logic that felt more and more like climbing a greased rope. I would only ever get so far before I lost my grip.

How could witnessing a childbirth remedy his rage?

I hoped there would be a surprising depth to his response, some long thought-out philosophy. Finally, a real regret followed by a flicker of remorse. Maybe his past really did burden him, and he was trying to find ways to live with himself.

"Maybe it might've changed me," he said. "But the idea is, if you don't see it, maybe you don't have that much feeling toward people."

I wanted to tell him I had never witnessed childbirth yet still managed to care a lot about people, even him, to some degree. But instead, I told him, "I imagine a person still would [kill]." The truth was I didn't believe anything would have changed him. Even if his own son had been born naturally rather than through a cesarean, and he had been standing beside Marcia the whole time, when she left him years later, the same rage would have consumed him.

I wanted to tell him it was more likely that he was born this way, that his brain wasn't the same as other people's, limiting any empathy he could feel for another person. But I didn't have the heart. I had already said enough, and I felt bad about it. I didn't have it in me to destroy any more of his hope. I guess that was what made us different. I knew when to stop, to let up on a person.

CHAPTER TWENTY-FOUR

Media About Him

Every so often Gary would remind me of the competition I was up against: writers, journalists, podcasters, news anchors, psychologists, and TV personalities from all over the world had been vying for an interview with him since his arrest in 2001. Without giving any of them a second thought, he would throw each letter into the trash.

"I get a lot of mail from people that want to come out and see me, [but] I don't see anybody because I couldn't fill up the calendar with all the people who want to come out and see me," he boasted, as if to remind me that I should be grateful he was giving me the time of day. As much as I wanted to know his reasons for choosing me, a novice freelance writer from New York, to share his story, I didn't dare ask.

"I talked to lawyers, [and] they wanted to ask me some questions about my numbers . . . but I'm not really interested in anything like that," he said, contradicting himself and gaslighting me at the same time. A few months prior, he had been adamant in telling me he had killed thirty-two to forty-two more women, and now he was acting as if it didn't matter, like that conversation never happened.

"In what? Stating how many victims there were?"

"Well, stating how many victims—because there's always going to be somebody out there that wants to do more than me." He spoke like he was trying to defend a crown, except there was nothing honorable about the title he was protecting.

"Yeah, that happens," I agreed. "Someone will always want to do more." I mean, he wasn't wrong.

"Yeah. Well, Bundy was the same thing as my cases, ya know, and they went and asked him anything he [knew] to catch me. [He knew] probably somebody would write a book about it. And what he did was a bunch of bull crap," he griped. I was used to his calm voice, but I began to sense agitation at the mere thought of Bundy. It was hard to fathom, but he saw Bundy as a competitor, as if killing women was a sport and he aspired to be number one.

"Wasn't he trying to get off of death row, so he said he would help profile who you were?" I asked, curious about their rivalry.

"I think it basically could have got him off the death penalty for one thing, and I think basically that he just wanted to take the highlight, the limelight, basically, of being the worst killer in Washington," he answered. It was obvious he had spent some time thinking of Bundy's motives.

"He felt threatened by you, right?"

"Yeah. I think that basically he just wanted to get some credit so it would keep him in the news, ya know, because he likes that, he likes his name in the highlights."

"He was very much into the attention of it all," I affirmed.

"Yeah."

"But you don't like the attention?"

Gary wasn't one to seek out notoriety, that much was true. However, he seemed to bask in the idea of his own infamy. Still, I couldn't help but wonder, *why now* and *why me* and *what exactly did he want*, especially since he seemed to lose interest in discussing any of his unsolved cases.

"Basically, I don't want to have it. I don't want to have people saying, 'Mr. Ridgway, the Green River Killer, I'm gonna kill more women than he did.' That's how they do it; 'because I'm learning from him, how he did it.'"

"But you never wanted—not even for that purpose—you never wanted to tell your story to someone, from your perspective?"

"Well, I want to, but the idea is—they want to know how many I did and where."

"But aside from that, what about sharing your perspective about why?"

"Well, everybody's gonna have their own opinion, and they want to throw in a lot of stuff to be able to get you—ya know, I had somebody ask me did I eat anybody," he said and chuckled. "Stupid things like that. 'Did you torture them?' [But] why torture them, ya know?"

By how often he brought up torture, especially what could be done to me, I doubted that last statement. Even if he didn't think so, being placed in a chokehold or having a ligature strangle the life from you was a torturous way to die. He failed to understand that, comparing himself to "worse" killers who had dabbled in cannibalism and prolonged torture, rather than the neutral ground of not hurting anyone at all.

"Like they want to make it more horrible than what it is, make it worse, basically," I said, placating him.

Even though he rarely engaged with the media, he seemed to enjoy the attention that went along with it. "There's a lot of books out there about me," he said before running off a list of the ones he had and hadn't read. "I read the first one on Judith, the book on Judith . . . she wrote another one this year . . . it's a second book on me, on herself, and her life," he said, showing no reaction to the content of it, which mostly focused on the enormous pain he caused her.

As he continued to run through the catalog of titles about him, I was surprised he remembered all of them. "I didn't read *Green River Red*—that's Ann Rule's book . . . I read the one *Searching for the Green River Killer*—that was it. I did read Sheriff Reichert's book, it's called *Chasing the Devil* . . . it was basically about him," he said mockingly.

"And what did you think of those books?"

"People write to . . . talk themselves up, basically," he said.

He was not entirely wrong. Some people did only wish to gain fame for themselves through telling a sensationalized version of his story. His primal instinct to detect one's true intentions granted him with the innate ability to see people clearly, maybe even more clearly than they could ever see themselves.

But if he really feels this way about all writers, why has he given his consent for me to write a book about him? If his agenda was unclear before, now it had been entirely blurred. It was impossible to know the direction we were going in or why we were on the route he had chosen. Although he could see people around him with perfect clarity, he was an expert at concealing his own objectives, and I wondered how well he *actually* understood himself.

It seemed like he wanted some control over what was said or written about him, or at least the opportunity to try to alter some of the public perception of him. The problem was no one would listen to him and let him control the conversations; everyone put their own priorities first, which often included fishing for as many grisly details of his crimes as possible. So, he would end up dismissing anyone who tried, but it didn't stop them. TV shows, books, articles, and podcasts would emerge time and again, and he detested them all.

When I had scheduled a visit with him, one of the main deterrents that made him rethink meeting me was a show about him that happened to be airing on A&E that same weekend. As a result, he became hyperfocused on everything that could go wrong, forcing me to change the date of the visit.

"A lot of fights happen all of the time, so I don't think it's a good idea for you to come and see me," he said. He sounded defeated, as if what he was imagining had already come true and he had been brutally beaten.

Disappointed as I was, I tried to understand his sudden change of heart. I had never heard him like that before. His words were weighed down with despondency, like he had been dreading breaking the news to me all day.

"I don't want you to come at all because during that week they got that damn program, and it'd be dangerous for me to be out there," he explained.

"Wait, I'm confused. It's dangerous for you to go to a visit?"

"It is," he said defensively. "Because I'm—that is right to the population . . . where all the visits are. So, I don't want to be over there because I don't want to cause a riot because it would be on the news and on TV. Normally, they don't give A&E, but now that program's gonna be on A&E, and somebody told me it was on next month, and basically, I want to be locked in my cell."

He was afraid. Because of his notorious serial killer status, he would always be a target in prison. Whenever his face flashed across a television screen, threats against him would escalate. Another inmate would love to make a name for himself by being the one to murder him, like Christopher Scarver had when he beat Jeffrey Dahmer to death in 1994. The threat was always looming over Gary, so he had come to appreciate the security of his cell. In there, it didn't matter that he was the most well-known person in the prison. I couldn't blame him for not wanting to leave. His cell was the only place where he had any control over his own fate.

During his interrogation, he once reflected on his "ability" to kill a woman whenever he felt like it. "I've got the power to do it. I have the power not to do it, too," he reasoned. But now beyond his four walls he had become powerless, unable to do anything when anyone even spoke his name.

CHAPTER TWENTY-FIVE
Recidivism

Seeing the Walla Walla phone number light up on my phone screen, especially around dinnertime, no longer felt surprising. Gary's voice became familiar like other parts of my day, like the smell of freshly brewed coffee in the morning or the way the sunlight invaded the living room by noon. However, what I had not been expecting was to be met with opposition after sending him an article I had written for *The Crime Report* about New York's Elder Parole Bill.

After discussing the possibility of me writing a book about him, I felt it was crucial to show evidence of my work, to prove I would be capable of such an undertaking. Gaining his trust was a slow process, like painting hairline details within a portrait. I assumed I could find common ground with him by sharing this article that involved freeing older people from prison.

Although I never shared my position on whether people over fifty-five years old should have the opportunity to face a parole board as long as they had served fifteen years of their sentence, I thought he would appreciate that I considered the possibility, even if I wholeheartedly believed he should never be released. I couldn't have been more wrong.

"What [are] the chances of ninety percent of them going back to crime after they get out of prison?" he demanded.

"So, I take it you read my article?" I tittered, unsure how to respond.

"Well, what do you think about more time in prison? Is a guy in prison—he's sentenced to fifty years in prison, and he's already in [for] forty-nine years—is it worth it to let him loose?"

I was shocked. He seemed bothered that I would even suggest such a ludicrous idea, people getting released from prison, as if he was not in prison himself. I hesitated to answer his question out of fear that he would hang up on me for disagreeing with him—this was early in our correspondence, and I wasn't sure yet how far I could push him before he might stop speaking to me altogether.

"It depends," I said, my voice shaky. "In my opinion, if someone can prove they are able to return—but I feel they would need some sort of family. There would have to be psychological evaluations. I think it's all circumstantial."

"Yeah," he agreed. "But the crime doesn't [always] match—you got a guy out there that steals a thousand IDs, and he profits. Maybe he made a million dollars off it. He gets about five years in prison, when you got a guy [who] killed the guy and he's in there for life. He hurt a hundred people, [so] why should he get out in five years where the guy who has hurt one person—who killed one person—why should he get life then in prison?"

I understood, in theory, what he was implying. It was simple. Whoever brings the most harm to the most people should receive the worst punishment. However, what he failed to consider was the value of a life. Those with stolen identities would always have the chance to repair the damage bestowed upon them, but a murder victim had no chance at anything.

My article had focused a lot on rehabilitation, but he seemed to be glossing over that part. Did he think it was possible for anyone to change? Most importantly, did he feel that he had changed at all over the past twenty-plus years?

"What about places like Norway, where their whole goal is to provide more rehabilitation than punishment?" I asked.

"Some people are hardwired to be—to not get reformed. So what works in Norway probably would not work here in the United States because their father was a criminal, their grandfather was, and their grandfather—it's a tradition for them to be bad guys."

I wondered if he was really referring to himself. Did he feel that he was hardwired to kill?

"Where do you think you fit into that?"

For a few seconds, I was met with silence before I heard him exhale a long sigh. He fumbled his words before finally forming a coherent thought. "You send somebody out there like me, [and] they're most likely going to get killed by the public rather than get killed by the coronavirus, basically. Who's going to take you on—sponsor you when you get out? You gotta have somebody sponsor you or get you a job. Who's gonna hire somebody like me?"

Although he didn't reflect on his own rehabilitation, or lack thereof, it seemed we were getting somewhere. Until that moment, I wasn't sure he possessed any real awareness, but he was completely and utterly cognizant of how much people hated him beyond the prison and how alone in the world he would always be.

It didn't seem to matter to him when I informed him of companies that specifically hired formerly incarcerated people. He remained steadfast, holding onto the idea that most people would return to a life of crime if given the chance of freedom. To prove his point, snickering, he recounted a story he had heard of a man who was pardoned due to Covid and lasted only a week before killing again. Although he was talking about someone else, it felt like he was telling me a truth about himself, that killing would always be inevitable for him.

Although I disagreed with his idea that no one should be released from prison—after all, there were many success stories of people capable of living crime-free lives—one thing we did agree on was that the system was terribly broken. But we believed this for different reasons. He was under the impression that many people confessed to crimes they didn't commit to "get more kills on [their] record." Although he was not wrong, he overlooked the idea that many people were coerced into confessing to crimes they didn't commit due to a faulty and traumatic interrogation process, that many people were not motivated by the desire to advance their credit as a killer; sometimes people were actually innocent.

"A guy confesses to a crime. Don't you think we should take him out to the spot where he killed somebody and prove it? [Ask him] where was the body laying?" he proposed.

He seemed to be referring to when he led the police to several bodies as part of his plea deal, and by doing so, many cases were solved. But he didn't describe his own experience. He continued to speak as though he were providing commentary on a news story he had heard. But it was obvious everything he said was about him; I learned it was always about him.

"Maybe you're trying to help people get out of prison . . . [but] you can help somebody to find out why they go into prison," he suggested.

Couldn't he see that's what I was trying to do?

* * *

Gary routinely revisited whether anyone should ever become freed from prison, a topic he had been obsessing over since I sent him my article.

"They got rapists in there, and when they get released he's gonna go out there and do it again because he's still got a penis, and he's still gonna want to have sex with somebody." He argued that almost anyone released would commit the same crimes again while indirectly referring to his own behavior. He seemed to suggest confinement in a prison cell was the only thing preventing him from killing, and then he confirmed it.

"Well, I can't go out and kill anybody now because I'm in prison."

That meant if he could, he would. I considered his honesty, the ugliness of his heart, like a house full of bad memories I wished to burn to the ground. I couldn't hate him for telling the truth, although I wanted to.

"Let me ask you a question," he continued. "In the Bible, Jeremiah 13:23 says, 'Can a leopard change its spots?'"

"Can a leopard change its spots?" I repeated, contemplating a response.

"I know a person who was a prostitute . . . and she says she got out of prostitution, but how can you tell that somebody gets out?"

"How can you tell? Well—"

"How can you tell? If they got out, did they not use sex as a bargaining tool to get a job?"

"You really don't believe that people can change?"

"I think some people can," he said. "But if you're a bank robber, let's say, he's not gonna rob banks [anymore], but he's gonna go work for the banks, stealing money for people because he can do it. He can find a way of taking money from somebody without getting caught for something. But he's just doing it for other people [now] . . . Some people can't change their spots."

I wondered if he knew the true meaning of that particular Bible verse suggests that people were capable of changing for the better only when they accept Jesus into their lives. Gary left that part out, reading the passage in its literal, black-and-white context. Or perhaps he was ignoring the true meaning on purpose since it did not fit his agenda. I began to think about his behavior and how deeply rooted it could be. I thought about his marriage to Judith and the way the media had made the ridiculous claim that love changed him, preventing him from killing. In reality, he had never changed. In the same way a leopard can't change its spots, he continued to kill during those years.

No matter his intention or interpretation, I was certain he was telling me that he also lacked the ability to change, and if given the chance, he would kill again.

CHAPTER TWENTY-SIX
Remorse and Memory

The way a friend would confide in another about happenings in their everyday life, Gary began to do the same with me. In a letter, he told me about some of the mail he had received, one message in particular grabbing his attention. Since he didn't retain a lot of what he read, it seemed this letter had impacted him to some extent because he remembered it long enough to share it with me. A woman who once worked as a prostitute wrote to him, berating him. "They are not trash. They never were trash. They are God's [children]," she scolded, defending the women he killed.

He contemplated her perspective, telling me the women he killed were the "same as us," meaning they were no different from him or me—the two of us now a sacred coalition—as if he had been wrong about them his entire life. But like always, his change of heart was fleeting, and as if that letter had been erased from his mind, the next time we spoke he resumed his true feelings, that the women were at fault, not him. Over the course of my correspondence with him, I noticed his remorse was never permanent but instead fluctuated in sudden waves like the fickle emotions of a child.

No matter how much he claimed to repent or that he was reformed, besides his words that were empty as air, there was never any evidence to support he had changed at all. But he seemed to accept his punishment, even believing he deserved to be in prison for the rest of his life. As long as he never killed anyone again—something only being in prison could ensure—he would be absolved of his past, or at least he hoped. It never occurred to him that what resided in his heart—every violent, vile thought and fantasy he had each day—also needed to be expunged.

In past conversations, he alluded that he would kill again, that no one could ever truly change. *A leopard can't change its spots* replayed in my mind like a mantra.

To set the record straight, I had asked if his heart had really undergone any alteration from the years he spent reading the Bible.

But the only true regrets he seemed to have were for things he *didn't* do while he was free, not for anything he *did*. He recounted one such story to me from the early 1980s, right before Marcia left him.

The wet street glistened under the white glow of the headlights from Gary's pickup. It was after midnight, and the quiet streets of Federal Way seemed even more soundless, as most of the houses he passed were shut in darkness. Working night shift for so long, he had grown accustomed to coming home to a deserted neighborhood. But tonight was different. Something caught his eye.

A couple blocks from where he lived, a Ford pickup, identical to his own, was parked in the driveway of a vacant, newly built house. Gary assumed whoever was parked there was most likely a thief, attempting to break in. As he got closer, he noticed the truck's wheels were spinning but going nowhere.

When Gary stopped, the man ran out to approach him, as if Gary's presence was the embodiment of an answered prayer. The man explained that his pickup had gotten stuck in a ditch and asked for Gary's assistance. Gary surveyed the situation and saw the driveway appeared rather slippery. It would not be easy to pull him out. As he stood there, contemplating his decision, the man made him an offer that would be hard to refuse. "Come back and tow me out of here, and I'll let you have sex with my girlfriend."

Free sex? Now, that was something that didn't happen to him every day. For the last few months, he and Marcia had barely had sex anymore, making him seek out prostitutes, a habit that wasn't exactly cheap while also paying a mortgage and basic necessities for his four-year-old son. His marriage was already in shambles, so did it really matter if he had sex with a random woman before going home and climbing into bed with Marcia, who probably was already sleeping?

Gary thought about driving home to retrieve chains from his garage, and multiple scenarios flooded his mind. If it all went well, he would tell the guy to park somewhere across the street while he took the woman somewhere a few blocks away. He would find a desolate spot and fuck her in his own truck. Then he would bring her back. He'd be damned if the guy was going to watch them. What if he would want to have sex with him, too? Some kind of erotic threesome? The only kind of orgy he would ever be interested in was if he was the only man surrounded by multiple women.

Worse, what if the guy was full of shit? The second his truck became free from the ditch, his tires would skid as he sped off out of sight in the opposite direction. Would a guy really allow another guy to fuck his girlfriend, all because he needed a favor? It seemed too good to be true.

Then another possibility crossed his mind: the guy could have a pistol concealed somewhere. If he was robbing the house, as Gary assumed, then of course, he would have a weapon. He could shoot Gary if he felt like it. Was the possibility of free sex really worth dying over? He could always set his own terms and conditions, tell the guy to turn over his gun before he helped him. But then he figured the guy would just punch him in the face. Not worth it.

So, he drove home. In his driveway, he thought one more time of finding his chains and bringing them back. He really wanted to have sex with a woman. But he unlocked the front door and took a shower. He then climbed into bed with Marcia, who pretended like he wasn't even there.

* * *

In his cot, barely big enough for a grown man, he tossed and turned. Night was almost over, and he had not gotten a minute of sleep. Tormented by this decision he made over forty years ago, he couldn't get it out his mind. *Why in the hell did I pass up free sex? Why in the hell didn't I do it?*

Just as he did then, he considered all the possibilities, everything that could have gone right and wrong. But still, it was free sex. The regret of not having sex with that woman weighed on him like all the remorse he should have felt but didn't.

But no matter what, he couldn't put the memory out of his mind. He longed for sleep to the point he even got down on the floor on his knees and prayed to God. "Help me sleep, Lord," he pleaded, as he leaned his arms into the thin, flimsy mattress that was like a cheap pool raft. Another reason why he could never sleep. It dug into his back and gave him bed sores on his hips whenever he slept on one side for too long.

His mind was the bigger culprit, though, as it jumped from one thing to another. But this was nothing new. Since high school he hadn't gotten a decent night's sleep. His mind, chaotic as a riot, was seldom quiet.

When he told me all this the next day, even confessing that thoughts of me and talking to me had also kept him awake, I was not surprised. He seemed to always be thinking of my eventual rape and murder. Of course, I was on his mind.

But I'd be lying if I said I didn't think that when he mentioned feeling troubled by something that had happened while he was married to Marcia that he was going to express regret for hurting her or his part in the marriage falling apart, some form of acknowledgment of wishing he had done something better, that he had been better. But that was wishful thinking.

Instead, I listened to him ramble on about why he would pass up free sex over forty years ago. What was wrong with him?

We both lost sleep wanting to know.

* * *

True remorse didn't exist in his tiny, boxed world, no matter how much he prayed or read the Bible. I couldn't understand why he thought he was forgiven by God if nothing within him had changed.

"We compromise," was something he said a lot. "Anybody, even Hitler, can go to heaven, [and] Hitler killed a lot of people," he asserted. Although he had uttered this ridiculous statement to me before, now it felt more poignant, as though he really believed it. By comparing the eighty-one to ninety-one women he killed to the millions who died under Hitler's Nazi regime, he suddenly became less of a monster and could even pass as a decent person. So what if it was still in his heart to kill more women?

"If you do something bad, you can still ask God for forgiveness, but it's a matter of how—it's a matter of what's in your heart, like how you go and live your life after the fact, I guess, no? I mean, that's what I've always thought," I said.

"Well, you have to basically pray to God, and there's some verses in the Bible like John 3:16. You gotta ask God to forgive you. You can't just—these women went out and had sex with the guy . . . and all of a sudden, right after, the man asks for a blow job, and she just gives one. Well, she's not going to go to heaven because she didn't stop."

I was stunned by his rationale, the superiority he believed he possessed. According to his logic, since prison had stopped him from killing and participating in any other nefarious behavior all these years, that made him a potential candidate for forgiveness, but any woman engaging in casual sex would be damned to burn in hell.

"Words in the Bible are great, but you got to have action with those words. If you say I'm not going to speed anymore, and then you go out and you get yourself killed, and you're speeding, God's not going to forgive you for that," he continued, making himself appear more righteous than he ever could be. "It's in your heart . . . you can beg for forgiveness from God because John 3:16 talks about that . . . God will forgive you . . . and like it says, He could forgive Hitler," he repeated, as if the more he said it, the truer it would become.

"So you feel at this point in your life that you've made your heart right with God, then?"

"Yeah. Basically, you have to believe in your heart and believe in your mind, and then what you want to do is like—prostitutes were already going to go out." He paused, sighing before finishing his thought. "[And] have sex with more men, and then she does it," he said, annoyed by the very idea.

The thought of women having sex and living afterward to do it again the next day seemed a difficult truth for him to accept. It was quite possible this loss of power over prostitutes might've been the most tragic for him, more than anything else that had been taken from him.

"Do you regret killing?" I prodded.

"Yeah. You can't go back, and you can't change it. But you can just, like I said, you can change the way you feel in your mind and yell to God about it."

Although he claimed to regret his actions, he refused to *live* in regret, which I supposed was a somewhat healthy approach to accepting his life in prison. In fact, that was probably one of the most sound statements he had ever made to me throughout our entire correspondence.

"So, it's just a matter of going forward and living the best way that you can?"

"Well, the best way that you can, and also to talk to people about God. One thing . . . if God can save Hitler, He can save anybody, basically," he repeated like a slogan.

"So, judge the sin, not the sinner?"

"Yeah, basically [if you] tell God you're not going to sin anymore, He won't hold you accountable for it. If you screw up, then you're—all the women that have been out and have sex and they told Jesus that they won't do it anymore and then they went out and did it anyway. They spoke to God . . . the property of the devil, basically," he ranted.

Rather than take accountability for his own actions, he continued to blame his victims, as if killing them was a punishment he inflicted on behalf of God. Not only that, but he was judging them for having sex, those that had sold their bodies to *him*.

However, since he claimed to have forgotten most of their faces, it was as though he had also forgotten what he should be sorry for. "The women's faces don't mean anything to me . . . They were bodies, if they had a pussy, I would screw and that was it," he once told detectives.

But not remembering them was also intentional. Nearly every woman willing to sell herself to him would end up with their backs turned to him, which he preferred. Avoiding looking at them while they suffered at his hands until they took their last breaths made it easier for him to disassociate from his actions, as if seeing them could possibly change his mind. Instead, he stared at the back of their heads until he came inside of them, the moment a ligature or his arms snared around their throats.

"He's behind you, so ya know, in a way—" he stumbled over his words to explain his method. As usual he spoke in third person as if another man had killed them and he only witnessed it.

"So, that removes the intimacy behind it or depersonalizes it, right?"

"Yeah, that," he agreed.

Even though he spoke a lot about forgiveness, I knew he would never be truly remorseful. How could he be when he argued the women he killed were damned, not even worth remembering?

DEATH AND WHAT COMES AFTER

CHAPTER TWENTY-SEVEN

The Afterlife

When the task force interviewed Gary for six months in 2003, he only agreed to it to avoid the death penalty. Although it was easy for him to take life after life, when it came to his own death, he feared the unknown, the possibility of facing never-ending torture in hell.

It wasn't until he converted to a Seventh Day Adventist in prison that his vision of hell transformed into a place he coaxed himself into believing could be tolerable. He believed God would never torment anyone for eternity. It would be a fast fire, like dousing a piece of cardboard in gasoline and throwing a lit match to it. The wicked would burn to ashes, a quick eradication, and their souls would cease to exist anywhere.

He seemed to think heavily about this conclusion, explaining, "In the Bible, it talks about when you go to hell you're burned up. You're not in there forever," he said. "God is love. God did not put you, His people, in hell to burn forever." All the time he spent in his cell had forced a new kind of introspection on him, one that gave him no choice but to contemplate outcomes he didn't want.

But at the time of his arrest, he exchanged his confessions for his life, hoping to stay alive as long as possible. I didn't have the kind of collateral the task force had. I could not barter with his life or threaten him with punishment to force the truth out of him. At any point, he could have ceased communication with me and faced no consequence.

So, I listened to him describe again and again some horrific death that was promised to me like an inheritance, something I'd have no choice but to accept one day. But other times, he discussed his own ending, what awaited him beyond the physical world.

"Purgatory is an in-between place. It's bullshit. When you die, you go in the grave, then you pass that by in your sleep," he preached.

He spoke with such confidence, you'd think he had died and been reborn several times.

The science of how to get admitted into heaven consumed him. He obsessed over the steps to get there, this place of peace so far away from his current realm in a cramped prison cell. But it was more than that. If he believed he was forgiven by a higher power—in this case, Jesus—he did not have to be accountable, and the nearly hundred women who died by his hands could be erased, like sweeping leaves from a path and then forgetting any memory of them. At least that seemed to be his plan as I listened to him profess his beliefs, which he regarded as bonafide facts.

He seemed determined to persuade me that he *could* go to heaven when he died, that he would be forgiven, even though I never disputed the possibility. What did my opinion matter? I couldn't quite figure out why he wanted my reassurance, as if it would somehow increase the probability of him not burning in hell.

But I said nothing.

Instead I listened intently, waiting for the word "remorse" to fall from his tongue, expecting to dissect the heart of it and all its veins pulsing into forgiveness and what that meant. But he never mentioned it. Considering his beliefs, I thought he would be required to feel sorry for killing close to a hundred women, not just believe in Jesus and accept Him in his life.

But his quest at reaching spiritual redemption didn't end with himself. I had somehow become included in his plans. Although he had thoughts of killing me, my soul's final destination really seemed to matter to him. He seemed to like me enough that he thought I deserved a pain-free afterlife, a place he was sure we would share together, where he'd no longer want to hurt me.

Answering his calls began to feel more and more like I had opened my front door to a group of Jehovah's Witnesses on a Sunday morning in Brooklyn. There was no way to get them to leave except slamming the door in their faces.

"Not everybody takes a chance, and if you don't take it, you lose it, basically. You choose the honest people to talk to about God, and here I am, given my history, and why am I talking to you about God? If He can forgive me, and I love Jesus, what in the heck can He do for you?" he asked.

It was rare for Gary to acknowledge that killing scores of women was wrong, especially when he always found ways to justify his actions. But there he was, putting me on some kind of pedestal, while he stood below me, admitting he was not a good person. He seemed desperate for me to listen.

"All you have to do is pick up verses and then get down on your knees and say a prayer to Jesus, you're sorry for what you did, and maybe everyone has a different saying when you're talking to God, and you add your own words to it. You will feel a lot better because then you don't have to worry about going out and getting raped," he said, trying to put my mind at ease. "Well, you're gonna die anyway. It's better to die when you're saved than when it is when you're not saved . . . You're gonna be good all your life . . . but being good is not going to get you into heaven."

He talked about heaven as though it was an exclusive club that he had learned the way inside, a secret handshake at the door followed by the right password. He was confident of his own pathway to forgiveness, that nothing could stand in his way. His embarkment to the afterlife would be smooth, and heaven would be a common space he hoped we would someday occupy together. The walls and bars and barbed wire and glass and the nearly three thousand miles separating us would no longer exist, according to his vision.

"If you read Matthew 22:30, when you go to heaven, you open the door to marriage in heaven . . . and you will basically be like one step down from an angel, basically, when you go to heaven," he explained with the same certainty of knowing the sky was blue. "You can do your book probably about me, too, because you're already in heaven, and you'll be married, and you're not gonna—I don't think you can have sex in there, in heaven," he said and laughed. I don't think—you won't need [to] in there," he said, envisioning an eternal life with me.

"People don't have sex in heaven?" I said and laughed.

"Yeah, I don't think you need it because everything is going to be fulfilled for you anyway."

For a moment, I thought about his vision—him and me sitting around on a cloud-carpeted floor while I still continued to interview him for this book, an endeavor that I would have eternity to complete.

But the more I considered it, I wondered if he really longed for a retreat from this world, not just prison, to be free from his obsessions. In his mind, heaven would be sexless, where he would be unchained from the desire for a woman's body. In this utopia, he would have peace by simply speaking with me and telling me about the life he lived. Trying to have sex with me or killing me, or any woman—urges that had consumed him for most of his life—wouldn't even be a thought in his mind. I wondered if this brief fantasy was the closest admission of remorse I would ever witness from him.

As unsettling as it was to think about sharing eternity with Gary, this vision he had for both me and him was probably the nicest thing he had ever expressed to me. It was also a testament of the respect he seemed to have developed for me, in his own convoluted way.

While he expected most women to burn in hell, I would exist with him in his heavenly world, alongside him, where he would no longer be a threat, and I would no longer be a target. That had to mean something.

CHAPTER TWENTY-EIGHT

Death and Necrophilia

During my first trip to Seattle, Asher and I wandered into the Ye Old Curiosity Shop, a recommendation made by Gary. He had raved about the shrunken heads that were on display there and thought it was hilarious that someone's head could be "shrunken down to size like a fist," making this attraction, if you would call it that, at the top of his list of suggestions.

Just as he said, in the back of the store, glass cases took up most of the wall. Inside of them were several heads, most of them small as coconuts, some slightly bigger. Their eyes were swollen shut, as if horrified by whatever they had seen last, and their mouths held somber expressions as if they writhed in agony before their final breaths. Their brown skin appeared dry and wooden like the bark of a tree. Black hair rested on some of their heads, full and soft, the kind easy to run your fingers through, while others were nothing but scalp.

A sign propped next to them explained that they were the heads of enemies decapitated by wild head hunters of the Amazon rainforest in Ecuador. Afterward, their bones were removed, and pebbles were heated in "sulphur, alum, and lime," and then shaken into the head for a day, a process that led to the head shriveling and deflating like a ball that had been kicked around too much.

Resting beneath one of the heads, another sign read, "Smallest shrunken head in the world. Extremely rare." However, the fact that

Gary Ridgway, one of the most prolific serial killers in the nation, had made this recommendation to me felt stranger than anything found within the shop, even the shrunken heads themselves.

I stood there for a while gawking at the heads, imagining that Gary once did the same thing in the same exact spot. However, I didn't laugh as he did. I remained quiet, fathoming if the heads were real—apparently some of them were, according to the store owner. I thought about the bodies they once belonged to and the lives these people might have led, running wild along the Amazon, and how brutal their deaths must have been, what they could have left behind, maybe at least one person who loved them before they were reduced to a prop in an oddity shop. But Gary didn't give their lives a single thought.

He regarded his victims in the same careless way. Even once they were dead, he still wanted to hurt some of them. For instance, in 1982, after he killed Linda Rule in a vacant lot by Northwest Hospital, he took matches from her pocket, lit them, and started to burn her hair, a final act of rage. But then he stopped himself, realizing the singe could permeate the air and draw attention to the site.

When he picked up Constance "Connie" Naon in June 1983 at the Red Lion Inn, he drove her to a vacant lot south of the airport. Outside, about twenty feet from his truck, they had sex. As his hands pawed at her breasts, she pushed them away, forbidding him from groping her. To him, that was more of a reason to kill her. Like all the others, after he came, he choked her, but this time his rage did not subside once she died. Leaning down to her chest, he sunk his teeth into one of her breasts. Red indentations formed, marking her pale skin. Still not satisfied, he picked up a rock, staring at her naked body on the ground. The triangular shape of the rock made pushing it inside her easy. Now he was relieved. He pulled a shovel from the back of his truck and dug a grave, burying her under about three inches of dirt, enough to conceal her and dissuade him from returning to use her body again for his pleasure. He had become too disgusted with himself and needed to control his urges. Besides, a warm body always felt better.

I suspected he remembered what he had done to Connie as he wrote in a letter to me about no one in particular, "Ate her breast." But maybe it didn't even make sense to him, why he defiled some women and not others after killing them. Why bite Connie's breast, why burn Linda's hair, why push rocks deep inside any of them?

And what about the victims that either were never found or he was never charged with their murders despite admitting to them? Rose Marie Kurran came to mind. During his interviews with detectives, he admitted to killing her in August 1987 and dumping her body in a ditch off 188th and Military Road, close to where he lived at the time. However, since he was not precise enough when describing the condition her body was left in, detectives were not convinced he had actually killed her. The true perpetrator had poured a liquid in her vagina, something Gary either couldn't or wouldn't accurately identify.

Yet, he recalled in detail, "I just got done getting my house searched, and I didn't want to get caught picking up any women, but I must have picked this one up somewhere on PAC Highway and killed her in the back of the truck and took the cleaner and put it inside her . . . I thought for sure I carried her in, but I must have drug her in and just left her in the ditch . . . there wouldn't be anything other than I know I did it. [The liquid] had to have been either cologne or cleaner . . . something to wash her out . . . put in her to kill the sperm . . . to get it out of her 'cause I didn't use a rubber. If I used a rubber I wouldn't of done anything, I would've just . . . put her out there . . . [but] I'm quite sure I put it in her vagina and either pushed it in hard . . . I know for sure I put . . . either my fingers or whole hand in her to . . . mix it up so wouldn't have the sperm way far up inside her."

Upon learning these details, I was instantly reminded of the letter he had written to me in which he listed a multitude of rape and murder scenarios. In one of them, he described pouring bleach inside of a woman's vagina, and I now wondered if he was remembering what he had done to this victim specifically. But it didn't seem like any of the former or current detectives would ever verify it. Most times when I asked about specific cases that had not been solved, I was either met with silence or some vague explanations that answered nothing.

As for Gary, he rarely retold stories of what he did directly, making it all the more difficult to potentially solve any of these cases. Instead, he would rely on sermonizing Biblical stories or inventing fantasies and hypothetical situations to create distance from his past. But his own experiences always resurfaced.

When he summarized the story of Lazarus, not only was he wishing to convince me of what happened in death, he seemed to be remembering all the times he was left to dispose of women's bodies, a chore he considered a "burden."

"So, you're just sleeping? Like nothing's happening?" I asked.

"No, you die—Lazarus, when he died, he was in the grave for four days."

"So, it's an unconscious state?"

"Yeah, kinda like an unconscious state, and when Jesus went over, he woke him up, and took him out of there, and four days in a hot—there's no air, so it's pretty hot, and there's probably a lot of odor because of the body," he explained.

Even though he was telling a story from the Bible, his knowledge of a rotting corpse went beyond that. I knew he would revisit some of his victims sometimes for two or three days after he killed them. He confessed to detectives he would "get on top of her . . . put her feet over my shoulder . . . [try] to spread [her] legs apart . . . until there was a smell or maggots . . . I got to tell my mind I only went back to two or three, but thinking about it, I went back to a lot of them and screwed [them]."

By imagining the physical environment of Lazarus's grave and the stench that must have penetrated the enclosed air inside it, I was positive he was drawing on his own memories of his sexual encounters with women he killed, thinking of the grotesque details in real time.

I cringed at the idea, but on the surface, I showed him only indifference. I carried on with the conversation, pretending his death anxiety and his apparent knowledge of the scent of a rotting corpse was as normal as discussing the weather. It was the only way to win him over, to inch closer to the truth of all the secrets I was certain he was keeping.

"But [when you're waiting for Jesus], where do you go in the meantime?" I asked, acting like he really knew all the answers.

"[Lazarus] didn't come back from heaven. He didn't come up from hell. He didn't have any memory of anything. He didn't talk about God in heaven, Jesus in heaven. You tell anybody this, and you start to sound crazy—'Oh yeah, I met God in heaven'—he's probably smoking something," he said and laughed. "That's a bunch of bull crap because when you die, nowhere in the Bible does it say you come down from heaven. You're dead for fifty years, a hundred years, God brings you back to life, [and] you're not going to have any memory at all. It's just like you go to sleep; you don't have a memory," he described.

"But when you sleep you dream, no?"

"Well, when you're dead you don't know nothing . . . when you die . . . you just move on."

Some faces of his victims flashed in my mind. I contemplated their final moments when they realized the danger they were in, sudden as a scream breaking a long silence. He left them only a few seconds to comprehend their ending—as his arm or a ligature wrapped tighter around their throats—before they slipped away and began to "know nothing," like he believed would happen.

"[That's] your super imagination," he mocked. "You wait till Jesus wakes you up," he said, dismissing all other possibilities.

"So, it's like a dreamless sleep, then, what it's supposed to be?"

"Basically, but you don't remember anything . . . The devil can bring people to life—not people—but [he] brings bullshit to you."

Anyone who believed they had a near-death experience and visited heaven for a brief period, according to Gary, was corrupted by the devil.

"When Jesus comes back, that's when the graves open, and the dead and Christ go to God first, and then the people that are still alive will go to Christ after, that are saints. So, if God saves you, you will go to heaven, basically. You gotta be saved to go to heaven," he reiterated.

Although he proclaimed that he was "saved," I was not entirely convinced that he believed it. He said it so many times, but his words lacked conviction.

"Your soul goes to heaven, but your body waves are not coming back," he said as he moved on to explain why cremation was acceptable. "If you know anything about getting buried, the worms in the ground eat you up, basically."

Although it was common knowledge that maggots feed on dead bodies, I knew he was speaking from his own experience again. Not only had he buried some of his victims in shallow graves, but he had witnessed the decomposition of some of their bodies over the course of several days.

Later, as I'd spend many nights reading the unredacted transcripts of his interrogation, often until sunrise, I'd try to grasp the reality of his words and reconcile them with the person I spent nearly two years attempting to understand. "I was in control. She could just [lay] there . . . and I could have sex with [her] . . . that was my gratification. And I could do anything I want with [her] . . . after two days . . . the flies were around there . . . that's when I buried her," he described. Even when he didn't speak about his victims directly to me, he seemed to always be remembering them.

Whether he was happy, sad, excited, regretful, or any other feeling as he thought about the things he did, like burying a body, it was impossible to tell. Since his demeanor never changed, the surfacing of those memories were like segments of home movies he recalled from someone else's life, holding no personal meaning for him. Yet, they seemed to always be on repeat in his mind.

I wondered when he would finally share the full memories he had hinted at to me. Whether those memories would be confessions already made or truths still untold, I was certain he'd make me wait. Until he decided it was time for me to know another part of him.

CHAPTER TWENTY-NINE
Finding Religion

Before Gary went to prison, practicing any religion was something he did to fulfill an obligation. Catholic, Baptist, Methodist, the Christian Christ Center—he'd frequented all these churches around Seattle, depending on the woman in his life and what she wanted.

"You grew up Catholic, so what made you change from that?" I asked.

"Well, I changed that because for one thing, I got divorced from Marcia, and she was Catholic."

The Catholic church also did not truly follow the teachings in the Bible, something he didn't appreciate. Only God was supposed to hear your sins, not a priest, who Gary assumed had the same exact desires as he had.

"Tom with his joystick. He was enjoying himself listening to the prostitute talk about her sins," Gary laughed. "It's just a joke, and it might be true," he concluded.

I couldn't disagree. During my twelve years of Catholic school education, I heard stories and witnessed what could only be described as corruption, but more so involving the nuns rather than the priests.

For most of his life he had been taught that sinning, specifically breaking any of the Ten Commandments, would lead to an afterlife of eternal damnation, your soul roasting within the flames of hell. Growing up Catholic, I was able to relate to his concern. Until I turned eighteen, it was drilled into my brain that committing any mortal sin—murder, adultery, blasphemy, and idolatry, to name a few—would lead to an afterlife tortured in hell.

Gary was brought up to believe the same. However, his list of sins was longer than the average person's. Killing close to a hundred women forced him to question what kind of eternal life awaited him. If there was any truth to the Catholic beliefs branded in his brain since childhood, he would be cast out of heaven the same way he had been cast out of society.

When members of the Seventh Day Adventist church would visit the prison, they would often stop by his cell to speak with him about the Bible. Curious, he listened attentively to what they had to say, the "news" they claimed to have for him.

He found their presentation to be more authentic than the Catholic faith he was brought up on. "The Catholics, [they have] all those guys in the Mafia, and they go to the Catholic church because they donate money to it, and they buy their way and have their name on a hospital wing. And they commit sins on Friday and Saturday, but on Sunday they go to church, and they get all their sins washed away."

He agreed with the Seventh Day Adventists, that was not how forgiveness or salvation worked. And he worried about forgiveness—not from the people he had hurt, but from God. His Catholic beliefs had vexed him with a death anxiety that filled him with dread. What would happen to him when he died? Somehow he had to secure a better eternal fate.

Members from the Seventh Day Adventist ministry college base in Walla Walla provided him with four books detailing the religion, and Gary grew more committed to learning about it. The idea that you could "give your heart to Jesus," be saved, and go to heaven, even if you had committed murder, relieved him. That hope, even if it was driven by self-interest, inspired him enough to make the decision to get baptized as a Seventh Day Adventist.

Usually, he would only leave his cell each day to take a shower or go to the yard for an hour, but on that day, officers led him out of his cell to a tub of water. Unlike a Catholic baptism in which a priest sprinkles holy water on a person's forehead, Seventh Day Adventists followed the Bible in the most literal way and believed a person must be "fully immersed and lay down with God and lay down in the water with Him." And that was exactly what Gary did.

With a pastor orchestrating a brief ceremony, Gary climbed fully clothed into the tub and submerged himself. When he came back up and breathed air again, he was reborn. As he rose to his feet, his heart pounded, and he shivered from the shock of the frigid water. Drenched from head to toe, he couldn't wait to return to his cell to change into dry, warm clothes. There, within those same four walls, he would bask in the hope that he had found a way to avoid hell and maybe even become a better person.

Another inmate finding God in prison, what a cliché, I thought. However, reading the Bible and being a practicing Seventh Day Adventist consumed a lot of his time while locked in his cell; his devotion appeared authentic, however disingenuous his motivations were.

What was Gary trying to accomplish by making religion a cornerstone in his life? To fool people into thinking he was a good person? Maybe while he was free that worked, but I already knew what he was, a serial killer capable of murdering close to a hundred women. He had also told me that he was incapable of ever truly changing. So, what was the point?

On some level, he seemed to possess a desire to be decent, a hope that if he dedicated several hours each day to copying passages of the Bible onto a notepad, he would miraculously shape into another person altogether. But could reading the Bible really stop the inherent evil within him from overflowing, or was there just too much of it, like trying to fit a pitcher of water into a single glass?

The more I spoke with him, the more I began to understand the different parts of him. In some instances, I even crossed the line into naivete, as I still tried to find the humanity he promised me was there within him.

In many of our conversations, he expressed he knew killing was wrong, but I'd never seen him display true remorse. He had immersed himself in a tub of water, but could that make up for anything? It seemed to only be an attempt to protect himself from hell, so if anything, his conversion was his way of avoiding penance for what he had done.

His argument was always that "If you break one of the Ten Commandments, you break them all." According to him, missing weekly Mass or lying equated to murder, so every person walking this earth was in the same mortal danger of someday burning in hell. But no matter what he had done, he would be saved, he kept telling himself.

When he asked me what I would do if I ever won a million dollars—one of many hypothetical questions he would ask to decipher my goodness—I witnessed the hypocrisy of everything he preached and the malfunction of his understanding of real morals.

I told him I'd help my family and maybe donate some of it to charity. Before I could elaborate anymore, he cut me off midsentence.

"Oh—I got exactly what you want," he said. "What would you think God would do if you gave it all to . . . well—okay, Saint Jude, or you gave it to, well . . . LoveShriners? If you gave all the money to them, do you think God would answer your prayers?"

"No, I don't think it works like that."

"I bet it [doesn't] work like that, but He's most likely going to answer your prayers more if you're good and do that, and you gave the money because you're helping," he argued.

If he truly believed this, then he always expected something in return, meaning that nothing he did was ever genuine. All of his "good" acts were for the purpose of obtaining a reward, whether from God or elsewhere. He was the opposite of kind.

Although I tried to explain it to him, he couldn't seem to grasp that not every exchange was meant to be transactional. Sometimes you just gave—whether money, love, food, anything—for the sake of giving without a desire for reimbursement. Gary couldn't understand this, regardless of anything I said.

"The thing is, though, if you donate money, right? It's one thing if you do it out of just being generous, out of the goodness of your heart, but if you're doing it and you have in the back of your head, 'I'm going to get something out of it,' then I feel that's not the right intention. Do you know what I'm saying?" I asked.

"Right. Even then, you get the money from God and He's testing you."

He was still stuck on the idea that if he "passed the test" then he would be rewarded, and if he didn't, then he would either receive nothing or be punished. Selflessness remained untranslatable, like a foreign language he would never know.

I began to doubt any good intentions he claimed to have toward me even more. I couldn't help but question, if everything was transactional to him, then what were his reasons for talking with me and allowing me to write about him? What was he getting or hoping to get out of this exchange?

During each call, he moved through his barrage of questions like categories in a game show, never staying on one long enough for a meaningful discussion, his words, like water disappearing down a drain, lost forever. Until we landed on a topic he wanted to explore. This time it was the interlacing of intuition and conscience.

"Well, you got senses, your body. God gives you something—okay, you're a woman, you don't go to a—have you ever been to a topless bar?"

I actually have. But he answered the question for me.

"You probably didn't go to one, but God tells you in your mind, you walk by one, usually you want to go there, and you know God wouldn't want you in there," he described as though drawing on a familiar experience—knowing it was wrong but doing it anyway.

Maybe when he'd drive on PAC Highway looking for a woman to kill.

"You have a sensor . . . you're going someplace, and you shouldn't go there, but you go there anyway, and of course, you get robbed . . . or you pay too much or something like that, but you had that sense. That's God probably, most likely God telling you stay out of there."

The sheer terror and pain he inflicted on some of the most vulnerable women, you'd think his conscience didn't exist at all. But as I listened to him overlap intuition with conscience, it became clear he understood what it meant to possess a guiding voice, one that tries to steer you from making bad decisions. How often had this voice tried to talk him out of killing someone? What would it take for him to listen to it? These were complex questions, and the answers he gave barely skimmed the surface.

As if these were the key factors in all decision-making, he asked, "Do you worship God? Do you love your God, or do you love the devil? Do you hate God, or do you hate the devil? [If] you know that, your heart in a bad place, that's supposedly the devil," he said, trying to give meaning as to why he killed. "You can't be a friend of God, and you can't be a friend of the devil," he spieled, as if concluding a homily drawn from the outcome of his life. You were either good or evil, according to him; nothing in between.

As if forgetting the murders he had committed, he easily contradicted himself, acting as if he was actually a good person and had abandoned all the evil that resided within him while he commented on the state of the world. One hypothesis after another, he predicted in a letter to me what would happen if religion was ever outlawed in America. "The whole nation [would go] to hell. No moral value in it.

Fathers and daughters [would have] children, brothers and sisters [would have] children, and some mothers and sons [would have] children. Babies [would be] thrown in carts [a]live or dead to the city dumps. No birth control. No 10 Commandments. No God," he wrote in a fear-mongering frenzy.

Before closing the letter with "Your friend in Christ Jesus" and signing his name, the only word in cursive—on the same line—he included a sentence he labeled as a joke: "Maria, shortage on Vaseline, butt lotion. Buy at least one case." *Jesus and butt lotion both on the same line, now that's quite the fucking contrast.*

But he lacked the ability to recognize his hypocrisy and seemed to rely on the fact I would never question what didn't make sense, as if he was God himself and I was supposed to follow blindly. He seemed to always be trying to make the point that there was more to him than just being a serial killer.

"Well, I did basic good things [too], ya know . . . but they don't think that about anybody, somebody doing any good," he reflected. He almost sounded defeated.

A rare occurrence, he narrated a story I could visualize as he told it. So much of what he had told me prior to this—the murders, the women, random details of his life—had been fragmented and disjointed.

Later, I would dissect his motives and come to understand that he was most likely trying to gain my trust, to make me see him as someone other than a serial killer, a real person I could even like.

He relayed a memory from either 1982 or 1983—he wasn't entirely sure. The beginning of his "career" as a serial killer, as he would describe it sometimes. On an early Sunday morning, with seven- or eight-year-old Matthew in tow, Gary drove to McDonald's on Pacific Highway South where they would eat breakfast, a ritual on the weekends Gary had custody of him. As they walked into the familiar restaurant and waited in line, Gary stared out the window, watching the cars pass by. A woman or a teenager—he could never be sure—wearing a dress caught his eye as she began to cross the street. His eyes followed her, and as he studied her movements, a car sped toward her, plowing right into her and knocking her to the ground. Did the driver not see her? He wasn't sure. But when the driver didn't stop, Gary assumed he had just been in too much of a hurry.

Without thinking, he left the restaurant, leaving Matthew there, and went to his truck. Unlocking the trunk, he grabbed a folded blanket and made his way to where the injured woman lay on the wet, cold blacktop. Crouching down, he asked if she was okay, and she moaned an inaudible answer. He then wrapped the blanket around her body to keep her warm.

In the distance, sirens belted their long wail and grew louder with each second. Someone in the McDonald's must have called an ambulance, he assumed. As cars continued to pass along PAC Highway, he rose to his feet and stood in front of the woman to prevent any cars from swerving into the lane where she was sprawled out. He waited with her until the ambulance arrived. As the EMT workers rushed to the scene, he explained what had happened and then retreated back to McDonald's, where he had breakfast with his son.

I wanted to ask him what he had done with his son for the rest of that day. Did they go to a park or return home? What about after he dropped him off? In a previous call, he had told me he would kill mostly on the weekends. During his interrogation, he told the detectives the same thing, elaborating that he would often pick up a prostitute on the drive home from dropping off Matthew. I wondered if that Sunday was any different, if his act of kindness set the tone for the rest of the day, maybe making him not want to kill, or did it do the opposite?

What had propelled him to help that woman in the first place? Was it that she was vulnerable, and he saw another opportunity to take control, to seem trusting and kind, to fool her and anyone watching? Or was it purely instinct? How could he care about this woman but none of the others he had killed? Weren't they also in dire need of help? The questions flooded my mind, and before I could ask any of them, the call ended, cutting him off as he recounted his good deed, midsentence.

I imagined a scale weighing this good deed alongside his atrocities. If he prayed enough and confessed all his wrongdoings to Jesus, he seemed to believe the scale would balance out, promising him admission into heaven. But I wasn't sure. The shift to killing to kindness was abrupt, like the hit and run he described, and it unsteadied me, as if I was there alongside him, watching him help one woman while strangling another.

CHAPTER THIRTY
Murder House

On a cul-de-sac, rambler-style houses lined both sides of the street with driveways creating some distance between them but not enough that neighbors would ever be strangers. Sidewalks didn't exist, discouraging outsiders, so only the people who lived there you'd expect to run into sometimes. By this secluded design, it was easy to keep secrets.

After living in an apartment for a few months following his divorce from Marcia in 1981, by the fall, Gary had purchased a house on that street, 32nd Place South, right off Military Road and only a minute from Pacific Highway South, his main hunting ground.

Aside from the freeway that ran behind the houses and the airplanes coming and going from the airport only ten minutes away, it was quiet. *A decent place to live and befitting the unassuming persona he presented to the world*, I thought as I turned onto Gary's former street.

If I hadn't known he had killed about thirty-six women there—his estimation—the heaviness that hung in the air as I got closer would probably have been easy to ignore. But instead, I felt bogged down as I recalled the number of bodies he dragged from his bedroom and lifted into his truck, the dead weight of them, and now whatever lingered of them—beautiful spirits—suspended in the orbit of where they took their last breaths.

I parked alongside the chain-link fence that blocked off the yard, the same one he had leaned against to hide his scratched arm from the cop that had shown up to question him about Marie Malvar's disappearance. I had seen the house—his "killing house," he once called it—numerous times in photographs and it once seemed a fictional place, every inch of it contaminated with an untraceable evil where nightmares manifested a monster too great to tame. It felt surreal to be only a few feet away from it.

Through the years, the color of the side paneling had changed from brown, to green—of all colors—to presently, tan, like the sand of a warm beach, as if trying to prove in its transformation that it was now a pleasant home and the vile history Gary gave it could be forgotten. A door replaced windows in the front, creating another entrance I figured was once the garage that had been converted into another living room. But everything else appeared the same—the large tree shielding a portion of the front window and the black mailbox at the end of the driveway that had once been smudged with Gary's fingerprints. Grass that carpeted the front yard stretched all the way to the back, which was big enough for a game of long-toss catch, the same grass he once told me he spent the day mowing, raking, and pulling weeds from after calling out sick from work and finding it impossible to rest.

It was as though I had stepped through a portal that had transported me directly to his past. Everything I had learned of the depravity that occurred in that house—some of it real and some of it fantasies he wished were real—flooded my mind.

He once told Sheriff Reichert that in a perfect world, he would have spent more time with each of the women he killed. In that very house, he wished he could have kept them naked and chained to the bed. Before he'd leave for work, he'd have sex with them, and when he'd come home from work, he'd do it again. "That would be a terror for her," he fantasized. "At the time, I'd probably just tell her, 'I'm gonna kill you' every time I see her . . . the devil was pretty far into me," he reflected. Nothing I hadn't heard before. Several times, he had expressed to me he believed the devil could invade a person's mind and influence their decision-making.

But when he reasoned the logistics of keeping a hostage, he thought it would be too much of a risk. He always had a girlfriend, and if she ever came over and discovered his sex slave, she would not be able to look past it, he figured. He also worried the neighbor kids would break in like they had once before and have sex with the woman tied to his bed. He hated the idea of anyone making good use of *his* possessions. "I could've got a chastity belt and put it on her. Always keep the key," he reasoned. Then that would have prevented anyone from using what belonged to him.

The idea never left him, even after forty years. "Maria, can you order a lockable chastity belt?" he once asked me. I laughed until I realized he was serious. According to him, a woman's vagina was the most valuable part of her, something that needed protection from other men and something he wished he could control and have unlimited access to.

His words knotted my stomach, and I was sure I'd throw up right there by the front yard. I closed my eyes for a moment, pretending I was somewhere else.

But when I opened them, the driveway still met the front door, where he would reverse and park his truck all those years ago. Most times when he brought a woman home he had planned to kill, he would do this on purpose, that way it would be easier to conceal carrying her body out later, especially at night when he didn't feel the need to wrap her in the throw rug he'd keep by the front door. The women probably never considered why he would park that way except that it would be easier to pull out later.

If a woman ever was hesitant about going with him to his house, he would offer her more money and assure her that if she still felt uncomfortable continuing the encounter inside, he would allow her to keep some of the money for her trouble and would drive her back to where he picked her up. It worked almost every time. A woman on the street rarely turned down a chance to make extra money. When they got to the house, he would encourage her to walk through it and check out the rooms, convincing her he had nothing to hide. It always appeared ordinary—each room was furnished and seemed lived in, and overall, was cleaner than most places where single men lived alone. Pictures of his son hung from the walls, making Gary appear as any other loving father. She felt safe.

Because I knew none of them were safe, I began to cry. I stared at the front door, where each one walked in with him as he followed behind, leading them to his bedroom. As if they were blindfolded and being directed toward the edge of a cliff, they walked, never expecting to stop feeling the ground beneath them.

The front door remained shut, reminding me of everyone who walked in but never walked out. I cried harder, and the house became a blur.

"What the fuck, Gary," I said to no one, rubbing my fingers over my eyes. "What the fuck."

The faces of his victims flashed like a montage in my mind, and then stopped on Debbie May Abernathy, as I remembered once standing on the same corner where she worked and now close to where she took her last breath.

I thought more about what had led her there and recalled my first time visiting Seattle with Asher. We had gone to a restaurant located on Pine Street between 8th and 9th Avenue. From my research, I knew Debbie had worked mainly on the corner of Pike and 8th, what had become the place of her livelihood for four weeks since moving from Texas with her son and boyfriend.

I began to walk in that direction, forgetting about dinner entirely.

As cars bustled past me, I watched as some Ubers pulled over to the side of the street, just like Gary probably parked his pickup there and hundreds of other corners through the years, beckoning a woman to leave with him. When I got to the corner I paced back and forth, thinking of Debbie's last moments.

That afternoon in 1983, she left her home on Rainier Avenue to work this corner, but she wouldn't make it there and was never seen again. Instead, Gary pulled up beside her in the Denny's parking lot on PAC Highway, although some reports suggest she really went missing from Rainier Avenue.

Later, when Gary was questioned about her murder by police, like many of the others, he couldn't remember specific details. He didn't even recall that he had killed her on his son's eighth birthday. All he cared about was the opportunity to find a woman, have sex with her, and kill her while remaining undetected.

With the day off from work, Gary had extra time. As soon as he left the house, he filled his truck with gas and took out money from an ATM. He knew he wouldn't spend it, but he would need it as a prop to lure a woman to go with him. If he flashed enough money at them, they'd usually go anywhere with him and do anything he asked. In this case, she agreed to accompany him to his house.

Years later, when he tried to give an accurate confession, like most of the other women, he couldn't remember specific details, whether she fought him in an effort to save her life, but he assumed they had oral sex and then sex from behind until he choked her with his arm. One of the few things he could recollect with certainty was that she resembled a "schoolgirl type" because she wore glasses. Later, when she took them off, he told her that she looked better without them.

He also remembered the tedious chore of carrying her body into the steep woods along Highway 410 near the Weyerhaeuser Mainline, one of the first bodies he dumped there and then throwing her driver's license out the window while he drove away.

Looking out onto Pike Street and then 8th Avenue, I wondered if any of his words to Debbie appeared as thoughtful as they sometimes were with me, as if he cared about the day I was having or the future that awaited me. I tried to imagine her fear when he began to squeeze all the breath she had left. But I couldn't.

We walked two different paths, although both led to him. I knew the sound of his voice like a song I could hear even when the music wasn't playing, all of his inflections, stutters, and sighs, the weight of his breath, heavy enough to keep me quiet and still, as I anticipated the horror of what he'd say next. Our two experiences were not the same, and I could never imagine what she experienced.

When it came to her fear, there was no way out of it, to make him stop. But I could always hang up, although I knew I never would. Just like some people habitually display their ignorance and say, 'Well, she got into his car,' blaming her—all of them—for what *he* did, I expected the same kind of criticism for staying on the phone as he subjected me to what amounted to mental torment.

The evil he was capable of knew no limits. I finally came to terms with this as I got out of the car and stood where the driveway met the street, an equator I knew he had walked over, but I was careful not to cross. Other than a brown dog that laid still on the grass, unbothered by my presence, it didn't seem anyone was home. As tempting as it was to stand closer to the house or hop the fence and wander into the backyard, I worried someone would see me and call the cops. So, I stayed in the street, the same ground that had also felt the soles of his feet.

In the distance, a car door slammed, and I thought it had come from the house next door, the same house Gary once contemplated burning down with the family who lived there still inside. A justified act of revenge, he tried to explain to me. Sometime in late 1984, he had gone to Bellevue to meet a woman he had been dating for dinner at a "fancy" restaurant. "I drove home at ten o'clock, and that's when I found out the house was broken into," he recalled.

In his bathroom, he immediately noticed the open window. He walked through the house and found no one, but when he opened the closet, his toolbox and some other belongings were gone. Since the window was small, he reasoned only a kid could fit through it. The neighbors "didn't care about their shitty kids," so he assumed they had to be responsible.

He called the cops, and when they arrived, he explained to them what had happened as if he was an innocent person, someone that could only be a victim and never the perpetrator. The fact he had killed over thirty women at that time, most of them in that very house, seemed to escape him as he made his complaint, pissed off that he would have to replace his tools. Although he suspected the two teenage boys next door, he kept it to himself.

Within the following weeks, he made attempts to catch them. He changed the time he left and came home from work and parked his truck down the block to make it seem as if he wasn't home. He didn't turn the lights on when he was home at night, hoping they would mistake the darkness for his absence. But they never came back. "I never had the balls to beat the crap out of them, the neighbor kids," he admitted to me.

If he did get revenge in that way, it would have been a bad idea, he concluded. "The police would be at my door for beating up the kids, and then I'd go to jail for six months . . . So, you gotta stay out of the limelight," he said. Attention was the worst thing imaginable for a serial killer.

He plotted other, unassuming ways to get revenge instead. "Burning the neighbors up was just constantly on my mind . . . I had dreams of walking around, of putting oil and gas around his house and burning the house up with the family in it," he told detectives, and then me, years later, still obsessed with the idea as if he had been robbed yesterday. He seemed to regret not doing it.

Thoughts of killing and the act of killing consumed him. Prostitutes were always his main targets, but passive-aggressive revenge on anyone he felt deserved it was never out of the question. When he couldn't afford his mortgage in the spring of 1982, he welcomed a Mormon family—a man and woman and their two young daughters—to live with him and pay him rent. They lived in the main part of the house, and he moved into the room that once was a garage. However, by October, they had fallen behind on their rent and owed him money, enraging him. To get even, when they were either sleeping or not home—he couldn't remember—he poured plaster into their flour, hoping the next time they cooked with it, they'd become sick.

After that, the idea of poisoning people appealed to him, and he experimented with other ways of doing it. Sometimes he would go to Wendy's and sprinkle rat poison over the condiment bins. At Larry's Market, he'd mix rat poison with the trail mix and birdseed, or anything that was out in the open for people or animals to consume. He never stayed long enough to monitor if anyone became sick, but just the idea of it, that he could cause pain or possibly kill one person after another with little effort, was satisfying to him.

He never knew if his tenants became ill from the tainted flour, but they moved out shortly after. Completely alone again, he had a secure and comfortable place to kill. For months he had been forced to have his encounters with women and choke them in the back of his truck or outside where someone could see him.

For a few more minutes, I stood in front of the house. Somewhere toward the back was the bedroom where his secret wars occurred, where screams were never heard. "There's a curse on the house," he once told me.

I recalled listening to Gary talk about ways to ward off spirits, a topic that had come out of nowhere. Candles, garlic, sage, holy water—he ran off a list before elaborating, "A priest goes through, and he puts his holy water around, and that's supposed to get rid of spirits, and the Indians burn sage in the house."

At some point during the 1980s in the midst of his killing frenzy, he had grown concerned about spirits lingering throughout the house. Just like he wanted to choke the life from those women, he wanted their ghosts gone. But eliminating spirits was not as easy as taking lives. What proof existed that a spirit was even present, let alone whether it had left? Yet, Gary sought a solution.

"That house that I had that I killed . . . the idea is I asked a guy named Al how to get a mirror, [but] he didn't know. He was spiritual, he was a witch, which is, we call it a warlock, that's a male witch," he explained.

Gary was referring to the superstition that a mirror could ward off evil spirits by scaring them away with their own reflections. He expected a warlock would know the right kind of mirror to obtain for such a task, but he was wrong.

Gary wouldn't elaborate on the specific havoc, if any, spirits created for him, but he did explain the power he believed they held: "You can get sick, or it [can cause] you to be angry with your wife . . . some people . . . they think somebody's watching you all the time."

The fact he worried—even briefly—whether he was haunted by the women he had killed to the point he tried to find a solution, made him appear more human, that perhaps this concern meant he knew what he had done was wrong, that there was a conscience buried within him that wasn't always defunct and out of order, that some kind of tormenting aftermath followed him, a twinge of morals.

At the time, I wasn't sure if I believed him about his house being cursed or haunted, but standing in front of it, the air felt suffocating, like a bag had been pulled over my head. I wondered how anyone could live there, but apparently, the same family had been living there since the 1990s, long before his arrest. It didn't make sense why they would continue living there once information about the murders became public, but they did not move nor destroy the house, even if spirits were present. He couldn't understand it, and I was just as perplexed.

"They probably will make all kinds of money off of it," Gary concluded. "It's like my car. I had a car, it went for I don't know how much, five thousand dollars, and it was only worth about three."

It was the same thing that happened with his letters, envelopes, and practically anything he owned—it was all worth a ton of money due to his notoriety. In a way, it seemed to fuel his ego, even though he tried to act modest about it and pretend as though he didn't understand why anyone would pay hundreds of dollars for his signature or why officers in the prison were constantly confiscating his mail. He seemed annoyed by it and had even told me he didn't want the attention, but I sensed he reveled in how much his dishonor was worth to others.

Yet, Gary complained the house wasn't knocked down years ago. I couldn't figure out if his intentions were pure or purely selfish. Did he want the house destroyed as a way to heal the community from the terror he had inflicted upon it? Or did he simply want the attention that would go along with bulldozing his former house and at the same time depriving the public the chance to gawk at it, like I was now, to keep the memories of what he had done in there entirely for himself?

He remembered Ariel Castro, the man who held three young girls in captivity for years in Ohio and recalled, "They destroyed the house. They knocked it down. But they didn't do that with my house. I remember getting my lawyer to ask them why in the heck they didn't."

But as I stood there, it seemed that wouldn't be enough. Even if the walls were torn to dust and debris, each room bulldozed to open space, and the foundation broken apart, mixing and turning into the earth below, his memories would exist. Only so much of the past could ever be erased. The fragments of his memories he shared with me would haunt me long after he was gone. *Until the day I die*, I thought.

"I can't sin anymore because I'm locked up," his words echoed in my mind. Perhaps that was the most honest thing he had ever said to me. If he could kill again, he would. The only things that stopped him were the stone walls surrounding him and a locked door he didn't have the keys to open. He had never changed. The person he was all those years ago when he escorted a woman inside and shut the door behind them, knowing those moments would be her last, was the same person I spoke to for those two years.

I turned around and walked back to the car. I took a deep breath and looked toward the sky that seemed larger than it ever did before, a blue vastness that spoke of all the beauty he tried to destroy, calling me to leave.

CHAPTER THIRTY-ONE
Fading Strength and Memory

The weather in Walla Walla became unbearable most days, with temperatures falling close to zero, keeping Gary shut in his cell even when he didn't have to be. In December 2021, he began to call less, complaining it was "too damn cold" and it was "a hassle" to stand in the yard for an hour, or whenever an officer came back for him. Such an excursion required him to wear coveralls layered with a jacket that wasn't heavy enough for a cool spring breeze, never mind the frigid temperatures that awaited him. Even though the yard was an enclosed concrete box, technically inside, the walls lacked insulation. So, it was more like an unfinished basement. I couldn't blame him for wanting to stay inside.

However, when a month went by with only a few letters and without a single call, I contemplated if there was more to his silence. This time his brooding didn't feel like a punishment, though, like how it did for the few weeks after I returned from Seattle when he seemed bothered by the time I spent with Asher. This time, right before he went quiet, he had even let his dinner get cold to remain on the phone, professing, "I don't care because I'm talking to you." Nothing had happened to make his silence feel personal. But Gary was far from reasonable, and his logic oftentimes only made sense to him. In the back of my mind, I was disquieted by the idea that he might have decided to toss me into the same graveyard as his imaginary friend, Arthur.

By January, Covid lockdowns had barred his entire unit inside for long stretches, so using the phone wasn't even an option some weeks. That was another variable, elongating the dead air that sat between us like a thick fog; it had to clear away eventually, I hoped.

By the end of January, the phone rang around dinnertime, just as it had for nearly two years. He talked as if no time had passed at all. He never had any concept of time other than how it pertained to his schedule. Morning yard, evening yard. Shower days, phone days. If I had not acknowledged his monthlong absence, I doubted he would have.

"I don't go to the yard in the morning, and basically I don't go too much in the evening because it's too damn cold out here," he grumbled.

There was nothing wrong beyond that. I had not been disposed of yet.

After that, Covid lockdowns shut down almost the entire prison. In March, I finally received a letter, and at the top, he scribbled he lost my phone number and asked me to include it in my response. Another logical explanation for the silence. But I wondered if his memory had been failing him more. All the times early in our correspondence he thought I had visited Seattle, even though I told him I never had. Either he wasn't listening to me, or his memory was failing. There hadn't been any call in which he didn't consult a list he had written beforehand to remind him of what he wanted to discuss with me. I wondered if these lapses were symptoms of his dyslexia, or the onset of dementia. Solitary confinement also didn't help. In time, old age would ravage him, turning him into a forgetful, feeble man. There could even come a point when I could lose access to him, that he could forget who I was.

I couldn't shake the feeling that some catastrophe was lingering on the horizon. Reminiscent of when I first began communicating with him and I just *knew* I was meant to hear some form of his story, I now had the same feeling gnawing at my gut, except it promised a coming end to our conversations. I tried to imagine the possibilities, and all I could think was he was about to die.

But I ignored my bad feeling and wrote a response to him, including a litany of questions, the same as always. I expected him to answer the ones he felt like, the same as always. He had become more open to discussing the women he killed, so I hoped we were finally on the verge of a breakthrough to try to piece together some of the cold cases. But one month went by, and then another. The bad feeling I had grew like a tumor and contained the same foreboding outcome. There would be no more time left. I remembered the last time we spoke in January, the last thing we said to each other. The robotic woman counted down the remaining sixty seconds and then thirty seconds, cutting off any other words we had to say.

"I hope you get my letter and enjoy reading it," he said. He had never expressed anything like that before in which he considered what I would like or wouldn't like. *That's oddly genuine of him*, I thought.

"Are you still there?" he asked.

"Yeah, I'm still here," I assured him.

But I wasn't sure if he had heard me. The inevitable disconnect followed, and just like the first time we ever spoke, I held the phone to my ear anyway, listening to nothing.

I had never spoken anything more true.

* * *

The letter Gary sent to me in March remained atop my desk for months. I removed and stuffed it back into the envelope to read those four pages again and again until I had unintentionally memorized his words and they lost their meaning. It was as though he had died, and I was clinging to the last thing he would ever say to me. *But it would be on the news*, I reminded myself.

Each time my eyes fell on his rushed, scribbled print, I hoped I would find a clue, something I had missed that would tell me why I still had not heard from him. It felt the same as trying to decipher the mixed signals of a man after a date I was certain had gone well. It had been almost two months since I had responded to him. Something was wrong.

When I could no longer shake the bad feeling that had settled into my gut like some incurable malady, I decided to call his counselor at the prison. In the past, Gary had advised that I should do this if several days had passed without hearing from him. "They leave you in the dark here sometimes," he said. *It had been almost two months.* I was not overreacting. Besides, in the letter, he had mentioned that he was going to mail out a few books to me, but I never received them, indicating they were either lost, or someone at the prison had stolen them. *Even more of a reason to call.*

I dialed the number and held my breath as if I was underwater. His counselor picked up, mumbling his name and title in a hurried greeting that could have easily been mistaken for annoyance. I explained who I was inquiring about and was met with such a long pause I thought he had hung up on me.

"Hello?"

"Yes, ma'am. He's in the hospital."

"The hospital?" I repeated. I had expected him to tell me anything else—another Covid outbreak in IMU, a lockdown, broken phones, construction in the yard. It was hard to believe Gary could ever be brought to such a weakened, bedridden state requiring him to need around- the-clock care. As much as I tried to always see the human in him, in my mind, he was hardly human. He was indestructible like a monster. He had evaded capture for nearly twenty years, and then when he was caught, he evaded the death penalty, too, all the while toying with the police and anyone else who ever tried to squeeze the full truth from him, me included.

"Yes, the hospital. It's been a few weeks," his counselor said without any emotion.

"Well, is he okay?"

"I think he might be okay."

"What happened to him?"

"I can't tell you that, ma'am, due to HIPAA laws."

"Okay. Well, does his family know?"

"His family? I didn't even know he talked to his family. He doesn't have a release on file to call anyone."

After I hung up, I stood in the same spot in my kitchen as if my feet had sunk into the linoleum.

Broken or fractured bones, shingles, Covid, an infection—I considered everything non-life threatening that could have happened. But then I remembered something Gary had told me, what had happened to him a few years before we started communicating. "They [gave me] tuna fish, and I had a stomachache, and they took me out on a wheelchair. Now that I think of it, I think I walked down, but I got so sick I laid down. I sat on the floor. Then the nurse came in there in the middle of the night, and they took me in—and they figured it was a stroke, a mild stroke . . . I could have had a stroke. I don't know," he said, as if he disputed the diagnosis. His nonchalance about the ordeal never made me question it any further. As far as I knew, he was considerably healthy, except for back pain and sinus issues he complained about sometimes. He still woke up every morning and walked back and forth for hours.

But they didn't keep you in the hospital for weeks over nothing, especially in prison. I knew whatever happened to him—possibly another stroke—must have been somewhat serious. I wondered if that meant I would never hear from him again, but I couldn't grasp that outcome. First, I had to find out what was wrong.

I contemplated if he would want his family to know that he was in the hospital, and I replayed different scenarios in my head. On one hand, I knew he favored his privacy, whatever was left of it in prison. However, after years of talking with incarcerated people, I knew that many of them did not receive the best healthcare. If the prison suspected an inmate had no one on the outside looking out for them, they could get away with doing the bare minimum, if that. Gary had already confided he did not receive the greatest of treatment from the nurses. Only a few months ago, when he discovered mold growing inside his drinking glass, he had requested a new one. After a couple days, a nurse brought him a new glass, but it had been sprayed with bleach-like chemicals. When he drank from it, it made him sick, something he believed was done on purpose. "The nurse didn't like me because of my past," he explained. According to him, she had it out for him. In prison, this was not a farfetched idea.

If Gary's family got involved, the medical staff would at least be held accountable. My mind was made up. After perusing the internet for their contact information, with the best intentions, I wrote an email to his older brother explaining the situation. However, when he responded a few days later, I was met with hostility, the last thing I expected. Since I was a writer, that made me an instant enemy. I didn't know how this tempestuous interaction with his brother would affect Gary, but I assumed the worst. He would never talk to me again.

The only thing I could do was write to him while he remained in the infirmary. For months, I dropped cards and letters into the mailbox, which felt more like an abyss. I had no idea if he read anything I sent, or if he was even capable of doing so. For nearly two years we had been in such close communication, it never dawned on me I could have overstepped a boundary by finding out his health was in decline, information he probably didn't want me to know. On top of that, contacting his brother without his permission could have angered him even more.

But I wasn't about to give up. In the past, I had always gotten him to talk, even if that meant unleashing his depravity on me. I knew subjecting myself to whatever he had in store for me—violent fantasies, lies, manipulation—was the only way to see him for what he was, a sacrifice of sorts for even a sliver of truth. I regretted nothing, and I was not ready for it to end. There were still a multitude of questions I never got to ask, information I needed to sort out, women that were missing that needed to be found, a box of evidence that had to be unearthed. I couldn't bear the idea of never having answers.

By the end of May, I decided to take my chances and call the prison infirmary. HIPAA laws prevented the doctor from telling me anything, but he offered to pass Gary a message, something I never heard of anyone doing in a prison before. What did I have to lose?

When I called back for an update, the doctor told me that Gary had taken the paper with my phone number and held it in his hands. *As if it mattered*, I thought. Maybe it did. Maybe he didn't crumple it into a ball and throw it into the trash bin.

School was about to end for summer break, and for once I was not thrilled. I had thought I would be heading to Washington to find Gary's treasure box and finally sit face-to-face with him.

A few days later, sitting in an empty classroom during lunch, the metal frame of the desk rattled. I glanced at my phone, staring at the familiar caller ID as though a ghost had entered the room. I listened to the robotic woman announce the call was from him just as I had done hundreds of times before. With trembling fingers, I pressed five and said "hello." I awaited the sound of his voice like an antidote I desperately needed to remedy the anxiety that had kept me awake each night to ruminate over every word I had said to his brother, counselor, and doctor until I regretted even the act of breathing. "Hello," I said again, but I was met with silence.

I pictured him holding the phone to his ear, listening to my eager voice that must have reminded him of a plea for mercy. "I'll let you go," he used to tell the woman as she begged him to live, trying to persuade him that she was "too young to die." But he never cared. Then I heard a click. He had hung up.

He'll call back. He always does.

I glared at the black screen of the phone. *Come on. Come on.* I tapped my fingers against the desk in an offbeat rhythm. The bell rang, signaling the end of lunch. Then another bell rang and another, and school was dismissed for the day; then more days passed, and school was dismissed for summer. Still, he had not called back. By September, I knew I was waiting for what would probably never happen again.

I called the prison a few more times during the summer, trying to piece together what had happened. On some days I was lucky to talk with a CO who either had no regard for HIPAA laws or had no clue a law was being violated, and I was given fragments of information. I learned Gary was unable to walk and had been transferred to a handicap cell large enough for a wheelchair, he had been going on routine trips to the hospital in town to see a specialist, he had become incontinent and had a catheter, and he had most likely suffered either a stroke or heart attack or both. I convinced myself his illness was the reason he hadn't called back, and a CO corroborated it, confirming that in order to use the phone in IMU, Gary would have to go up and down a couple of steps, something he could barely do. A stroke could have impaired his right arm, preventing him from writing a letter. It made perfect sense. Perhaps his silence wasn't deliberate.

But by the end of September, I began to see notes he had written to various departments within the prison for sale on murderabilia websites. That meant he was able to write and was *choosing* not to respond to me. His notes being taken and sold also meant his feeble condition had left him vulnerable to those around him. Someone had been stealing all his notes, which were primarily simple requests such as a new address book or an enforcement of the quiet-after-ten PM rule in the unit. Each one sold for hundreds of dollars.

The following month I came across a note in which he was begging for medical attention. Since I was reading it on a murderabilia site, I knew it had never reached anyone in the infirmary. He had been left helpless to suffer alone in his cell. If he did not see a doctor, it was possible he could die.

My first instinct was to dial 911, but then I remembered his emergencies didn't matter to the outside world. His emergencies didn't matter to most people in the prison, either, so I knew better than to tell a CO. So, I called the chaplain, the one person at the prison I knew he had positive interactions with sometimes. I explained that Gary's notes had surfaced on murderabilia sites, and I even forwarded screenshots of them to him. I demanded that Gary receive immediate medical attention.

Most people would hate the decision I made to help him, believing he deserved to suffer and die. I also knew if the situation was reversed, he probably would help me die, killing me if he could. But a life would always be a life to me, no matter who it was. While his compassion was a dry well, mine had always carved a path for me, leading me to whatever I needed to do. Now was no different. The next day, I learned that he had been transferred to the infirmary, where he would remain for the next year. I never saw any of his notes on sale again.

If he knew I was the one who had intervened to help him, I didn't expect any acknowledgment. Yet, I wished for a *thank you*, a *fuck you*, anything. Even though I knew he was in the infirmary, his sickness didn't feel like closure. Each time I called for an update, I was told he had access to a phone. "But was he well enough to get there to use it?" No one knew.

The journalist in me longed for answers. Had he cut me off deliberately, or was he truly incapable of speaking to me or anyone? This question lingered in my mind. I knew I would ruminate over every possibility, no matter how much time passed. The only thing I could think of that would confirm his ability or inability to use the phone was to obtain his call records.

Within a couple days, an email appeared in my inbox, revealing the truth. I expected a short document, evidence to confirm that I was the last person he called, six months ago.

He would call if he could, I had convinced myself. Even if he was too sick to ever talk again, he would tell me. I was certain of it. I thought of Ted Kaczynski, the Unabomber. In Kaczynski's last letter to me, he had apologized for no longer being able to correspond when he was diagnosed with cancer and had become too ill. *If Ted had the decency to inform me why he could no longer communicate and we didn't even talk frequently, Gary would do the same, right?*

But when I opened the document, months of calls he had made and attempted to make filled the pages. Granted, they were infrequent, not every day like when we would talk. They were mostly to his brother and a few to a friend he would tell me he called when I was working, when he knew I couldn't answer. I noticed a jumble of numbers similar to mine that he dialed during the summer, proof his dyslexia had worsened. He seemed to have given up after a few times.

I wanted to throw up and punch him and scream all at once. For reasons I couldn't even begin to contemplate or understand, he had discarded me like he had so many other women before.

As I stared at the numbers, I knew our communication was over for good. I would never have the opportunity to ask him anything again. Pages of questions that sat on my desk beside his last letter would remain just that, questions with answers he'd probably take to his grave. In his mind, I had become dead to him, forgotten like any other face not worth it for him to remember.

Epilogue

For the first half of 2023, I mulled over what I would do with the nearly two years of information Gary had given to me. Fragments of stories that would never be finished taunted me until I believed I was a failure, and I barely got out of bed on most weekends. Any hope of finishing the book I had wanted so badly to write, what I had been so invested in, had been destroyed. I had convinced myself it was my fault that Gary had cut me from his life.

I contemplated the reasons why, but I never landed on anything definitive, just endless possibilities that all seemed plausible when considering how Gary's mind operated: he was too sick to exert the energy he once did when we'd spend sometimes hours talking on the phone; he was embarrassed that I had found out about his illness; he wanted to preserve his image as a formidable serial killer rather than confront his own body that was betraying him and breaking down; he was angry I had taken control of the situation; he had lost his identity and manhood once a catheter had been inserted inside him, in turn, rendering me useless since he no longer had the need to fantasize about me; he was irrational and blamed me for his illness; he was employing whatever control he had left by removing me from his life, the next best thing to killing me.

Months passed, and I hoped I would forget about him, but even if we never spoke again, and even if he didn't prefer that I finished what we had started, I knew I had no choice. I never gave up on anything.

To prove to myself I was serious, I booked a trip to Seattle for an entire month. I had no idea what kind of book I would write, but I vowed to work with the information he had given me. I would never understand him from three thousand miles away; I wouldn't until I was retracing his footsteps and breathing the same air he once did.

* * *

Down the road from where he once lived in Auburn, I stopped at Lake Geneva Park, the first park on my list where I suspected he had buried his box of souvenirs. It met all the requirements: it was on his way to work, it was desolate, it had a paved walking path, a bench was bolted to the ground a few feet away, the shrubbery, grass, and trees were tall enough to hide a person, and some of the ground closer to the lake sloped in what could be considered a bank hill, just as he described. It was worth a shot to search it, and I decided to follow his advice and ask someone to help me. One person could dig while the other looked out for any joggers or hikers, he had once advised.

One of my oldest childhood friends, Marlo, agreed to the bizarre adventure and flew into Seattle a few days later. We rented a metal detector and drove to a Walmart to buy supplies: a "big scoop" aluminum shovel, a small garden shovel, and garden gloves printed with pink flowers filled the cart. To anyone we passed, we looked like we were about to embark on a gardening project rather than trying to dig up a serial killer's keepsakes.

As we exited the store, a wall full of photographs—mostly young women and teenagers—caught my eye. As I got closer, I saw that they were all missing persons. I scanned the dates, checking if Gary could have been responsible, but all of them were recent, within the last few years. I remembered his question after the first time I had visited Seattle, if I had seen any posters of missing women, as if excited by the idea.

I stared at the faces of women on the wall, knowing most of them were probably dead. I had to at least try to find his box. The pictures he claimed were shut inside it could help identify women that were still missing, bringing some closure to the people who still loved and missed them.

At the end of 46th Avenue, along the curve toward Military Road South, Lake Geneva Park appeared almost hidden, tucked away from the road like Gary's house down the street. At one end, an empty playground and a few picnic tables glistened in the sun, and behind it, a long grassy field. The rest of the park was canopied by trees that created comfortable shade along the walking path. The entire park seemed desolate, as if anyone who lived close by had forgotten it existed.

Marlo and I dragged the shovel and metal detector behind us, trying to find a spot that matched Gary's description. About halfway down the path, the grass became taller alongside it and patches of dirt encompassed the trees. The ground sloped as we got closer to the lake. It seemed like a good place to start the search. I hovered the metal detector over the ground as I walked, waiting for a sound like an alarm clock's relentless ring. But I heard nothing except the crackling of dirt under our heels.

If I was Gary, where would I hide this thing? I glanced around, hoping to recognize another hint he could have left me. Something from our conversations that only I would know, a reference marker, an unobtrusive detail like the shape of a tree that I might suddenly remember if I looked hard enough. But nothing came to mind. I could only recall the few clues he provided in his letters, and they didn't seem to be enough.

We walked and walked, skimming all the ground about a foot away from the paved trail, like he said. Then, at the base of a tree, an incessant beeping cut through the silence.

"Could this be it?" Marlo asked, smirking.

The closer I suspended the metal detector over the small plot of ground, the louder and more consistent the alarm became, as if screaming to unbury whatever was there. "Maybe we should start digging here," I said.

We both took turns shoveling the dirt away. The hardened earth barely moved at first, as if it had been frozen. It required a lot of force to make a dent, as we both stabbed the ground with the tip of the shovel over and over, like breaking through ice. The mound began to crack, dust blowing in our faces, and it became easier to lift piles of dirt, throwing it behind us. The more dirt we removed, the louder the metal detector rang, as if we were getting closer to something.

"A little bit more. He said seven to eight inches," I instructed Marlo.

We were both growing tired. This was not easy work for two petite women.

Sweat glistened on our faces and our clothes had become covered in dirt. *Probably the way Gary looked after dumping a body.* Marlo continued to plow the shovel into the earth, a bigger hole forming at our feet. As she pushed the shovel down again, the metal whacked against something hard.

"You hear that?" she asked, leaning her body against the shovel.

"I did. It sounded like a crack."

We both stared at each other in disbelief. I imagined the metal lockbox only a few inches away, buried under a thin layer of dirt. It was something I could physically touch and hold, something that would restore my faith in Gary, proof that not everything he said was a lie, that he did have some good intentions. For a moment, he became more human, and I thought of his kindness as a real part of him, like his heart or legs or fingers, something tangible that I could feel once this box was freed from the earth. In that moment, I was certain of its existence. My heart fluttered at the thought of all the possibilities that would follow after finding it, until I felt like I was drowning, breathing in the dirt I believed he had once touched and wiping tears from my irritated eyes.

Marlo smashed the ground with the shovel again and again, trying to loosen whatever was there. All we could see was a whitish surface, which I thought was the plastic he said he wrapped around the box to keep out any water.

"Fuck. Fuck," she seethed. Since she was the one digging, she noticed it first.

A flattened Budweiser can wrapped in a thick, rusty chain. We were back to square one.

By this time, our arms were sore, our backs ached, and our hands burned, despite wearing gloves. We had only covered a sliver of ground in the entire park, and there was still so much that remained untouched. Across the walking trail, there was an entire lot where grass grew as high as our waists. It was possible he could have buried it on that side in the '90s when the grass was shorter. How could we ever walk through that? We would need machetes to cut it all down.

"I hate to say this, but I wish we had a team of big men," Marlo blurted out.

"Me too," I said and sighed. We both knew it would be impossible for us to dig as much as we just did again. If we tried, we would keel over from the pain. "We need better equipment, a bulldozer even," I said.

"Let's take a break and figure something out," she said.

We dragged our feet, pulling the shovel and metal detector behind us. At the end of the walking trail, there was a wooden dock that led to the lake. We walked to the edge and sat down, gazing at the water below us. There was barely a ripple as far as I could see, making the entire body of water resemble a mirror with perfect glass. I wondered if this water had ever held the reflection of Gary's face like it did ours. He had never mentioned spending any time there, which was another reason I suspected it could have been the burial ground of all his secrets. He would never make anything easy for me.

The thought of searching the other seventeen parks on my list crossed my mind and seemed unfeasible. There was no way we would be able to do it with two mediocre shovels and one metal detector. We either needed more people or better tools. We also needed a lot more time, which we were running out of, since Marlo would be on her way home in two days.

"You think I should tell Tom, the detective I met with?"

Weeks prior, when Tom and I met, I contemplated telling him about the box, but I was wary. Since 2003, it didn't seem like much effort was exerted in trying to find any other victims, and he didn't seem to believe it would ever be possible. Besides, I had promised Gary I would try to find his box of treasures on my own. Since it was harder than I thought, I began to reconsider.

"Maybe. The police would have men and equipment," she said and laughed.

But I wasn't ready to admit defeat just yet. I contemplated visiting all the parks on my list and at least trying, even if it killed me. But I knew going through with it was impractical. I would never be able to dig up seventeen parks all by myself.

"Time's almost up on the metal detector. We're gonna have to head back," I said, as we both struggled to our feet, every muscle throbbing from hours of digging and walking.

On the way back, a man no older than forty years old emerged from behind the trees and crossed our path on the walking trail, stopping us in our tracks. Marlo and I looked at each other, startled. He was the only person we had seen in the park that whole day, and I wondered if he had been there the entire time, watching us. I immediately thought of Gary's premonition: it was inevitable that I would be raped and killed. My hand clutched the shovel, ready to slam it over his head.

A beach towel was tied around his waist as if he had just gotten out of the shower, and he wore no shirt. A snorkel hung from his neck like an oversized necklace. He held a rusty dagger in one hand while his other hand rested at his side. "You guys out here looking for treasure, too?" he asked, eyeing the metal detector.

"Something like that." Marlo chuckled nervously.

"I found so much today, you wouldn't believe," he gushed. "Want to see?"

Marlo and I looked at each other, our eyes trying to communicate what we should do next: bash his head with the shovels and run past him, run in the opposite direction, or scream for help. "Well, see, the thing is you're holding a dagger, and that's not making us feel too comfortable to check out anything you found," Marlo said.

"Oh, of course!" The man placed the dagger down on the ground in front of us and raised his hands in the air, trying to convince us he was not a threat. He then reached into his towel and opened his hand to us, revealing an emerald ring and a few coins. "Found all this snorkeling today," he said. "The dagger was a bonus." We both looked at the display on his palm, nodding. "You never know what you'll find out here," he said. "How'd you guys do?"

"Came up empty," I said. "We're kinda new at this."

"Well, keep at it. You're bound to find something."

I was not entirely convinced he didn't pose a threat, but since he had been disarmed and we still held our shovels, I was certain we could do more damage to him than he could to us. So, I asked him more questions about hunting for treasure in this park. Apparently, he had lived in the neighborhood since the '90s, around the same time Gary moved there. In the 1960s, he explained, the park had been a resort and then after that turned into a fishing camp. He figured all his findings came from that time. When he didn't mention unearthing a box containing pictures of naked women and notebooks of Gary's summaries of murder, I was satisfied all of Gary's secrets were still undiscovered.

We told him we had to get home and stepped cautiously around him, making sure he didn't pick up the dagger. Once we passed him, we bolted to the car. I imagined him running up behind us, the rusty blade at my throat, our bodies never being found in those woods, and our bones disintegrating into the same dirt I still believed Gary had touched with his bare hands. I picked up speed, and Marlo followed.

When we got to the car, we threw everything into the trunk and jumped in our seats, locking the doors. The man was nowhere in sight, but we knew he was still somewhere nearby. We could barely catch our breath, but our hearts beat violently with life.

* * *

Before I left Seattle, I made one last attempt to visit Gary. The prison had already denied my request months prior, even though my name still remained on his visiting list. They stuck to their rule: only immediate family members were permitted into the infirmary, where he was now living indefinitely. But while strolling through a flea market in Fremont one Sunday morning, an idea popped into my mind that I regretted not thinking of sooner: maybe Tom would be able to help me arrange a visit with Gary.

I chucked the fistful of costume jewelry I was about to purchase back into the bins, and I walked to the corner to email him to plead my case. He knew more than anyone how important it was to build rapport with Gary, and I had been successful. It would require a lot more dedication and energy from the detectives that had recently shown up at Walla Walla to ever get any information from Gary. Why not let me try?

Tom didn't hate the idea. In fact, he ran it by the Major Crimes Scene Unit, but it seemed they barely gave it much thought. A few days later, he passed along their decision: "It was their consensus that we (KCSO) cannot have you act as an agent for law enforcement without compromising any information that you might obtain. Hence, you may do as you wish with regards to further contact with Ridgway, and you may report what you learn at your discretion, but you will not be doing so with the encouragement of law enforcement."

It took all the restraint I had not to throw my phone off the hill in Gas Works Park, where I read the message. I failed to understand why they wouldn't want to try anything that would bring closure to families that had been waiting for decades. What did it matter who Gary confessed to as long as he confessed? He was already serving forty-nine life sentences, so nothing else could be done to punish him. This was about providing closure to families who still had no idea who had murdered their loved ones. By working together, there was no telling what I would have been able to find out, but they didn't seem to care.

* * *

When I returned to New York, I continued to brood over the idea of telling Tom about Gary's mystery box. The detectives in the Major Crimes Scene Unit were the ones against working with me, but since Tom was retired, he seemed more open to the idea of at least listening to me.

I knew if I kept this information to myself forever, then I would be no better than the detectives refusing to work with me. The most important thing was trying to find answers, and how those answers were found didn't matter.

Although Gary had denied it, Tom, along with most of the original task force, always believed he kept souvenirs hidden somewhere. Everything that he claimed to stash into the box matched with what he admitted to Tom years ago. Tom didn't believe that Gary had ripped up the Polaroids he claimed to take of his victims. The night Constance Naon went missing, she drove her Camaro to the Red Lion, so it would make sense that Gary kept the key emblem, like he claimed. The room keys from the Three Bears Motel also seemed a plausible keepsake, since prostitutes often stayed there. Since Gary loved making lists, the journals cataloging details of his victims were not hard to believe.

Tom agreed that the pictures, especially, could serve as evidence and verify confessions Gary made that had yet to be proven. After listening to the recorded conversations I had with Gary about it, Tom was convinced Gary had mumbled he had buried the box in a "dog park," but I wasn't entirely sure. To me, it sounded like he muttered an "uh" before saying "park." However, if the park was located along Gary's work route, it didn't really matter what kind of park it was. All of them were worth searching.

Tom compiled a short list of all the dog parks Gary could have passed on his way to work, and I compared it to my longer list. Some of the parks matched up. A good sign. In December, Tom said that once the weather improved, he would visit some of them and see what he could find.

But when over a month passed and I didn't hear from him, I wondered if any search had been conducted at all. By the end of January, he informed me that some detectives had gone to Walla Walla to ask Gary about the box. *A stupid idea.*

According to Gary, he claimed he made up the whole story, which could have been true. The box could have been just another lie he told for the sake of getting a reaction as he watched from afar while I traipsed around all of Washington in search of it.

But I also knew he would never confide in them about a secret he didn't want to share. What was worse, any trust he had in me was most likely destroyed. If they had allowed me to follow up with him months ago, there was a chance I could have retrieved more information. After all, he had confided in me, not them. Instead, Gary told them nothing. His advancing dementia didn't help, either.

The only information they obtained was the reason Gary stopped communicating with me. Since he no longer had a use for me, he lost interest in speaking with me, something I had already suspected months ago when I learned of the condition of his health, specifically that he had to keep a catheter inserted in his penis at all times. Of course, that would render me useless to him.

But when it came to finding the box, Tom made it sound promising. New metal detectors had been issued to KCSO, and their first practice mission would be searching some of the parks in the spring. I knew they would probably never show me the contents of the box if they found it, but I didn't care. If even one case could be solved, it would be worth it.

But after several months, there still was no news to report. No one in KCSO had even tried to find the box. Since Gary claimed he lied to me about it, they took him at his word. Tom was far from convinced, but since he was retired, he was powerless in the situation. The only way the box would ever be found was if I returned to Seattle and dug it up myself.

* * *

The list of unsolved cases I had compiled and shared with Gary in 2021, what seemed like a never-ending inventory of his killing, was still saved on my computer. Although my communication with him had ceased, I returned to the list often, hoping to connect something he had told me to any of the names that had become just as familiar as people I knew. In most of the cases, the women nor their remains were ever found, but that was not true for Nicole French and Sarah Habakangas. Since their bodies had been discovered and identified, it didn't make sense why their cases had gone unsolved.

Both women had been involved in prostitution and went missing from the same corner where Gary picked up several other victims. Habakangas was last seen alive in 1991 at the Three Bears Motel, and a year later French disappeared nearby, on the corner of South 216th and Pacific Highway South. Both women were strangled and found in North Bend, not far from where Gary placed several other victims. In 1983, after killing Tina Thompson, April Buttram, and Maureen Feeney, he placed their bodies around the intersection of I-90 and Highway 18, and by the end of that year, he continued his spree, killing Delise Plager, Kim Nelson, and Lisa Yates, all of whom he left by Exit 38 in North Bend. Both locations were only a few miles from where French and Habakangas were discovered.

The more I researched these cases, I was reminded of what Gary had told me. During the '90s when more bodies of women were discovered, KCSO informed the media that these cases did not resemble the Green River killings, blaming another serial killer they suspected to be in the area. In my conversations with Gary, he protested this idea. How could another serial killer be choking women and placing them in his dump sites? He asked this over and over, demanding an answer from me. When I finally asked him what he thought it meant, he admitted, "They're all mine." If a woman was working as a prostitute and was found strangled in or near one of his dump sites prior to his incarceration, it had to be his doing. That would explain the thirty-two to forty-two more victims he claimed to have killed.

Nicole French and Sarah Habakangas fit into his theory. The closer I examined the cases, I learned that like Wendy Coffield and Opal Mills, Gary had also left Nicole's pants tied around her neck, used as a ligature. "If I had any problem . . . sometimes I'd left it on there . . . if it was really tight on there, then I would just leave it on her. Others . . . I 'll take them off at the site," he explained to detectives. It was not unheard of for Gary to use a ligature or leave it noosed around his victims' necks.

Old newspaper clippings only revealed so much, though. So, I asked Tom why Gary had been ruled out as a suspect. He explained that Gary had denied responsibility for both cases, something I wasn't sure I believed. Although Gary had never actually been ruled out, there was no physical evidence to charge him, according to

Tom. With advancements in technology since then, I began to wonder if evidence collected at the scenes could be retested. But when I brought this up to Tom, I was met with silence.

When I spoke with Nicole's mother, I was not surprised to hear her anger over the lack of closure. She explained that the medical examiner, Dr. Michael Dobersen, had been the one to deliver the news of Nicole's death, only two days after her remains were discovered by a hiker in November 1992. Since Nicole's case was so similar to other Green River cases, he told her, "Your daughter died in his hands, and the autopsy proves it."

"He was not in the least bit undecided," she recalled.

But the police department never called her to discuss their investigation. "When they disbanded the task force, they washed their hands of it . . . they felt these women were disposable," she said. I remembered Gary had told me something similar. Since the police did not seem to prioritize investigating crimes against prostitutes, he was able to continue killing and remain undetected for nearly twenty years.

During Gary's interviews with police in 2003, Tom had even told him, "[The official Green River list] has been somewhat politically manipulated over the years . . . to I think stay at number forty-nine," the number of victims Gary was convicted for. Detective Mattsen then interjected, "There were other reasons [why] that number stayed at forty-nine."

I began to wonder how many cases had gone unsolved on purpose just to fill some political quota that I suspected most likely had to do with the sheriff's office protecting its reputation.

When Nicole's mother visited Seattle to speak with the detectives directly, she described that she was met with heartlessness and indifference. At first, they told her she should go home, but she protested that she wanted to visit the site where Nicole had been found. They acquiesced and directed her to wait for a detective at the location. After waiting an hour, finally someone showed up and led her into the woods. They couldn't provide her with much information about the investigation, but she did learn that whoever killed her daughter also took her jewelry, another detail consistent with the Green River cases. After that, KCSO never had any further communication with her, but she wasn't surprised. She felt they had not been thorough in their investigation at all.

Sarah's brother recounted a similar experience with KCSO when it came to the investigation of his sister's murder. "I don't think they investigated it very well because she was a prostitute. They weren't interested in investigating it. They said that two people killed her, and that the handprints on her neck did not match with Ridgway . . . but they never provided us with documentation," so he was never convinced that what they told him was the truth.

When I brought up the idea of retesting the evidence found at the scenes, both families gave me consent to retrieve the autopsy reports. In my conversations with the medical examiner, Dr. Dobersen, who completed the autopsy report in Nicole's case, he was able to confirm that the sweatpants used as a ligature to strangle Nicole should still be on file as evidence. "Assuming he wasn't wearing gloves or anything else like that, I would think that would be a pretty good place to start looking for trace evidence," Dr. Dobersen validated. "You should never be throwing away any potential evidence like that."

He went on to explain that even though there was no evidence of spermatozoa found in her vagina or anus, sexual assault could not be ruled out. "If I was on the stand, the attorney would probably ask me something like is this consistent with what you would see in a sexual assault, and I would say yes," he confirmed.

Abrasions had been found around her anus, indicating sexual activity. But these injuries were also consistent with Gary's explanation, that most of his victims ended up with scratches on their backside after he would drag them through the woods. "My last ones . . . any one that you found fresh . . . there'd be scratch marks on her, on her back and buttocks from dragging [her]," he detailed to detectives. I couldn't understand why they seemed to gloss over this detail of her autopsy while they were questioning him, never mentioning to Gary the abrasions that were discovered on her, which could have helped jog his memory.

When I asked Dr. Dobersen the reasons he believed Nicole had been killed by Gary, he explained, "It just fit the pattern. Strangulation, the victim had a lot in common with the other victims, and the cause of death, the fact the body was put in a remote area certainly fit the pattern. I can't think of anything that doesn't fit the pattern."

I agreed that everything was consistent except the autopsy had proven that at some point Nicole had been tied up with rope. Gary had never done that in any of his other cases, but that was not to say it didn't happen. He did have a nearly lifelong fixation with exerting dominance over women. His former girlfriend Nancy attested that Gary had tied her hands and feet to stakes in the woods, and his ex-wife Marcia recalled that Gary had tied her up before as well. So, it was not much of a stretch. It was also proven that the piece of rope found at the scene matched the exact rope Gary used to keep in his truck. During his interview with detectives, Gary concluded, "I'm quite sure I did that one because if I had rope like that in the back, maybe a piece fell out . . . when I drug her up there." He continued, "It's possible I tied them, [but] I don't remember tying any up. If these are around my dump sites then every one of them up here has a woman tied up in it, then somewhere along the line, I started using ropes to tie them up. I don't remember tying them up, though," he said. Like always, it was difficult to decipher the truth from the lies.

Later, he denied killing Nicole and Sarah, but he also denied killing a lot of women he eventually admitted to. I couldn't understand why the detectives seemed satisfied with him flip-flopping on these cases. I certainly wasn't.

Since technology had advanced so much since then, Dr. Dobersen confirmed that even the vaginal and anal swabs that were taken could be retested today. "DNA techniques are sensitive and getting better all the time," he said. I couldn't understand why KCSO had not done this already—perhaps the number of cold cases exceeded the manpower they had—but Dr. Dobersen agreed that they had nothing to lose.

Othram, a company specializing in forensic genetic genealogy to resolve unsolved murders, seemed like a good place to start. When I contacted them and explained the details of these two cases, they were more than willing to help. But my elation on hearing this news was quickly destroyed. In May 2024, Othram received a response from KCSO, stating, "This is an open/active case, and is still being worked on," and that they had nothing to add at this time.

Dr. Dobersen shared my confusion. "It certainly is suspicious. I don't see why they can't be more forthcoming," he agreed. When I asked Tom about their decision, I was met with more silence. It seemed as though I was being shunned for giving attention to these cases. I didn't understand it.

I decided to go directly to the source, the detectives of the Major Crimes Scene Unit, Sergeant McNabb and Sergeant Miniken, to ask why they refused to work with Othram and why Gary had been ruled out as a suspect. After sending three emails, I finally received a response.

As if reciting a memorized line that held no true meaning, Sergeant McNabb responded that these cases were open investigations "and as such we will not discuss any of the facts of the investigation." Since it had been over thirty years, I wondered if they were investigating anything, but if they were as dedicated as they claimed, it didn't make sense why they were not interested in hearing from someone who had conversed with their main suspect for two years. Wouldn't they at least want to know what Gary had told me?

By that point I was disgusted enough to contact an attorney who specialized in public records requests. Since the cases were considered "active investigations" and had not been closed, all the records associated with them could be denied indefinitely. That meant for years on end, investigators would never have to face any accountability, and all the records containing important information could be concealed from the public without any expiration date.

Since the attorney I contacted believed I was trying to do a good thing, he provided me with free legal advice. The last resort would be to sue KCSO for their records, which included the scene notes at the time the bodies were discovered, something that would have helped Dr. Dobersen remember more about the case. In court, a judge would ask the detectives to prove they had been actively working on each case as they claimed. If they weren't be able to produce decades worth of work, the judge would most likely rule in my favor, according to my new attorney friend. It also would help that the victims' families were on my side. But it would cost me a couple thousand dollars. Giving me advice was one thing, but taking a case in which he would have to represent me in court would require a lot of work.

Before we pursued a legal case, he advised that I should tell KCSO what I was planning in the hopes that they would be rattled enough to speak with me. He also advised that I should contact the detective who had worked the cases in the 1990s. There was always the chance he would be willing to share his case files with me. But when I reached out to retired detective Randy Mullinax, he refused to speak with me.

The only other option before resorting to legal action was to make another attempt to visit Gary to try to retrieve any information I could. I knew his health had declined significantly, but as long as he was still breathing, I felt it was worth a shot. This time I contacted the person with the most authority in the chain of command, the superintendent of the prison, Rob Jackson.

However, it would take nearly two months of me calling every day before he realized I was never giving up, and he got on the phone with me. He told me I would have to be on Gary's visit list if I wanted to see him. When I told him I already was on his list, he then said infirmary visits were only permitted for immediate family members. He didn't care that I had built a rapport with Gary or that I was trying to solve two cases or find out about his box of souvenirs. As the superintendent, he was responsible for Gary's safety, and he concluded that my presence would somehow disrupt that along with the security of the entire prison. The only way he would ever consider granting me access to see Gary would be if someone from KCSO escorted me, and even then he wasn't sure if he would.

By the end of August 2024, I followed my attorney friend's advice and sent an email to the sheriff, informing her that I was planning to take legal action within the coming weeks. Her assistant responded, with the same tired script.

A week had passed, and as I was about to move forward with the lawsuit, a recent mugshot of Gary on social media caught me off guard. His face appeared thin, like he had not been eating, and a stubbly gray beard sprouted unevenly over his chin and above his jawline. Whatever hair he had left on his head was just as unkempt. But what alarmed me most was his pale complexion. It was not just from lack of sun; it reminded me of the faded color of someone who was dying. A white pillow encircled his head, indicating the picture was taken while he was lying down in bed. My heart raced at the unexpected sight of him, what appeared to be him on his deathbed.

But his expression didn't seem to translate into helplessness. He still smirked like in his previous mugshots, as if to say he was unbothered and still had a psychological advantage over everyone. His eyes stared at the camera, an intense, unbreakable gaze, as if he was plotting the death of whoever was behind the camera and anyone who decided to look at the picture later. But I couldn't look away.

After trying to process the photo, the headline and story that followed were just as shocking. On September 9, 2024, without notifying any of the victims' families as they were supposed to, Gary was transferred to King County Jail in Seattle, but authorities refused to provide the public with any further information. While people guessed the reasons all over social media—police found another body, they were bringing him around Seattle again to point out his dump sites, he was receiving medical care at a hospital—although I couldn't prove it, I wondered if my relentlessness had anything to do with it.

My lawyer friend was able to find out that the order to transport him had been created on August 23, the day after I had spoken to the superintendent of the prison. After my email to the sheriff on August 25, the following day a declaration to seal the documents was made, preventing me or anyone from retrieving any information for at least a year. The only information that existed was that Gary was brought to the jail due to a homicide investigation. That meant if I proceeded to sue KCSO for their records, I would most likely lose. They would now be able to prove they were actively working on unsolved cases.

I tried to get a concrete answer from Tom as to why Gary was moved to the jail, but he didn't respond to my email. All I had left were logical guesses that couldn't be verified. The only thing I was certain about was they wasted tax dollars to drive an ill man who could not even stand for a mugshot four hours to a jail in Seattle only to drive him back four hours by the next morning to Walla Walla. However, the media would be under the impression that Gary remained in the jail for a week. Since I knew his location would have to be updated as soon as he was returned to the prison, I continued to utilize their "inmate search." Just about every hour I ran his name, and sure enough before noon the next day, he was back in the prison. But months later, in March 2025, every news site would report that he was there for a week to accompany law enforcement on field trips to help locate some of his victims, a search that came up empty. When I showed the prosecutor's office my screenshot proving Gary was returned to Walla Walla after only one day, they could provide no explanation as to what had really happened.

Not expecting to hear anything else about Gary until he died, to my surprise, in December 2025, he was in the news again. I wasn't sure if he had been dying a slow suffering death, but the headlines made it appear that way, reporting he had been receiving end-of-life care.

Eager to share the news—after over a year of no communication—Tom wrote to me, informing me of the latest development, that Gary could be dying, but along with everyone else, he wasn't entirely sure. The only details he could verify was that according to the Department of Corrections, there had been no change in Gary's health.

This discussion also prompted him to share with me that during the "road trips" to Seattle Gary had been taken on in 2024, he had disclosed that his box of evidence actually existed; he had not been lying after all. Whether law enforcement tried to find the box during those road trips was unclear, but just as Gary told me, he also told them he buried and unburied it often, moving it to different locations through the years. The last place he recalled seeing it was in his house, asserting to police that it was there even during their search in 2001, but no one had found it. Then just like when he tried to convince the task force in 2003, he claimed he destroyed any evidence that had been inside it, contradicting himself like always.

As the story of Gary's impending death pressed on, Dave Reichert—the sheriff at the time of Gary's arrest—was quite vocal in the news, reflecting on what Gary's death would mean for victims' families. I was curious about what else he had to say and what he knew. When I was conducting a bulk of my research he had been running for governor, which I figured was the reason my interview requests at the time had gone unanswered. But with a political career no longer on the horizon, I thought I would have better luck getting a response from him, and I was right.

In mid-December 2025, we spoke on the phone, sharing as much as we both knew about Gary's health. Was Gary really days away from death? We discussed the probability, trying to form conclusions until I asked him the question that had been on my mind since I saw him on the news a few weeks prior. Was he planning on visiting Gary one last time in an attempt to retrieve answers about the unsolved cases?

The more we discussed the idea, the more enthusiastic he seemed to become about it. But he was unsure if he would be granted access into the prison—since Gary was in the infirmary and possibly on his death bed, the strict visiting rules would be more heavily enforced than before. But if he did somehow get approved, I asked if I would be able to accompany him.

Without hesitating, he said yes. I paced my living room, pinching the skin on my arm to confirm that his response was not something I had imagined. We continued to hypothesize the visit, the possibility of one of us, or both of us, retrieving answers that had been unknown for so long. With Christmas only a few days away, he assumed it might take a couple of weeks to get both of us approved; but he seemed confident that it would be possible and said he would call me with news.

All the hope that had burned out from years of disappointment reignited into a torch, blazing the darkness that had once shrouded this path. I might've been getting ahead of myself, but I couldn't help it: I began searching for flights to Seattle and hotel rooms in Walla Walla, and most importantly, I began penning the questions I had been waiting for Gary to answer for years. In which park did he bury the safe, and did he murder Nicole French and Sarah Habakangas? I knew if this visit did happen, my time with him would be limited, so I prepared to prioritize my questions.

The days passed, and I replayed the same scenario in my head: I envisioned an officer escorting me through one gate after another, the prison swallowing me like anyone else who walked further and further inside of it, the boxed up smell of sweat and metal burning my nostrils, and then the door I had been waiting years to pass through, where Gary would be on the other side, and I would finally face him. It all seemed so simple—one foot in front of the other, a few phone calls—what could go wrong?

But when I didn't hear from Dave after a month, and then nearly two months had passed without him returning any of my calls or text messages, I knew the visit was not going to happen for reasons I'd probably never know.

It's difficult to translate anyone's real intentions—at times law enforcement and I seemed to be on the same side, fighting for the same justice, but other times, I have felt entirely alone in this pursuit, their eagerness to help me seeming to rescind to disregard. And still, locked and sealed behind Gary's lips, the women he stole, hidden in places only he remembers—his cemetery-silence, like a fence walling us away from those pockets of earth to take back what was never his, to put names to the beautiful faces he has forgotten, to bring them back home.

Nicole French and Sarah Habakangas serve as only two examples from a long list of women where the truth seems to have been neglected. The other pieces of stories Gary had passed on to me—the woman Robin he possibly met in the hospital, the women he picked up on the way back from San Diego, the nine-year-old girl he mentioned who worked as a prostitute, the woman he told me he fingered against her will, and so many references of torture—point to more women and girls that could have been hurt by him.

When it comes to Gary, his truth and lies intersect so often, leaving behind only guesses as to what could have happened. The box he claimed to have buried serves as a prime example of his incongruencies. Its existence, or lack thereof, only speaks to his ability to manipulate any person who has ever tried to understand him, or worse, uncover his secrets. I'm sure now he will die with those secrets, coveting them until his last breath.

In Memoriam

Gary Ridgway's Confirmed Victims

Wendy Lee Coffield
Gisele Annette Lovvorn
Debra Lynn Bonner
Marcia Faye Chapman
Cynthia Jean Hinds
Opal Charmaine Mills
Terri Rene Milligan
Mary Bridget Meehan
Debra Lorraine Estes
Linda Jane Rule
Denise Darcel Bush
Shawnda Leea Summers
Shirley Marie Sherrill
Colleen Renee Brockman
Alma Ann Smith
Delores LaVerne Williams
Gail Lynn Matthews
Andrea Marion Childers
Sandra Kay Gabbert
Kimi-Kai Pitsor

Marie Malvar
Carol Ann Christensen
Martina Theresa Authorlee
Cheryl Lee Wims
Yvonne "Shelly" Antosh
Carrie Ann Rois
Constance Elizabeth "Connie" Naon
Kelly Marie Ware
Tina Marie Thompson
April Dawn Buttram
Debora May "Debbie" Abernathy
Tracy Ann Winston
Maureen Sue Feeney
Mary Sue Bello
Pammy Annette Avent
Delise Louise Plager
Kimberly L. Nelson
Lisa Lorraine Yates
Mary Exzetta West
Cindy Anne Smith
Patricia Michelle Barczak
Roberta Joseph Hayes
Marta Kalas Reeves
Patricia Ann Yellowrobe
Rebecca "Becky" Marrero
Wendy Marie Stephens
Sandra Denise Major
Tammie Charlene Liles
Lori Anne Razpotnik

Unconfirmed/Possible Victims

Keli Kay McGinnis
Kasee Ann Lee
Patricia Ann Osborn
Kristi Lynn Vorak
Angela Marie Girdner
Patricia Ann LeBlanc
Rose Marie Kurran
Darci Renae Warde
Deborah Yvonne Wims
Nicole Michelle French
Sarah Marshlene Habakangas

Gary Ridgway Timeline

February 18, 1949: Gary Ridgway is born in Salt Lake City, UT
1956/57: Sets a fire in a neighbor's garage in Pocatello, ID
1960: Moves to Seattle, WA
1961: Suffocates and kills a cat in an ice cooler
1963/64: Stabs a young boy but doesn't get caught
1969: Graduates from Tyee High School
August 18, 1969: Enlists in the navy
August 15, 1970: Marries Claudia Kraig
1971: Honorably discharged from the navy
January 14, 1972: Divorced from Claudia Kraig
1972: Allegedly chokes a woman for the first time
December 14, 1973: Marries Marcia Brown
September 5, 1975: Matthew Ridgway, Gary's son, is born
May 1981: Divorced from Marcia Brown
December 1981: Chokes woman in downtown Seattle, but unconfirmed if he kills her
1981: Chokes woman in Skyway and possibly kills her (potential first victim), but this is unconfirmed
May 1982: Arrested for solicitation
July 8, 1982: Wendy Coffield, first victim, goes missing after leaving foster home
July 15, 1982: Wendy Coffield is discovered dead in the Green River

July 17, 1982: Gisele Lovvorn is last seen alive
July 25, 1982: Debra Bonner is last seen alive
August 1, 1982: Marcia Chapman is last seen alive
August 11, 1982: Cynthia Hinds is last seen alive
August 12, 1982: Debra Bonner is discovered dead in the Green River
August 12, 1982: Opal Mills is last seen alive
August 15, 1982: Marcia Chapman, Cynthia Hinds, and Opal Mills are discovered dead in or near the Green River

August 28, 1982: Kase Lee is last seen alive; although Ridgway believes he might have killed her, it is impossible to search the site where he claims to have left her due to development of the area.*

August 29, 1982: Terry Milligan is last seen alive
September 15, 1982: Mary Meehan is last seen alive
September 20, 1982: Debra Estes is last seen alive
September 25, 1982: Gisele Lovvorn's remains are found in a wooded area near S 200th St and 18th Ave South
September 26, 1982: Linda Rule is last seen alive
October 1982: Shawnda Summers is last seen alive
October 8, 1982: Denise Bush is last seen alive
October 20–22, 1982: Shirley Sherrill is last seen alive

October 31, 1982: Kristi Vorak is last seen alive and has never been found; her case remains unsolved

November 1982: Rebecca Garde Guay is assaulted by Ridgway but gets away
December 24, 1982: Colleen Brockman is last seen alive
December 24, 1982: Sandra Denise Major, formerly identified as "Jane Doe B16," is last seen alive

1982: Lori Anne Razpotnik, formerly identified as "Jane Doe B17" is last seen alive

January 31, 1983: Linda Rule's remains are found in a wooded area at Northwest Hospital

February 6, 1983: Wendy Stephens, formerly identified as "Jane Doe Bones 10" is last seen alive

March 3, 1983: Alma Smith is last seen alive

March 8–17, 1983: Delores Williams is last seen alive

April 1983: Kimi-Kai Pitsor is last seen alive

April 10, 1983: Gail Matthews is last seen alive

April 14, 1983: Andrea Childers is last seen alive

April 17, 1983: Sandra Gabbert is last seen alive

April 30, 1983: Marie Malavar is last seen alive

May 1983: Angela Girdner is last seen alive

May 3, 1983: Carol Christensen is last seen alive

May 8, 1983: Carol Christensen's remains are discovered in a wooded area in Maple Valley

May 22, 1983: Martina Authorlee is last seen alive

May 23, 1983: Cheryl Wims is last seen alive

May 31, 1983: Yvonne Antosh is last seen alive

May 31–June 15, 1983: Carrie Rois is last seen alive

June 8, 1983: Constance "Connie" Naon is last seen alive

June 9, 1983: Tammie Liles, formerly identified as "Jane Doe B20," is last seen alive

July 18, 1983: Kelly Ware is last seen alive

July 25, 1983: Tina Thompson is last seen alive

June 28, 1983: Keli McGinnis is last seen alive; although Ridgway admitted to killing her, her remains have never been found

August 11, 1983: Shawnda Summers's remains are found in a shallow grave near South 146th Street and 24th Ave South across the street from a water tower

August 12, 1983: Patricia Ann LeBlanc is last seen alive; her remains have never been recovered and her case remains unsolved

August 1983: April Buttram is last seen alive
September 5, 1983: Debbie Abernathy is last seen alive
September 12, 1983: Tracy Winston is last seen alive
September 19, 1983: Gail Matthews's remains are discovered near Star Lake Road
September 28, 1983: Maureen Feeney is last seen alive
October 1983: Yvonne Antosh's remains are discovered about 25 yards downhill from Auburn-Black Diamond Road

October 1983: Patricia Osborn is last seen alive; although Ridgway believes he killed her, he couldn't provide details regarding where he placed her body

October 11, 1983: Mary Sue Bello is last seen alive
October 26, 1983: Pammy Avent is last seen alive
October 1983: Kelly Ware's remains are discovered near 25th South and South 192nd
October 27, 1983: Constance "Connie" Naon's remains are found in a shallow grave in a vacant lot at 25th South and South 192nd
October 30, 1983: Delise Plager is last seen alive
November 1, 1983: Kim Nelson is last seen alive
November 13, 1983: Mary Meehan's remains are discovered in a shallow grave in South Airport near Tyee Golf Course
December 1983: Lisa Yates is last seen alive
December 14, 1983: Kimi-Kai Pitsor's skull is discovered along Mountain View Drive
February 6, 1984: Mary West is last seen alive
February 14, 1984: Delise Plager's remains are discovered at Exit 38 off I-90

March 13, 1984: Lisa Yates's remains are discovered at Exit 38 off I-90

March 13, 1984: Cindy Smith is last seen alive

March 21, 1984: Wendy Stephens's remains are discovered behind the Highline Baseball Field (however, it would take nearly 37 years to identify her)

March 22, 1984: Cheryl Wims's remains are discovered near the Highline Baseball Field

March 31, 1984: Debbie Abernathy's remains are discovered near Highway 410 next to the Weyerhaeuser Mainline near the White River

March 31, 1984: Delores Williams's remains are discovered near Star Lake Road

April 1, 1984: Terry Milligan's remains are discovered near the northern, downhill end of Star Lake Road

April 1, 1984: Sandra Gabbert's remains are discovered in the woods near Star Lake Road

April 2, 1984: Alma Smith's remains are discovered in the woods along Star Lake Road

April 12, 1984: Detectives question Gary about the disappearances of Keli McGinnis and Tina Thompson

April 20, 1984: Tina Thompson's remains are discovered near the intersection of Highway 18 and Interstate 90

May 7, 1984: Gary is administered a polygraph, which he passes

May 26, 1984: Colleen Brockman's remains are discovered near Jovita Boulevard in north Pierce County

October 12, 1984: Mary Sue Bello's remains are discovered near Highway 410

November 14, 1984: Martina Authorlee's remains are discovered near Highway 410

December 1984: Rebecca Garde Guay reports 1982 assault

February 23, 1985: Gary is interviewed by Green River Task Force about the assault on Rebecca Garde Guay, but she does not pursue charges against him

March 10, 1985: Carrie Rois's remains are found in a swampy area near Star Lake Road

April 22, 1985: Angela Girdner's remains are found in Tualatin, OR, close to a site where Ridgway left other victims; however, her remains are not identified until 2009, and her case remains unsolved

June 1985: Denise Bush's and Shirley Sherrill's remains are discovered off a rural road in Tigard, OR. Ridgway moved their remains to Oregon as a way to confuse the task force.

September 8, 1985: Mary West's remains are discovered in Seward Park

December 30, 1985: Sandra Denise Major's remains are discovered near Mountain View Drive; she was not identified until June 2012

December 30, 1985: Lori Anne Razpotnik's remained are discovered near Mountain View Drive; she was not identified until December 19, 2023

March 1986: A human torso belonging to Tracy Winston is discovered in Cottonwood Park; however, she would not be identified until 1999 due to advancements in technology

May 2, 1986: Maureen Feeney's remains are discovered south of the intersection of I-90 and Highway 18

June 1986: Kim Nelson's remains are recovered in a wooded area off I-90 and Exit 38

October 17, 1986: Patricia Barczak is last seen alive

February 7, 1987: Roberta Hayes is last seen alive

April 8, 1987: Detectives search Ridgway's house, vehicles, and locker at work but find no evidence linking him to any of the murders; however, saliva samples are taken, which in 2001 link him to several murders

June 27, 1987: Cindy Smith's remains are discovered in a ditch alongside SE 312th Way near Highway 18

August 26, 1987: Rose Marie Kurran is last seen alive
August 31, 1987: Rose Marie Kurran's body is discovered in a ditch near South 188th St and Military Rd, but it is never confirmed Ridgway killed her

May 30, 1988: Debra Estes's remains are found in a shallow grave in Federal Way
June 12, 1988: Marries Judith Mawson
1989: Andrea Childers's remains are discovered near 25th South and South 192nd, also known as the South Airport site
March 1990: Marta Reeves is last seen alive

April 24, 1990: Darci Warde is last seen alive; her remains have never been recovered, and her case remains unsolved. Ridgway confessed to police he murdered a woman named "Darci" or "Dorsey" in the 1980s, and it's possible he was referring to Warde.

September 20, 1990: Marta Reeves's remains are discovered near Highway 410

October 25, 1990: Deborah Wims is last seen alive; her remains have never been recovered, and her case remains unsolved

September 11, 1991: Roberta Hayes's remains are discovered north of Highway 410

October 31, 1991: Sarah Habakangas is last seen alive
November 4, 1991: Sarah Habakangas's body is found in the woods near North Bend, but her case remains unsolved
November 6, 1992: Nicole French is last seen alive
November 7, 1992: Nicole French's body is discovered in a rural

area a few miles north from North Bend, but her case still remains unsolved

February 1993: Patricia Barczak's remains are discovered off Highway 18
August 1998: Patricia Yellowrobe is last seen alive
August 6, 1998: Patricia Yellowrobe's body is discovered in a gravel parking lot near an entrance ramp to Highway 99
November 16, 2001: Arrested for solicitation
November 30, 2001: Arrested on four counts of murder
2002: Divorced from Judith
June 13–November 25, 2003: As a result of a plea deal to avoid the death penalty, Ridgway confesses to 71 murders, but he's later only convicted for 48
August 2003: With Ridgway's assistance, partial remains belonging to Tammie Liles are recovered off Kent-Des Moines Road, but they wouldn't be identified until later
August 2003: With Ridgway's assistance, Pammy Avent's remains are discovered near Highway 410
August/September 2003: With Ridgway's assistance, the Green River Task Force recovers partial remains belonging to April Buttram north of I-90 and Highway 18 near Leisure Time Resorts
September 28, 2003: With Ridgway's assistance, the Green River Task Force recovers some of Marie Malvar's remains from a wooded ravine near 65th Avenue South in Auburn
November 5, 2003: Ridgway pleads guilty to 48 counts of aggravated first-degree murder
December 18, 2003: Ridgway is sentenced to 48 consecutive life sentences without the possibility of parole
January 6, 2004: Ridgway is transferred to Washington State Penitentiary in Walla Walla to serve out his sentence
February 18, 2011: Ridgway pleads guilty to the 1982 aggravated first-degree murder of Rebecca Marrero, his 49th conviction,

and receives an additional life sentence without the possibility of parole

May 14, 2015: Ridgway is transferred to United States Penitentiary-Florence in Colorado

September 2015: Ridgway is transferred back to Washington State Penitentiary in Walla Walla

August 2020: Maria mails first letter to Ridgway

September 20, 2020: Ridgway calls Maria for the first time

January 2021: The remains of Wendy Stephens, formerly identified as "Jane Doe B10" are identified

April 2022: Ridgway is housed in the prison infirmary for medical reasons

June 2022: Ridgway calls Maria for the last time

January 22, 2024: The remains of Tammie Liles, formerly identified as "Jane Doe B20," are identified

September 9, 2024: Ridgway is transferred from Washington State Penitentiary to King County Jail, but no one states why

September 10, 2024: Ridgway is transferred back to Washington State Penitentiary from King County Jail despite the media claiming he returned on September 13, 2024

March 8, 2025: The media reports Ridgway was transferred to King County Jail in September 2024 to allegedly assist in the investigation of unsolved cases, which happened to be unsuccessful

December 1, 2025: The media reports that Gary is receiving end-of-life care; however, the Department of Corrections refutes this claim, stating there has been no change in his health.

*Bolded cases are unconfirmed.

Acknowledgments

The following people offered me comfort, support, insight, and endless conversations while I was researching and writing this book. Without them, this book would not have been possible.

I'm eternally grateful to my immediate family—my mother, Christine DiLorenzo (for always loving me, believing in me, and encouraging my creativity), and my father, Vincent DiLorenzo. Thank you to Janine and Michael Jichetti for so many hours of conversations around your dining room table. To Lucas and Gianna Jichetti, for bringing light and joy to my life.

I'm grateful to my agent, Austin Miller, for the unwavering belief in my work and for taking a chance on me. Thank you to Rebecca Silensky, Jan Miller, and the entire team at Dupree Miller & Associates. I'm grateful to my editor, Rebecca Nelson, for providing invaluable insight and advice that helped bring this manuscript to fruition, to my copyeditor, Elizabeth Oliver, and to Laura Apperson, Marcia Markland, and everyone at Crooked Lane Books who helped make this book a reality.

To my family, especially my uncle, Ronald DiLorenzo, and my cousins—Frankie DiLorenzo, Michael DiLorenzo, Diane Weidler, and Joe Latona. To Viki Pedrotty—thank you for the long messages that have uplifted my spirits. Thank you to Nicole Cannilla for the coffee, makeup, and long talks in the car.

To my dearest friends—Emily Santoro, Arathi Reddy, Joann Maldonado, Geoff Shields, Daisy Calidonio, Laura Larsen, Chrissy Plotkin (RIP), Thomas Sobolow, Meaghan Galileo, Anthony Sica, Lou LaRocco, and John Goncalves—for always listening. A special thanks to Marlo Savino, for helping me dig up a park in my quest for truth and justice, Vincent Punziano, for literally helping me gain clarity, and Michael Mazzeo, for the continuous support and accompanying me on various parts of my journey. I am grateful to Christopher Robinson and Amanda Knox for giving me a voice on Crime Story Media years ago and listening to the ideas I had for this book in the midst of my research in Seattle.

To Dr. Rose Soussan (RIP), I would not have made it through without your kindness, understanding, empathy, and incredible insight into the human psyche. I will cherish your words and guidance for as long as I live, and I will always miss you.

To Mark David Chapman, for the long letters, phone calls, unique perspective, and lemon jokes.

To those I have worked with who have helped me grow as a writer—Stephen Handelman, Audrey Nielsen, Zoltan Lucas, and everyone else at *The Crime Report*, and Jenni Savin from *Cosmopolitan*, for giving me a space to share my perspective. Thank you to Joseph Diaz from ABC, for caring about my work and listening to my ideas.

I would never have grown as a writer if not for my time in the MFA program at Hunter College. I am especially appreciative of Donna Masini, Jan Heller Levi, and Tom Sleigh, for their guidance. I am grateful to Cate Marvin, who noticed the potential of my words when I was an undergraduate student and pushed me to never stop improving my craft.

To everyone who entrusted me with their story on Beyond the Crime and elsewhere, especially Max Gelman and Keith Jesperson, for always sharing my work from behind the walls.

I am grateful to Jay Wilkinson, and Dr. Michael Dobersen, for helping me in my pursuit for justice. I am also grateful to Tom Jensen, Sue Peters, and David Reichert for taking the time to speak with me.

To everyone from the Streetwise generation who took time to speak with me and entrusted me with their stories, especially Angela Herr—for the coffee and foot cream when I was in Seattle, but more than anything, for helping me understand. I am grateful to Judith Magnan, Charles Habakangas, and Nick Habakangas for entrusting me with memories of their loved ones for the sake of pursuing justice.